London
2008

WHAT'S NEW | WHAT'S ON | WHAT'S BEST

www.timeout.com/london

Contents

London by Area

Essentials

Published by Time Out Guides Ltd
Universal House
251 Tottenham Court Road
London W1T 7AB
Tel: + 44 (0)20 7813 3000
Fax: + 44 (0)20 7813 6001
Email: guides@timeout.com
www.timeout.com

Managing Director Peter Fiennes
Editorial Director Ruth Jarvis
Deputy Series Editor Dominic Earle
Business Manager Gareth Garner
Editorial Manager Holly Pick
Accountant Ija Krasnikova

Time Out Guides is a wholly owned subsidiary of Time Out Group Ltd.

© **Time Out Group Ltd**
Chairman Tony Elliott
Financial Director Richard Waterlow
Time Out Magazine Ltd MD David Pepper
Group General Manager/Director Nichola Coulthard
Managing Director, Time Out International Cathy Runciman
Time Out Communications Ltd MD David Pepper
Production Director Mark Lamond
Group Marketing Director John Luck
Group Art Director John Oakey
Group IT Director Simon Chappell

Time Out and the Time Out logo are trademarks of Time Out Group Ltd.

This edition first published in Great Britain in 2007 by Ebury Publishing
A Random House Group Company
Company information can be found on www.randomhouse.co.uk
10 9 8 7 6 5 4 3 2 1

For further distribution details, see www.timeout.com

ISBN 13: 978-1-846700-25-5
ISBN 10: 1-84670-025-6

A CIP catalogue record for this book is available from the British Library

Printed and bound by Firmengruppe APPL, aprinta druck, Wemding, Germany

The Random House Group Limited makes every effort to ensure that the papers used in
our books are made from trees that have been legally sourced from well-managed and
credibly certified forests. Our paper procurement policy can be found on
www.randomhouse.co.uk

London Shortlist

The **Time Out London Shortlist 2008** is one of a series of guides that draws on Time Out's background as a magazine publisher to keep you current with everything that's going on in town. As well as London's key sights and the best of its eating, drinking and leisure options, it picks out the most exciting venues to have opened in the last year and gives a full calendar of events from September 2007 to December 2008. It also includes features on the important news, trends and openings, all compiled by locally based editors and writers. Whether you're visiting for the first time in your life or the first time since 2007, you'll find the *Time Out London Shortlist* contains everything you need to know, in an easy-to-use and portable format.

The guide divides central London into five areas, each containing listings for Sights & Museums, Eating & Drinking, Shopping, Nightlife and Arts & Leisure, and maps pinpointing their locations. At the front of the book are chapters rounding up these scenes city-wide, and giving a shortlist of our overall picks. We include itineraries for days out, plus essentials such as transport information and hotels.

Our listings give phone numbers as dialled within London. To dial them from elsewhere in the UK, preface them with 020; from abroad, use your country's exit code followed by 44 (the country code for the UK), 20 and the number given. We have noted price categories by using one to four £ signs (**£-££££**), representing budget, moderate, expensive and luxury. Major credit cards are accepted unless otherwise stated. We indicate when a venue is NEW, and also give **Event highlights**.

All our listings are double-checked, but places do close or change their hours or prices with no notice, so it's a good idea to call a venue before you visit. While every effort has been made to ensure accuracy, the publishers cannot accept responsibility for any errors this guide may contain.

Venues are marked on the maps using symbols numbered according to their order within the chapter and colour-coded as follows:

❶ Sights & Museums
❶ Eating & Drinking
❶ Shopping
❶ Nightlife
❶ Arts & Leisure

Map key	
Major sight or landmark	▇
Railway stations	▇
Underground stations	⊖
Parks	▇
Hospitals	▇
Casualty units	✚
Churches	✚
Synagogues	✡
Congestion Zone	Ⓒ
Districts	MAYFAIR
Theatres	●

Time Out London Shortlist 2008

EDITORIAL
Editor Simon Coppock
Copy Editors Ismay Atkins, Jonathan Derbyshire, Lesley McCave
Researcher Carol Baker
Proofreader Patrick Mulkern
Indexer Carol Baker

DESIGN
Art Director Scott Moore
Art Editor Pinelope Kourmouzoglou
Senior Designer Henry Elphick
Graphic Designer Gemma Doyle
Junior Graphic Designer Kei Ishimaru
Digital Imaging Simon Foster
Ad Make-up Jodi Sher
Picture Editor Jael Marschner
Deputy Picture Editor Tracey Kerrigan
Picture Researcher Helen McFarland

ADVERTISING
Sales Director/Sponsorship Mark Phillips
Advertising Manager Alison Wallen
Advertising Sales Ben Holt, Alex Matthews, Jason Trotman
Advertising Assistant Kate Staddon
Copy Controller Declan Symington

MARKETING
Marketing Manager Yvonne Poon
Sales & Marketing Director, North America Lisa Levinson
Marketing Designer Anthony Huggins

PRODUCTION
Production Manager Brendan McKeown
Production Co-ordinator Caroline Bradford
Production Controller Susan Whittaker

CONTRIBUTORS
Simone Baird, Martin Coomer, Guy Dimond, Emma Howarth, Cathy Limb, Sharon O'Connell, Chris Parkin, Holly Pick, Lisa Ritchie, Andrew Staffell, Zoë Strimpel, Neville Walker and Natalie Whittle. Thanks also to contributors to the *Time Out Guide to London* and *Time Out* magazine.

PHOTOGRAPHY
Photography pages 2 (bottom left), 25, 28, 33, 45, 51, 53, 70, 95, 114, 124, 125 Michelle Grant; pages 7, 23, 66, 89, 103, 163, 188, 191 Alys Tomlinson; pages 8, 9, 11, 49, 82 Andrew Brackenbury; page 13 Avery Associates Architects; page 14 Scott Wishart; page 18 Rogan Macdonald; pages 20, 46, 48, 55, 56, 61, 74, 103, 114, 118, 130, 131, 136, 148, 165, 177, 184, 193, 209 Britta Jaschinski; page 29 Oliver Knight; page 37 James O Jenkins; page 63 Leon Chew; pages 65, 87, 113, 120, 121, 127, 162, 182 Ming Tang Evans; pages 90, 194, 201 Olivia Rutherford; page 72 Abigail Lelliot; pages 76, 170 Martin Daly; pages 78, 79, 93, 100, 159 Heloise Bergman; pages 109, 146 Gemma Day; page 128 Ed Marshall; page 141 Silvia Petretti - Sustiva, Tenofivir, 3TC (HIV) © Mark Quinn, 2005, Courtesy Jay Jopling/White Cube (London) and Wellcome Trust; page 155 Michael Franke; page 160 Viktor Pesanti; pages 168, 169 Anthony Webb; page 207 Scott Chasserot.

The following images were provided by the featured establishment/ artist: pages 30, 35, 36, 39, 42, 52, 69, 81, 157, 175, 197, 204.

Cover photograph: Westminster Bridge, London, Credit: Taxi/Getty Images.

MAPS
JS Graphics (john@jsgraphics.com).

About Time Out

Founded in 1968, Time Out has expanded from humble London beginnings into the leading resource for those wanting to know what's happening in the world's greatest cities. As well as our influential what's-on weeklies in London, New York and Chicago, we publish more than a dozen other listings magazines in cities as varied as Beijing and Mumbai. The magazines established Time Out's trademark style: sharp writing, informed reviewing and bang up-to-date inside knowledge of every scene.

Time Out made the natural leap into travel guides in the 1980s with the City Guide series, which now extends to over 50 destinations around the world. Written and researched by expert local writers and generously illustrated with original photography, the full-size guides cover a larger area than our Shortlist guides and include many more venue reviews, along with additional background features and a full set of maps.

Throughout this rapid growth, the company has remained proudly independent, still owned by Tony Elliott nearly four decades after he started Time Out London as a single fold-out sheet of A5 paper. This independence extends to the editorial content of all our publications, this Shortlist included. No establishment has been featured because it has advertised, and no payment has influenced any of our reviews. And, for our critics, there's definitely no such thing as a free lunch: all restaurants and bars are visited and reviewed anonymously, and Time Out always picks up the bill.

For more about the company, see www.timeout.com.

Don't Miss
2008

Great Court

WHAT'S BEST
Sights & Museums

London's most exciting new buildings are currently all about infrastructure: a new Eurostar terminal brings high-speed Channel Tunnel trains from Europe to the marvellous Victorian red-brick St Pancras station from November 2007, while Heathrow's high-tech Terminal 5 opens for business in 2008. It isn't that the city lacks eye-catching headline projects – the extraordinary 10-storey glass pyramid extension to Tate Modern (p64) secured planning permission in summer 2006 – but they do seem mostly focused further in the future, as if the 2012 Olympics has become everybody's de facto deadline.

So instead of the fabulous new monuments that ushered in the millennium – the Great Court at the British Museum (p136), the Millennium Bridge, the London Eye (p57) – it's now time for steady renewal. In May 2007 the Peter Harrison Planetarium was due to open at Greenwich Observatory (p186), the refurbished London's Transport Museum (p129) should follow in November and the Museum of London (p152) has undertaken major improvements, not least a glass entrance that will be set into the museum's forbiddingly dark brickwork. Few of the major museums charge for entry these days. This not only keeps visitor numbers high, but also makes brief but intense visits to, say, the giant Victorian museums of South Kensington (pp83, 86) by far the best approach.

Consolidation at London's major attractions has tended towards internal improvement rather than dramatic overhauls – the reopened pagoda at Kew's Royal Botanic Gardens (p185), Gorilla Kingdom at London Zoo (p95) and the Sackler Wing at the V&A (p86) are some examples – but the problems presented to tourists by London's gnarled streets are also being addressed: witness how the new information centre (p148) beside a St Paul's (p152) beautifully spruced up for its 300th anniversary will complete the link across the river to Tate Modern. The new public space at the bottom of the Monument (p152) is also welcome.

On a smaller scale, there are plenty of exciting developments. In line with London's booming contemporary art scene, there are a handful of notable new art spaces: the long-awaited Charles Saatchi Gallery (p91) should reopen on new premises in November 2007, while

See London in a world of your own

+44(0)870 5000 600 or londoneye.com ⊖ Waterloo and Westminster

BRITISH AIRWAYS
London eye

Kinetica (p174) and the Louise T Blouin (p189) have held impressive inaugural shows. It will be intriguing to see how the populist Charles Saumarez Smith fares at the bureaucratic Royal Academy of Arts (p105), having quit as director of the National Gallery (p73) after widely reported internal conflicts.

The Wellcome Collection (p140) looks set to be the most impressive of a new breed of scientific and medical attractions, offering a provocative mix of modern art and historical medical artefacts. And we hope the glorious renovation of St George's Bloomsbury (p140) will be followed by an equally fine remodelling of St Martin-in-the-Fields (p74).

The lay of the land

This book is divided by area. The **South Bank** primarily covers riverside Bankside, home of Tate Modern and the revamped Southbank Centre. Over the river, **Westminster & St James's** covers the centre of UK politics, while the impressive Victorian museums of **South Kensington**, the Knightsbridge department stores, and the boutiques and restaurants of still-fashionable **Chelsea** lie to the west.

The **West End** includes most of what is now central London. We start north of unlovely Oxford Street, in the elegant but slightly raffish shopping district of

St Martin-in-the-Fields

Peter Harrison Planetarium p8

Making the most of it

Some tips for getting the best out of London in 2008. Don't be scared of the transport system: invest in an Oyster travel smartcard (p213) and travel cashless through the city by bus and tube. Buses are best for getting a handle on the topography. Some good sightseeing routes are RV1 (riverside), 7, 8, 11 and 12, along with the Heritage Route served by the last Routemasters (p73). Don't be afraid to wander at will: crime in central London is low, and walking can be the best way to appreciate its many character changes. No one thinks any the less of anyone consulting a map – so long as they dive out of the stream of pedestrian traffic. And most people will be happy to help with directions: Londoners' reputation for standoffishness is largely undeserved.

To avoid the worst of the crowds follow the tips given in the text, and try to steer clear of the big draws at weekends and on late-opening nights, when the population turns out in force. Aim to hit exhibitions in the middle of their run – or prepare yourself for crowds (an audio tour at least helps screen out the chat). Last entry is often a little before closing time, so don't turn up just before a place closes if you want to appreciate it fully. Some sights close at Christmas and Easter – ring ahead to confirm openings.

If time is really short, start with a stroll along the South Bank, from Waterloo to Tower Bridge. This is where you'll find 21st-century London's biggest draws, for both locals and visitors: the London Eye, the revitalised Southbank Centre, Tate Modern and the Millennium Bridge, and Borough Market, along with great photo-opportunities for the Houses of Parliament, City Hall and Tower Bridge.

Marylebone. South, between Marylebone and St James's, is **Mayfair**, as expensive as its reputation but less daunting, with inviting mews and pubs. Eastward is **Soho**, notorious centre of filth and fun, then **Covent Garden**, so popular with tourists that locals often forget about the charms of its boutique shopping. North lie the squares and Georgian terraces of literary **Bloomsbury**, home of academia and the British Museum; west across Tottenham Court Road is **Fitzrovia**, its elegant streets speckled with inviting shops and restaurants.

The **City** comprises the once-walled Square Mile of the original city, compelling for its long and still-visible history, and **Holborn** and **Clerkenwell**, whose great food and nightlife help them to feel much more lived-in.

Around these central districts **neighbourhood London** has interesting clusters of restaurants, bars, clubs and attractions, servicing what are mainly residential zones.

Arbutus

WHAT'S BEST
Eating & Drinking

London has, contrary to all expectations, established itself as one of the world's great centres of eating. Not only because the quality keeps improving, but because of the sheer diversity: how many cities can boast Afghan, Armenian, Burmese, Eritrean, Malaysian, Seychellois and Swedish restaurants within a few miles of each other? What's more, those seeking exotic tastes often have not just one restaurant, but a whole range, to choose from, clustered in a kind of gastronomic ghetto. There are at least ten Vietnamese places on the Kingsland Road in Shoreditch; a little further north you're spoilt for choice of Turkish *ocakbasi* grills. Head west and there's an unbeatable range of proper Punjabi cooking in Southall, go south to Stockwell and there are great Portuguese cafés.

In these culinary corners, old favourites prosper and new openings are scarce. Not so on the manic main stage of London dining, which sees gluts of openings (and closures) almost every week. And if there's one restaurant species whose population has exploded faster than any other in recent times, it has to be the gastropub. Hardly a week goes by without some old pub sanding down its floorboards, pumping weissbier into its taps, and ditching toad in the hole in favour of Cumberland sausage with a red-wine jus and truffled mash. To be sure, not all of these bandwagon-jumpers get on and stay on. But a few notable openings prove that it's still possible to deliver an inspired, sincere interpretation of a sound concept – a proper pub serving great food. Fine recent examples include the Hat & Feathers (p161), Charles Lamb (p170) and Great Queen Street (p129).

The menus at many of these gastropubs – as well as at a number of upmarket, self-styled 'British' restaurants such as Roast, National Dining Rooms (p77) and Smiths of Smithfield – remind us that we also have an illustrious, indigenous culinary tradition. One of the catalysts for its revival has been growing concern about the dangers of industrial farming methods and the effects of long-distance mass transportation of food, encouraging chef's to focus on using seasonal, local and well-farmed ingredients.

Two recently opened restaurants have put these ethical concerns at the heart of their operations. First was Konstam at the Prince Albert, which sources nearly all its ingredients from within the M25; not long after, nearby Acorn House was inaugurated with an even more ambitious manifesto including strict policies on recycling, transport, energy-efficiency and sourcing of ingredients.

For all that these restaurants set a laudable example, they are also canny enough to trade on their concept. And why not? A notable number of new openings now peddle a carefully crafted concept instead of just slotting in to some established – and cluttered – category: bistro, trattoria, curry house, tapas bar. So Ooze is the first 'risotto bar'; Mother Mash (p121) gives that East End staple, pie and mash, a minimalist, modern format. Asian cuisine seems the readiest grist to the restaurant-concept mill. 'Pan-Asian' is an increasingly popular genre, of which Gilgamesh, Tamarai and Haiku are the latest and most impressive examples; others have innovated by following a specific prototype, such as Nagomi (p111) and the eagerly anticipated Cha

SHORTLIST

Best new eats
- Arbutus (p118)
- Barrafina (p118)
- Bar Shu (p118)
- L'Atelier de Joël Robuchon (p130)
- Odette's (p171)
- Trinity (p187)

Star bars
- Dorchester Bar (p107)
- Gilgamesh (p170)
- Hawksmoor (p177)
- Lost Society (p187)

Old-school booze
- Gordon's (p129)
- Lamb (p142)
- Ye Old Mitre (p166)

New ideas
- Acorn House (p140)
- Konstam at the Prince Albert (p142)
- Ooze (p144)
- Tea Smith (p179)

Food with a view
- Galvin at Windows (p107)
- Plateau (p179)
- Roast (p67)
- Skylon (p67)
- Top Floor at Smiths of Smithfield (p164)

Best global
- Boteca Carioca (p144)
- Nahm (p88)
- Providores & Tapa Room (p100)

Oriental innovation
- Cha Cha No Hana (p79)
- Haiku (p108)
- Ping Pong (p67)
- Tamarai (p131)

Modern classics
- Anchor & Hope (p66)
- Hakkasan (p144)
- Moro (p163)
- St John (p164)

wagamama

delicious noodles
wine

bloomsbury | **borough** / l...
covent garden | **earls cou**...
knightsbridge | **leiceste**...
old broad street / **ban**...
vic...

p o s i t i v e

uk | ireland | holland | austral...

e dishes | freshly squeezed juices
ake | japanese beers

n bridge | brent cross | camden | canary wharf
leet street | haymarket | islington | kensington
uare | mansion house | moorgate / citypoint
utney | royal festival hall | soho | tower hill
| wigmore | wimbledon

ating + positive living

agamama.com

ubai | belgium | new zealand | denmark | turkey | usa

Cha No Hana (see box p77), both loosely based on the izakaya (the closest Japanese equivalent to a pub).

Not every opening on the hyped-up frontline of London restaurant openings presents a polished concept. Other places garner publicity by making a meal of whoever's behind the venture: this is, after all, the age of the celebrity chef, and known names get bums on seats. A common trick is to shoehorn the chef's name into the restaurant's own: so Tom Aikens opens Tom's Kitchen (p89); we get a branch of L'Atelier de Joël Robuchon, and Theo Randall at the InterContinental speaks – rather clumsily – for itself. Gordon Ramsay's prodigious reach continues to extend, but such is the hype he generates, no vanity-naming is required. His most recent ventures are gastropubs: the Narrow (p179) in Limehouse and, due as we go to press, the handsome Warrington in Maida Vale. Alain Ducasse's imminent arrival at the Dorchester (see box p105), scheduled for September 2007, is causing a stir, while St Alban (p80) was the hottest new opening of 2007.

While an original concept or association with a pre-eminent chef might guarantee some attention, these qualities alone cannot ensure a long and prosperous life for a restaurant. That requires the balance of an agreeable atmosphere, appropriate service and, above all, consistently high-quality cooking. After all, there's nothing wrong with a proven formula, so long as it's executed with aplomb: the popularity of the high-class, canteen-style chain is a case in point – witness Wagamama, Busaba Eathai (p118), Ping Pong, Carluccio's, even Leon and Itsu. By the time you read this, the latest addition to the genre, Wahaca, should have opened its first branch

St Alban p18

in Covent Garden, turning out classy interpretations of Mexican street food.

Canteen chains aside, any restaurant that gets the formula right, proves its place in the market and then keep standards up can count on years of undying loyalty. Moro, St John and Hakkasan are examples of veteran venues that remain so popular it's still necessary to book significantly in advance; some of these place opened a decade ago.

Some complain that the rise of the gastropub has sounded the death-knell for the traditional British pub, but it doesn't have to be this way: for one thing, the better gastros are perfectly deferential to their boozer heritage; for another, there are many properly historic, ungentrified pubs (the Lamb and Ye Old Mitre are, in their different ways, perfect examples). A more significant change to pub culture is promised by the smoking ban, which should have come into force in June 2007.

London's cocktail scene – still not as diverse or interesting as its restaurants – continues to improve, with recent high-class openings including Hawksmoor, Gilgamesh and Lost Society. The wine bar also seems to be cutting loose from its dowdy suburban image with a clutch of fine places in Clerkenwell (see box p162) and, in Fortnum & Mason, the superb 1707.

Neighbourhood watch

Covent Garden is full of mediocre, overpriced, chain bars and restaurants. Away from the main drag of Old Compton Street, adjacent **Soho** has a much better range of well-priced and interesting places to eat, including Busaba Eathai, Hummus Bros and Imli.

Prices in **Mayfair** are high, especially at its many hotel-based fine-dining establishments, but some of its more interesting restaurants, such as Maze, Chisou or Galvin at Windows, merit a splurge. Food-obsessed **Marylebone** has some top choices, including Italian Locanda Locatelli, the steak-frites-only Le Relais de Venise l'entrecôte and global fusion at Providores & Tapa Room.

Westminster and the **City** aren't great places to eat, but the latter abuts Clerkenwell where you'll find top venues such as St John, Smiths of Smithfield and Vinoteca.

Knightsbridge, **South Kensington** and **Chelsea** are also expensive, but there's no doubting the quality of some of their restaurants, old and new, such as the bistro Racine and double-Michelin-starred Pétrus.

On the **South Bank**, the Tate Modern has a couple of decent brasseries, but you won't regret heading to Table or, if you can

grab a table, the exemplary Anchor & Hope gastropub.

Shoreditch in east London is now the centre of London's bar scene and nightlife, but there's not much to choose between many of the identikit trendy bars there; Loungelover and Hawksmoor are notable exceptions. Shoreditch is also the heart of London's Vietnamese community: try Cay Tre or recent addition Thang Loi, but it's hard to pick a dud around here.

Surprisingly, **Brick Lane** is also lacking in the food and drink stakes: the street's 50-plus curry houses might be legendary and may be cheap, but they're unremarkable. Serious curry pilgrims need to head out of central London to Tooting for countless cheap, regional options; to Wembley's Ealing Road for Gujarati- and Mumbai-style food; or to Southall, a Punjabi home from home.

Dos & don'ts

Don't expect to be able to get a table at a buzz restaurant any day of the week without booking at least a week ahead. If you find yourself caught without a booking, try a gastropub, where at least you can wait indoors; otherwise head for one of the ethnic food neighbourhoods above or choose a walk-in only restaurant (see box p114).

Many restaurants add a 10 to 15 per cent service charge to the bill; check whether they have before leaving extra, and be wary of the common and despicable practice whereby a restaurant adds a service charge, then still gives the customer the option of adding a further tip at the credit-card payment stage.

As of July 2007, smoking is no longer permitted in any enclosed public place – which means all restaurants, bars and pubs.

Dover Street Market

Shopping

In spring 2007, the tailors of Savile Row – London's bastion of bespoke threads – held a protest against the arrival of US clothing chain Abercrombie & Fitch. The antithesis of buttoned-up English style, this new flagship is staffed not by deferential, besuited gents but – horrors – semi-clad 'store models'.

The winds of change are also whistling down Piccadilly. Having held firm against the whims of fashion for 300 years, the grande dame of department stores, Fortnum & Mason (see box p81), got a major nip and tuck for its big three-o-o birthday. While the impeccably mannered staff still sport tailcoats, the famous ground-floor food hall has been spruced up and extended into the basement, now all clean lined with its fresh food counter and fantastic wine bar. Even that creaky

repository of cashmere twinsets and embroidered velvet slippers, the Burlington Arcade (p112), is being restored to its Regency glory with such glamorous new tenants as posh Parisian cake shop Ladurée.

Yet, despite widespread style makeovers and the insidious influence of the chain stores, London has managed to hold on to some of its eccentric old specialist shops, and business is booming for fashion boutiques, fuelled by Londoners' obsession with designer labels and niche brands.

Fashion first

Influential design college Central Saint Martins produces some of the most exciting and mould-breaking talent on the international scene. The name on everyone's lips for 2007/8 is recent graduate

Christopher Kane, whose debut collection of bandeau dresses captured a sexy, body-con style with nods to the 1980s. Avant-gardist Gareth Pugh, who has a fondness for PVC and theatrical catwalk shows, has been gaining attention over the past couple of years. Percy Parker and Amy Molyneaux – the designers behind niche label PPQ, popular for staples such as drainpipe trousers and minidresses – opened a dedicated shop in Mayfair in autumn 2006.

To find items by the young stars of tomorrow, either head east, to the northerly section of Brick Lane and its offshoots (some shops only open later in the week to coincide with the Sunday market), or west to Notting Hill, where they set up shop at Portobello Green market (on Portobello Road, under the Westway flyover) on Fridays and Saturdays.

Green & pleasant

There are clear signs of eco-conscious consumerism in London. In addition to special lines in stores such as Bamford, M&S and H&M, the city now has a handful of dedicated 'eco-boutiques'. Concern about recycling has fed into the vintage craze: vintage sections are commonplace in department stores as well as the boutiques, and hybrids selling a mix of old and new clothing (Jaan) or customised vintage (One) mark the latest phase in the trend's evolution. Organic restaurants and food shops are cropping up all over town, including Pimlico's posh country store Daylesford Organic – rumours suggest a new branch will open in Notting Hill – and American giant Whole Foods Market (see box p86), which has taken over the site of Barkers department store on Kensington High Street.

SHORTLIST

Best new
- Daylesford Organic (p93)
- Jaan (p90)
- Marc Jacobs (p113)
- PPQ (p113)
- Sera of London (p192)
- Three Threads (p181)

Unmissable markets
- Borough Market (food) (p68)
- Columbia Road (flowers) (p180)
- Spitalfields (designers) (p181)

Cutting-edge concepts
- b store (p112)
- Dover Street Market (p112)
- Shop at Bluebird (p93)
- Weardowney Get-Up Boutique (p102)

Recycled chic
- Appleby (p191)
- The Girl Can't Help It at Alfies Antique Market (p100)
- Junky Styling (p181)
- One (p192)

Cool classics
- DR Harris & Co (p80)
- Liberty (p123)
- Margaret Howell (p101)
- Mulberry (p102)

Best of British
- Miller Harris (p191)
- Rupert Sanderson (p113)
- Topshop (p102)

Art of design
- Contemporary Applied Arts (p147)
- Labour & Wait (p181)
- Mint (p101)

Best for tunes
- Rough Trade (box p183)
- Sounds of the Universe (p123)

Best for words
- Cecil Court (p132)
- Daunt Books (p101)
- London Review Bookshop (p142)
- Skoob (p143)

LETS FILL THIS TOWN WITH ARTISTS
BEST CHOICE TOP BRANDS LOW PRICES

EASELS

75% OFF

£12.95
WINSOR & NEWTON
DART SKETCHING
EASEL
RRP £39.99

70% OFF

£9.95
DALER-ROWNEY
EDINBURGH
TABLE BOX EASEL
RRP £29.50

70% OFF

£49.95
DALER-ROWNEY
SALISBURY EASEL
RRP £200

PAINTS

£3.82
DALER-ROWNEY
SYSTEM 3
250ML ACRYLIC
RRP £7.65

HALF PRICE

UP TO 50% OFF

HALF PRICE

WINSOR & NEWTON 14ML ARTISTS
WATERCOLOUR UP TO 50% OFF
WINSOR & NEWTON ARTIST OIL 37ML
ALL HALF PRICE

BRUSHES

WINSOR & NEWTON ARTIST HOG BRUSH SET
RRP £26 NOW £12.95 HALF PRICE

HALF PRICE

CANVAS

HALF PRICE

WINSOR & NEWTON
ARTIST QUALITY CANVAS
ALL HALF PRICE

SETS & GIFTS

HALF PRICE

£4.95
FABER-CASTELL 9000
12 ART PENCILS
8B-2H IN TIN RRP £9.95

HALF PRICE

LESS THAN HALF PRICE

A4 - £3.95, A5 - £2.95
DALER-ROWNEY EBONY
HARDBACK SKETCH PAD
RRP (A4) £8.50, (A5) £6.25

REMBRANDT PASTELS
MANY HALF PRICE SETS

£9.95
WINSOR & NEWTON 8X14ML
DRAWING INKS SET RRP £19.95

HALF PRICE

HALF PRICE

PRESENTATION PORTFOLIOS
MANY HALF PRICE ITEMS

CASS PROMISE – CREATIVITY AT THE LOWEST PRICES. WE'RE CONFIDENT OUR PRICES CAN'T BE BEATEN

CASS ART LONDON

FLAGSHIP STORE, 66-67 COLEBROOKE ROW, ISLINGTON N1, 020 7354 2999
13 CHARING CROSS RD WC2, 020 7930 9940
220 KENSINGTON HIGH ST W8, 020 7937 6506
24 BERWICK ST, SOHO W1, 020 7287 8504
OPEN 7 DAYS WWW.CASSART.CO.UK

ALL OFFERS SUBJECT TO AVAILABILITY & PRICES SUBJECT TO CHANGE. ALL PRICES VALID 01/00/07. CASS PROMISE, ASK IN STORES.

Market up

London's exuberant markets are great places to sample street life while picking up some bargains. One of the most central is in Berwick Street (p123), where stalls displaying fruit, veg and fish are surrounded by shops selling cheap fabrics, CDs and the less wholesome wares of Soho's red-light district. Borough Market, on Thursdays, Fridays and Saturdays, is the foodie's favourite. Lush flower market Columbia Road is well worth a visit on a Sunday morning – and there are several interesting shops on the sidelines. Brixton's maze of indoor and outdoor markets pulsate with people and reggae. The jumble of wares, reflecting the area's large Afro-Caribbean population, includes plantains and pigs' trotters, Afro wigs and printed textiles.

Antique streets

Portobello Road Market has over 1,000 antiques and bric-a-brac stalls on Saturdays, but it sometimes feels uncomfortably crowded. If you want to avoid the crush, Alfie's (p100) houses high-quality dealers, and a clutch of interesting antiques shops, selling everything from vintage shop fittings to art deco china, has grown up around it in Church Street.

Culture with kudos

Despite fierce pressure from the chains, London has some magnificent book and record shops. Bibliophiles are drawn to Charing Cross Road, but even locals overlook the small antiquarian specialists on pedestrian alleyway Cecil Court. The beautiful Edwardian conservatory at Daunt Books has travel books and novels arranged by country.

Soho's Berwick Street, a longtime enclave of independent record shops, has recently seen several closures, including 24-year-old Reckless Records, but several survivors remain here and around Portobello Road. Defying the online behemoths, at press time Rough Trade, the indie label that first signed the Smiths, was due to open a megastore and in-store gig venue in the East End.

Neighbourhood watch

For a taste of retail past, St James's Street is lined with anachronistic specialist shops, including London's oldest hatter, an old-fashioned chemist and the royal shoemaker. The best of Mayfair's royal arcades is Burlington Arcade (undergoing a rolling refurbishment until summer 2008), where you can pick up classy cashmere or an authentic Globe-Trotter suitcase – at a price. Stuffy Savile Row has been given a shake-up in recent years by a handful of tailoring upstarts with modern design sensibilities – but it is now under more serious threat from encroaching chain stores.

Bond Street remains the domain of luxury international catwalk names, auctioneers and posh galleries. To the north, it's best to

DON'T MISS: 2008

Spitalfields p21

hurry across heaving thoroughfare Oxford Street, with its chains and department stores, and duck into pedestrianised Gees Court and St Christopher's Place – picturesque alleyways, lined with cafés and shops, that lead to the bottom of Marylebone. Hyped to the hilt and in danger of becoming a chi-chi village cliché, curving Marylebone High Street offers a varied selection of clothiers, perfumeries, gourmet food shops, design stores and jewellers, but it is in the equally meandering backstreet, Marylebone Lane, that more interesting newcomers, such as avant-garde shoemaker Tracey Neuls, are rubbing shoulders with time-honoured residents such as century-old deli Paul Rothe & Son.

A couple of London's most celebrated streets have recently been lifted out of decades in chain-dominated doldrums. That emblem of 1960s cool, Carnaby Street, had fallen prey to tacky souvenir shops and ersatz pop-culture emporiums, but it's been salvaged by an influx of quality youth clothing brands and by Kingly Court, a small shopping centre housing interesting independent boutiques (including vintage). Tucked behind Carnaby, cobbled, car-free Newburgh Street has a further cache of one-off jewellery and clothes shops.

Also synonymous with the Swinging London of Mary Quant, Jean Shrimpton and Terence Stamp, as well as later punk pioneers Vivienne Westwood and the Sex Pistols, the King's Road had morphed into shopping-mall mediocrity (although Viv's first shop still survives 37 years on at World's End). Fittingly, it's this end of the street that has been given a boost by a crop of hip stores, such as the Shop at Bluebird.

Nor should Covent Garden be written off as a tourist trap. North-west of the piazza, cobbled Floral Street and the offshoots from Seven Dials are fertile browsing ground: you'll find streetwear, arty erotica, niche cosmetics, quality coffee and British cheeses. Don't miss sweet little Neal's Yard, with its wholefood cafés and organic herbalist.

Unless you're looking to work the platinum AmEx in Sloane Street's international designer salons or marvel at the art nouveau food halls of Harrods, there's little reason to swing by Knightsbridge. To the south, however, pretty Elizabeth Street is one of central London's overlooked gems, with smart shopfronts containing cutting-edge footwear, rare perfumes, fine chocolate and artisan breads. For luxe designer labels without the crush, Notting Hill (especially where Westbourne Grove meets Ledbury Road) is overflowing with posh boutiques. On the other side of town, Brick Lane (around the Old Truman Brewery) and offshoot Cheshire Street offer a dynamic collection of offbeat clothing and interiors shops.

The sprawl of London encompasses numerous villagey neighbourhoods. If you have the time, Primrose Hill, Islington and Northcote Road in Clapham are all pleasant places to browse.

Shop talk

Most goods are subject to value added tax (VAT) of 17.5 per cent, usually included in the marked price. Books, children's clothes and food are exempt. Some shops operate a scheme allowing visitors from outside the EU to claim back VAT on goods over a certain amount (this varies) – you'll need to obtain a form in-store and have it stamped at customs. Central shops are open late (until 7pm or 8pm) one night a week (Thursday in the West End; Wednesday in Chelsea and Knightsbridge); some department stores are open late most nights.

93 Feet East p27

Nightlife

L ondon nightlife is a pale
imitation of what can be found
elsewhere in the UK – and indeed
the rest of the world. Blatant lie
alert! To be honest, it gets a little
boring waxing lyrical about London
ruling the world. Still, a fact's a fact:
London nightlife rules the world.

Clubbing

In the last year, nu-rave has gone
from a handful of inspirational and
highly creative kids in east London
to something that's a major Day-Glo
influence on the racks at Topshop
and Dorothy Perkins. Nu-rave
parties see skinny-jeaned indie folk
mingle with flamboyantly dressed
fashionistas and surreal cross-
dressers vogueing to pop classics,
filthy electro synths and 'rave'
(which is what they call any pre-1996
dance track). Want some? Bearing in
mind the fact that it's impossible to
overdress or look ridiculous, head
on over to Bar Music Hall (p181).

Illegal parties? We can't get
enough of them, despite many being
shut down by the police before three
records have been played out. Check
the hand-drawn posters at the north
end of Brick Lane and the corner
of Shoreditch High Street and
Commercial Street: they'll have
the crucial contact email addresses.
Myspace is another priceless source
of information for on-the-sly parties.

At the other end of the spectrum,
super-sized clubbing is another
trend. Not to be confused with
superclubs such as Liverpool's
Cream or the Ministry of Sound,
venues like Turnmills and the
Scala hold regular 'festivals in
clubs'. Every room is opened
up and the music policy takes
in just about everything – exactly
like a festival. There's usually a
dressing-up theme, and the chance
of hilarious sideshow encounters
with laughing gas or girls dressed
as housewives.

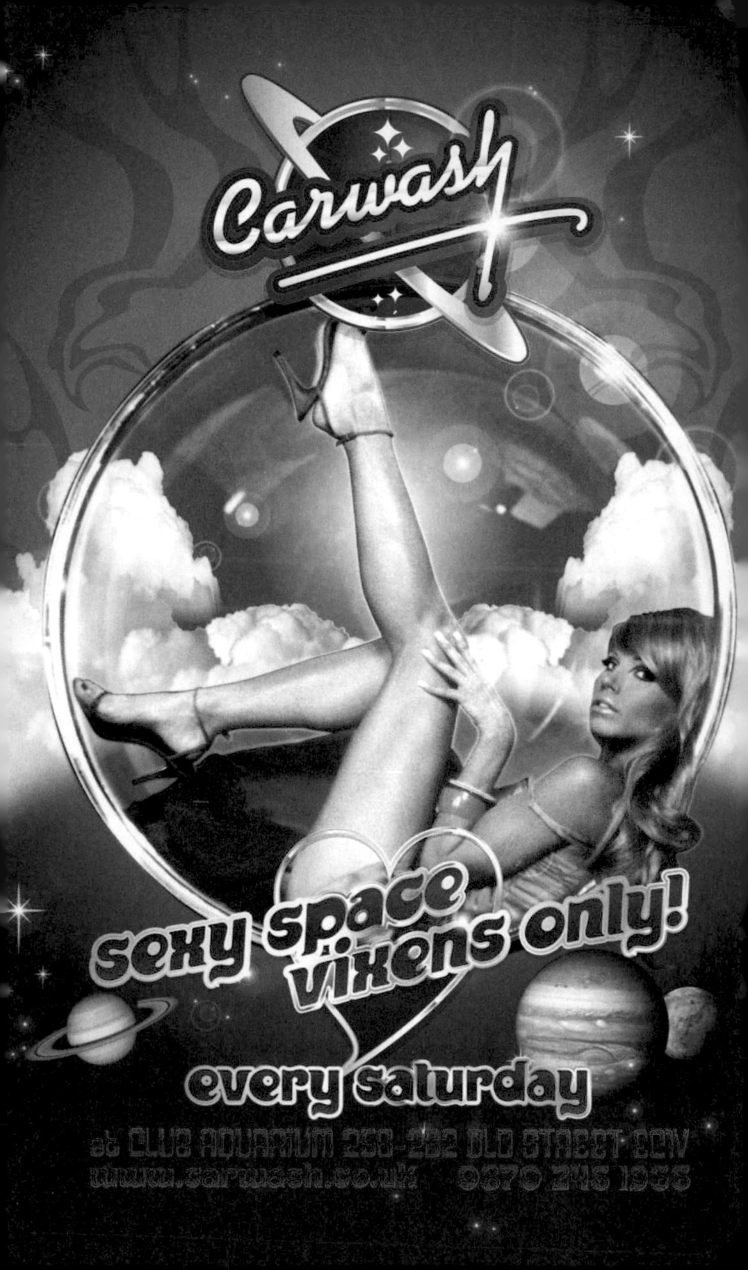
Carwash
sexy space vixens only!
every saturday

Adding a bit of class to proceedings are the new Mayfair members clubs. Not a member? No need to worry: they are being taken over for interesting soirées, for which a couple of quid on the door will get you in for the night. The impeccably battered Hedges & Butler is especially popular with the avant-garde nostalgists.

Shoreditch is still London's hippest area, but recently people have been heading north up Kingsland Road – try Melange, a great new pub where it always feels like a curtains-closed lock-in, even at 2pm. The area had, we thought, reached saturation point, so it's hats off to Favela Chic, who took a struggling corner site and turned it into a unique bar-club-restaurant. Fridays and Saturdays in Shoreditch are very much for those in from the 'burbs; for an authentic experience, it pays to visit Sunday to Thursday. If you do visit for the weekend, most places are free but you should expect one-in, one-out action from 10pm.

Soho has reappeared on the nightlife map with a new bijou space called Punk (p125) that's drawing in the young hyper-fashion kids. The Soho Revue Bar (p126) now hosts a mix of cabaret, burlesque and polysexual nights, while Jaded, London's most famous afterparty, shifted to the End (p133) to cause Sunday morning damage each week.

Finally, King's Cross is slowly cementing its reputation as a clubbing destination, despite still being dodgy right around the clock. The Big Chill House (p172) is a new three-floor venue, right near the station, which has a delicious sun-trap terrace and across-the-board line-ups. EGG, the Key, Canvas and the Cross have kept York Way a destination area.

SHORTLIST

New gig venues
- Fly (p143)
- O_2 Arena and IndigO_2 (p188)

Best indie mash-ups
- Barfly (p172)
- Chalk at Scala (p173)

Best leftfield dance action
- End (p133)
- Fabric (p167)

Best for jazz
- Black Gardenia (p124)
- Ronnie Scott's (p126)

Best small clubs
- Key (p173)
- Plastic People (p183)

New supper clubs
- Pigalle Club (p115)
- Volupté (p167)

Killer line-ups
- Cargo (p182)
- Notting Hill Arts Club (p192)

Best for dancing outside
- Canvas (p172)
- Cross (p172)
- EGG (p172)

Best for bands
- Bardens Boudoir (p181)
- Luminaire (p173)
- Roundhouse (p173)

Best for dressing up-up-up
- Bethnal Green Working Men's Club (p182)
- Café Royal (p124)

Best cabaret/drag queens
- Bistrotheque (p176)
- Hedges & Butler (p115)
- Royal Vauxhall Tavern (p188)
- Soho Revue Bar (p126)

Friendliest faces
- Favela Chic (p182)
- 93 Feet East (p183)
- Turnmills (p167)

DON'T MISS: 2008

Live action

Let's hear it for guitars! London's the best place in the world for live music (even if we say so ourselves), which means there are gigs every night of the week. Sure, you can pay through the nose and get a ticket for one of the major tours sweeping through town, but Wembley Arena could be anywhere, and where's the fun in that? The threatened closure of major mid-sized venues has led to smaller but often more interesting independent venues stepping in: Bardens Boudoir and the Luminaire have adopted the old 1970s New York trick of having bands as well as DJs. Scenesters have also been calling the Old Blue Last and the Hoxton Square Bar & Kitchen home.

Camden is the indie mecca, of course, but it isn't all sticky carpets and grotty glasses. KOKO (p173) is an opulent, balcony-tiered space that keeps Club NME kids happy every Friday; there's a more interesting selection of bands during the week. The Roundhouse is a mixed-use performance space that does London (and its own crucial musical history) proud with theatre, intriguing new collaborations and musicians firmly on the legendary list.

It's not just indie that's getting folk on to dancefloors. We're loving jazz clubs like the Black Gardenia, a new dive with a speakeasy feel, strict vintage dress policy and great bands, and are delighted to see Ronnie Scott's reopened – even if we're less impressed by some of the acts. We're also watching the development of the Dome with interest, especially purpose-built club/gig venue IndigO2.

Gay disco

Soho has gay bars and clubs aplenty, but it's Vauxhall that is now London's gay village. The self-professed beating heart of

Scala p27

that village is the Royal Vauxhall Tavern. Nearly lost to developers, it had been struggling along for years, but new management has invested blood, sweat and tears into bringing it back to full life. A good thing too, as it's been an essential gay venue since World War II. The RVT's strength is cabaret: Duckie has long been the Saturday night slot, but Thursday and Friday are also full of puppet shows, questionable lipsynchers and, of course, drag queens in beards. Fire (p187) is where the hedonistic go to play: boys with their tops off are dancing right through to Monday. Bistrotheque is east London's pride and joy, thanks to the drag-on-acid programming in its tiny cabaret room.

The laughter cure

For sure-fire bust-a-gut laughs, you can't go past the Comedy Store (p124). It's the venue every stand-up wants to play, for good reason.

Well worth seeking out, however, are the new breed of experimental comedy nights. Comedic jugglers and clowns join the stand-ups at nights such as Dr Dimaglio's Secrets, monthly at Euston working men's club St Aloysius, or the Popcorn Club at Holloway's Red Rose. And Grand Theft Impro at the Wheatsheaf (p147) is currently about the best improv night in town.

Supper clubs such as Bonobo Presents and the Flash Monkey's Cabaret Casbah offer a sit-down meal in lovely venues such as Café de Paris (p124) and the Café Royal's Grill Room before unveiling a bill of talent that might include famous comedians, burlesque starlets and hula-hooping spoken worders.

If you're visiting London in late July or August, it's worth bearing in mind the fact that most names head to the Edinburgh Festival, and most comedy venues close or run small bills. October, though, is great for fresh shows.

Making the most of it

Plan your weekend well in advance. Each summer, London hosts a crop of outdoor parties and festivals that you'd kick yourself if you missed. Over Christmas, New Year's Eve and the half-dozen bank holidays, things really kick off – in a good way. Check www.timeout.com/london to coordinate your visit.

Advance planning isn't, however, essential: in London there is always something going on, no matter the day, no matter the hour. Even long-in-the-tooth Londoners fall into brand new happenings just by taking the wrong street, and the best way to get a taste of 'real London' is to go with the flow.

Either way, be sure to get to grips with the transport system. The tube stops running at midnight (1am at weekends). Black cabs are pricey and hard to find at night, but safe. There are also licensed

minicabs; some bigger nightclubs run their own service, or you can summon one by phone. Beware illegal minicab touts. Far better to check out the Night Bus system before you head out (try the handy Journey Planner at www.tfl.gov.uk). A couple of minutes spent working out which Night Bus gets you home before you go out can save hours of blurry-visioned confusion later on. For more on London's transport options, see p211.

In addition to *Time Out* magazine and its website, www.dontstayin.com is excellent for on-the-ground clubbing news, and record shops are an invaluable source of flyers, tickets and advice. City 16 (1 Cheshire Street, 7613 5604), just off Brick Lane, is very friendly. To see what Londoners wore out clubbing last night, check www.dirtydirtydancing.com – Alistair Allan uploads his photographs every weekend.

And one last thing: smoking is to be banned in all enclosed public places (including clubs and gigs) from July 2007.

Roundhouse p27

Royal Festival Hall

WHAT'S BEST
Arts & Leisure

In spring 2007 the Arts Council announced grant cuts of £29 million in response to the government redirecting £112.5 million from the national lottery to preparations for the 2012 Olympics. It's no surprise, then, that new sports venues have been big news this year: headline openings of the blandly corporate Wembley Stadium (p174) and of Arsenal Football Club's much more dramatic Emirates Stadium, a new South Stand at Twickenham rugby stadium (p185), bigger seats at Wimbledon (p186)… even the Dome (now open as the O_2 Arena) promises boxing and NBA games alongside the stadium gigs.

Don't be kidded, though: this is no simple tale of sport flourishing at the expense of the arts. The O_2 and Wembley, for all that their Olympic roles are laid out, have been under development since long before the 2012 bid, and London's most significant reopening for visitors is all about the arts: the hugely exciting refurbishment of the various institutions that make up the Southbank Centre arts complex (p71) should have been completed in summer 2007. The acoustic re-engineering of its Royal Festival Hall, which received 80 per cent of the total £111 million budget, is keenly anticipated, although improvements to the riverside aspect and new restaurants may be of more frequent interest to the South Bank's many casual visitors.

Film

The first major part of the
Southbank Centre makeover to
reach completion was the National
Film Theatre, now rebranded the
BFI (British Film Institute)
Southbank. Visitors might be
confused as to what exactly a
'BFI Southbank' is – it's a three-
screen repertory cinema with café,
bookshop and the Mediatheque,
a room containing 14 viewing
stations where film and television
from the BFI archive can be seen.
Whatever the name, BFI Southbank
continues to offer the most
ambitious programming of
any cinema in London, placing
particular emphasis on new foreign
films and retrospective studies of
the work of individual directors.
It's also an important venue in the
annual London Film Festival (p36),
which is Britain's largest public
film event, screening more than
300 movies from 60 countries.

The cinemas around Leicester
Square continue to dominate the
blockbuster premières, but fans
of art cinema are increasingly well
catered for. Screening rooms are
springing up in the most unlikely
places. The Roxy Bar & Screen
offers a mix of free screenings of
classic movies and VJ nights (DJs
mixing visuals alongside their
records), while the Whitechapel
Art Gallery (p176) has opened the
Laboratory annexe specially to
show 'lens-based' artworks during
the main gallery's closure.

Outdoor screenings are an
established part of summer: check
www.timeout.com for the best of
them – the Somerset House (p159)
programme is always worth a look.

Classical music & opera

Apart from the acoustic refit of the
Royal Festival Hall, the biggest
news in classical music is John

SHORTLIST

Best new venues
- Arsenal Football Club's Emirates Stadium (p173)
- O_2 Arena (p188)
- Shunt Vaults (p71)

Best revamp
- Southbank Centre's Royal Festival Hall (p71)
- Young Vic (p71)

Biggest theatrical event
- Lord of the Rings (p34)
- Sam Mendes returns to the Old Vic (box p63)
- Ralph Fiennes and Juliette Binoche at the National Theatre (box p63)

New filmhouses
- BFI Southbank (p69)
- Roxy Bar & Screen (p71)

Best arthouse cinemas
- Curzon Soho (p126)
- Institute of Contemporary Arts (p80)

Best auditoriums
- Cadogan Hall (p94)
- Coliseum (p134)
- Lilian Baylis Theatre at Sadler's Wells (p173)

Best bargains
- Standby tickets at the Barbican (p157)
- Standing tickets at the Coliseum (p134)
- Standing tickets at the Proms (p43)

Best off-West End theatres
- Battersea Arts Centre (p188)
- Donmar Warehouse (p135)

Most innovative work
- London Sinfonietta at the Southbank Centre (p71)
- Royal Court Theatre (p94)
- Spring Loaded at the Place (p41)

Shunt p34

Tusa's departure in August 2007 from the Barbican arts centre, having steered it safely through its 25th anniversary celebrations. His successor as managing director is Nicholas Kenyon, who had been in charge of BBC live events – notably the annual Proms festival of classical music. In January 2007 the Barbican's resident London Symphony Orchestra began its ambitious programme, under principal conductor Valery Gergiev, of a dozen programmes each year – watch out for his version of Mahler's 6th in November.

There have been changes at the troubled English National Opera too, where Edward Gardner began his tenure in May 2007 hoping to inaugurate a period of stability after key resignations followed major refurbishments at the Coliseum. Along with artistic director John Berry, Gardner needs to consolidate the ENO's reputation for celebrating English opera (especially Britten) and promoting contemporary work – with all works performed in English, a visit to the ENO can be a great introduction to opera. Things are more traditional but still quietly excellent at the Royal Opera House (p135), where the massively expensive renovations of 2000 are holding up very well.

The city is also blessed with exemplary venues on a much more intimate scale. Cadogan Hall (p94), Wigmore Hall (p103) and LSO St Luke's (p183) are the pick of the bunch, but a number of London's ancient churches host fine concerts, some of them for free: St Martin-in-the-Fields (p74) continues to host recitals as it makes steady progress towards completing renovations, while the refurbished St George's Bloomsbury (p140), one of Hawksmoor's architectural gems, is now providing a fine setting for classical music.

Theatre & dance

Despite the imminent cuts, the city's theatrical scene remains vital. Much of the excitement is being generated on the South Bank, with a refurbished Young Vic already winning plaudits, and Nicholas Hytner securing headline coverage for the National Theatre (p71) with such splashy items as Ralph Fiennes' appearance as Oedipus and a dance/theatre collaboration between Juliette Binoche and homegrown star choreographer Akram Khan. The Old Vic (p71) isn't about to be overshadowed – it secured the services of stellar director Sam Mendes, returning to Britain for the first time in five years.

Dominic Cooke's regime at the Royal Court Theatre (p94), which has spent five decades as Britain's leading venue for new playwriting, has started with promise, offering the kind hard-hitting political pieces that you'd hope for from the UK's home of theatrical radicalism. We're also expecting more politically engaged work from the Soho Theatre (p127), with Lisa Goldman having been appointed the new artistic director in early 2007. Donmar Warehouse continues to draw in big screen stars, with a forthcoming Shakespeare due to feature Ewan MacGregor

In the commercial West End, it's hard to see beyond Kevin Wallace's massive production of the stage adaptation of Tolkien's *The Lord of the Rings*, which should have been running for a few months at the Theatre Royal Drury Lane (p135) by the time you read this. Previews were mixed, but a spectacle is guaranteed.

The last year has also seen a number of wonderfully offbeat shows in unusual urban venues – a trend we hope will flourish. Keep an eye on Punchdrunk's website (www.punchdrunk.org.uk) for any upcoming site-specific works (although their next production is in Battersea Arts Centre's regular theatre), and check what's on at Shunt – usually something odd in the field of theatre, spoken word, electronica or cabaret.

Allen Robertson, *Time Out*'s dance critic, has argued that 'contemporary dance is the most exciting cultural endeavour in London', citing the unique combination of different dance traditions and of cultures as disparate as Bangladesh and Israel. It helps that there are venues to suit all scales of performance, from the vast Royal Opera House through Sadler's Wells (p173) to the intimate Place (p143). You might just catch Hofesh Shechter's 'Uprising/In Your Rooms' piece in its last peformance at Sadler's Wells on 28-29 September; the show has been progressively adapted for the Place, the Southbank Centre's Queen Elizabeth Hall and now for Sadler's Wells.

London is also able to attract the best international dance companies due to the commitment of Dance Umbrella, whose annual autumn festival draws large audiences for often rather challenging work. The new Spring Loaded festival provides an unbeatable showcase for the city's most promising young choreographers.

What's on

We've included long-running musicals we think are likely to survive into 2009. However, a new crop will inevitably open through the year, along with seasons at individual venues. *Time Out* magazine and www.time out.com have the most informed and up-to-date listings.

Calendar

London International Mime Festival p39

The following is our selection of the best London events that had been announced as this guide went to press. To stay completely current with new announcements, buy a copy of *Time Out* magazine or check timeout.com/london; always confirm dates before making your travel plans.

Dates of public holidays are picked out in **bold**.

September 2007

2 **Regent Street Festival**
www.regentstreetonline.com

6 **Great River Race**
Thames, Richmond to Greenwich
www.greatriverrace.co.uk

9 **Brick Lane Festival**
www.bricklanefestival.com

15-16 **Mayor's Thames Festival**
Westminster & Tower Bridges
www.thamesfestival.org

15-16 **Open House London**
Various locations
www.openhouselondon.org
Free access to over 600 buildings.

15 Sept-13 Jan 2008
The Art of Lee Miller
Victoria & Albert, p86

15 Sept-30 Mar 2008
Henry Moore at Kew Gardens
Royal Botanic Gardens, p185

22 **Great Gorilla Run**
Mincing Lane, the City
www.gorillas.org/greatgorillarun
Fund-raising 7km run, in gorilla suits.

26 Sept-7 Oct **Raindance**
Various central London venues
www.raindance.co.uk
Britain's largest indie film festival.

October 2007

Ongoing The Art of Lee Miller (see Sept); Henry Moore at Kew Gardens (see Sept); Raindance Festival (see Sept)

7 **Pearly Kings & Queens Harvest Festival**
St Martin-in-the-Fields, p74
www.pearlysociety.co.uk
A 3pm service for the professional Cockneys, in traditional outfits.

11-14 **Frieze Art Fair**
Regent's Park
www.friezeartfair.com

17 Oct-1 Nov **London Film Festival**
National Film Theatre (p69) & other venues
www.lff.org.uk

27 Oct-Apr 2008 **Shell Wildlife Photographer of the Year**
Natural History Museum, p83

November 2007

Ongoing The Art of Lee Miller (see Sept); Henry Moore at Kew Gardens (see Sept); London Film Festival (see Oct); Shell Wildlife Photographer of the Year (see Oct)

2-4 **London to Brighton Veteran Car Run**
From Serpentine Road, Hyde Park
www.lbvcr.com

Bankside Frost Fair p44

5 **Bonfire Night**

10 **Lord Mayor's Show**
Various streets in the City
www.lordmayorsshow.org
A grand inauguration procession for the City's new Lord Mayor.

11 **Remembrance Sunday Ceremony**
Cenotaph, Whitehall

16-21 **London Jazz Festival**
Various locations
www.serious.org.uk

mid-late Nov **State Opening of Parliament**
House of Lords, Westminster
www.parliament.uk
Limited public access, but you can watch the Queen arrive by coach.

28 **Diwali**
Trafalgar Square
www.london.gov.uk
The Festival of Light is celebrated by Hindu, Jain and Sikh communities.

Nov-Dec **Christmas Tree & Lights**
Covent Garden, Regent Street & Trafalgar Square
www.london.gov.uk/www.covent gardenmarket.co.uk/www.regent streetonline.com

December 2007

Ongoing The Art of Lee Miller (see Sept); Henry Moore at Kew Gardens (see Sept); Shell Wildlife Photographer of the Year (see Oct); Christmas Tree & Lights (see Nov).

1 **VIP Day**
Oxford, Regent & Bond Streets
London's major shopping areas pedestrianised for the day, with promotions and exhibits.

12-21 **Spitalfields Festival**
Various locations
www.spitalfieldsfestival.org.uk
Classical music, walks and talks.

14-16 **Bankside Frost Fair**
Tate Modern & Shakespeare's Globe
visitsouthwark.com/frostfair

25 **Christmas Day**

Have a happy New Year

Simone Baird, editor of *Time Out*'s Social Club, explains how to get the most out of the festivities.

The trick with New Year is to make like a local – think beyond it. It's no mere eight-hour event like most clubbing nights on the calendar: for Londoners, it goes on for days.

On New Year's Eve, first line your stomach, then make for a reliable Soho boozer: maybe the Endurance (90 Berwick Street) or the Coach & Horses (29 Greek Street). The best boozers don't usually to stay open for midnight, so get a couple of quick boozes in before popping into the best off-licence ever, Planet of the Grapes (p133), to pick up a bottle of something stronger. Unlike other countries, you're allowed to drink in the street in England. A good thing – it's going to be cold and you'll need the fortification as you make your way back through the buzzing streets to the Thames.

The area along the Embankment gets crammed, but you'll want to be in amongst it for the fireworks as Big Ben chimes. Once the hugging and salutations are done, head back to your hotel – it's time for a few hours' kip. The tube

stays open until 4am and all public transport is free on New Year's Eve, so getting home should be easy.

It's now that the fun starts: fed up with paying inflated prices on New Year's Eve, Londoners have taken to going on New Year's Day like nu-ravers have taken to silly eyewear. The parties kick off from 5am and attract a cooler crowd who enjoy paying a third of the price for exactly the same DJs as were playing at midnight. Try the End (p133) and AKA (p129) – their Circo Loco all-dayer is legendary – or go east: the T Bar (p183) starts early and doesn't tend to stop.

If holding off until New Year's Day doesn't float your boat, try getting on one. You'll need tickets in advance, but whether it's feather boas and funky house or twisted electro you're after, there's an 'ahoy there, sailor' hat with your name on it. All of the boats make for the London Eye as Big Ben chimes in the New Year, so you'll be guaranteed a spectacular view of the fireworks.

Osatsuma

MODERN JAPANESE DINING

56 Wardour Street, London, W1 020 7437 8338
www.osatsuma.com
⊖ PICCADILLY CIRCUS LEICESTER SQUARE
Open M-T 12-11 W-T 12-11.30 F-S 12-12 Sun 12-10.30

Camden Crawl p41

26 Boxing Day

31 New Year's Eve Celebrations
Trafalgar Square
See box p37.

January 2008

Ongoing The Art of Lee Miller
(see Sept); Henry Moore at Kew
Gardens (see Sept); Shell Wildlife
Photographer of the Year (see Oct)

1 New Year's Day

**12-27 London International
Mime Festival**
Various locations
www.mimefest.co.uk

16-20 London Art Fair
Business Design Centre, Islington
www.londonartfair.co.uk

February 2008

Ongoing Henry Moore at Kew
Gardens (see Sept); Shell
Wildlife Photographer of the
Year (see Oct)

**5 Great Spitalfields
Pancake Race**
Dray Walk, Brick Lane
7375 0441/www.alternativearts.co.uk
Charity race, flipping pancakes from
frying pans as they go.

7 Chinese New Year Festival
Chinatown, Leicester Square
& Trafalgar Square
www.chinatownchinese.co.uk
The largest celebration of Chinese New
Year outside China.

mid Feb **Children's Literature
Festival**
Southbank Centre
www.southbankcentre.co.uk

March 2008

Ongoing Henry Moore at
Kew Gardens (see Sept);
Shell Wildlife Photographer
of the Year (see Oct)

**6-14 Human Rights Watch
International Film Festival**
Various locations
www.hrw.org/iff

16 (tbc) **St Patrick's
Day Festival**
Various locations
www.london.gov.uk
Irish music and dancing, arts and crafts.

21 Good Friday

24 Easter Monday

late Mar-early Apr **London
Lesbian & Gay Film Festival**
National Film Theatre, p69
www.llgff.org.uk

April 2008

Ongoing Shell Wildlife Photographer of the Year (see Oct); London Lesbian & Gay Film Festival (see Mar)

6 Olympic Torch Relay
www.london2012.org
The flame passes through the capital on its way to the 2008 Olympic Games in Beijing.

11-17 (tbc) La Linea
Various venues
www.imaginamultimedia.com/comono
Latin American music festival.

13 London Marathon
Greenwich Park to the Mall
www.london-marathon.co.uk

mid May-mid Apr **Spring Loaded**
The Place, p143
7121 1100/www.theplace.org.uk
Major dance festival showcasing nearly 30 choreographers over 21 nights.

14-16 London Book Fair
Southbank Centre & Earl's Court
www.londonbookfair.co.uk
Not just for booktrade types, some events are now open to all.

17-18 (tbc) Camden Crawl
Various venues in Camden
www.thecamdencrawl.com
A showcase of new musical talent, mostly of the indie guitar variety.

17-24 East End Film Festival
Various locations
www.eastendfilmfestival.com

19 Oxford & Cambridge Boat Race
On the Thames, Putney to Mortlake
www.theboatrace.org

May 2008

Ongoing Spring Loaded (see Apr).

5 Early May Bank Holiday

mid May-early June **Cockpit Arts**
Cockpit Yard, Bloomsbury, & Deptford Centre, Deptford
7419 1959/8692 4463/
www.cockpitarts.com
Series of open weekends at designer-makers' studios.

11 May Fayre & Puppet Festival
St Paul's Church Garden, Covent Garden
www.punchandjudy.com

20-24 Chelsea Flower Show
Royal Hospital grounds, Chelsea
www.rhs.org.uk

24 May-Sept **Kew Summer Festival**
Royal Botanic Gardens
www.kew.org

26 Spring Bank Holiday

June 2008

Ongoing Cockpit Arts (see May); Kew Summer Festival (see May)

2-20 Spitalfields Festival
See above Dec 2007.

5 Pride London
Oxford Street to Victoria Embankment
www.pridelondon.org
Huge gay and lesbian parade, culmination of a week of cultural events.

5-6 (tbc) Beating Retreat
Horse Guards Parade, Whitehall
www.army.mod.uk/ceremonialand
heritage/index.htm
An evening of Cavalry drumming.

6 June-17 July Watch This Space
Outside National Theatre, South Bank
7452 3400/www.nationaltheatre.org.uk
A lively free festival of music, street theatre and films taking place outside the National Theatre.

7-8 Open Garden Squares Weekend
Various locations
www.opensquares.org
Private squares opened to the public.

7-8 (tbc) Homefires IV
Conway Hall, Bloomsbury
7242 8032/www.eatyourownears.com
Alt-folk music festival.

June **Hampton Court Palace Festival**
www.hamptoncourtfestival.com
Big-name concert series, with mostly classical pops and hoary rockers appearing over three weeks.

Festival of architecture

Architecture is too important to be left to architects – that's the guiding philosophy behind the **London Biennale Festival of Architecture** (opposite), which in 2008 brings a month's worth of architecture-themed events, installations, guided walks and cycle tours to an increasingly receptive, design-savvy London public. Ever since the Millennium celebrations produced a string of popular successes – Tate Modern, the London Eye, the Great Court at the British Museum – architecture's ability to improve the everyday experience of the city has become more obvious; more recently the Gherkin proved that even commercial office developments could be beautiful and popular.

The current focus is on transport, long the capital's weak spot: the Channel Tunnel rail link is catalyst for the transformation of King's Cross, while Lord Rogers' soaring Terminal 5 is a revelation to a travelling public that increasingly regards airports as a hell to be endured. With the 2012 Olympics just over the horizon, the Biennale feeds off this new popular design consciousness. Sometimes quirky and attention-seeking (the Millennium Bridge, *pictured*, has featured in a variety of stunts), the Biennale is never less than thought-provoking, lively and fun.

Spurred by the success of the 2006 event – which attracted 75,000 visitors – the organisers are going for broke this time, with five hubs across central London, from South Kensington in the west to Canary Wharf in the east, including the original Clerkenwell hub alongside new ones in Covent Garden and on the South Bank.

Under the banner FRESH! the 2008 Biennale investigates and celebrates fresh ideas and talent, new communities and green themes. The associated LAB student festival is working with schools to create site-specific installations, and an international element should see embassies display work of young architects from their countries. While the hugely popular Open House (p35) celebrates the buildings that make London what is, the Biennale is all about what London could become.
■ www.londonbiennale.org.uk

12-15 (tbc) **O₂ Wireless Festival**
Hyde Park
www.o2wirelessfestival.co.uk
Major rock bands and dance acts.

14 Trooping the Colour
Horse Guards Parade, St James's
www.trooping-the-colour.co.uk
The Queen's official birthday parade.

mid June **Architecture Week**
Various locations
www.architectureweek.co.uk

20 June-20 July **London Biennale Festival of Architecture**
Various locations
www.londonbiennale.org.uk
See box opposite.

26 June-21 Sept **The Courtauld Cézannes**
Courtauld Gallery at Somerset House, p159

June-July **Jazz Plus**
Victoria Embankment Gardens, Westminster
7375 0441/www.alternativearts.co.uk
Free lunchtime concerts by contemporary jazz musicians.

June-Aug **Opera Holland Park**
www.operahollandpark.com

June-Aug **Coin Street Festival**
Bernie Spain Gardens, South Bank
www.coinstreet.org

late June **Meltdown**
Southbank Centre, p71
www.southbank.co.uk
A fortnight of contemporary music and culture, curated each year by a different musician – Jarvis Cocker in 2007.

23 June-6 July **Wimbledon Lawn Tennis Championships**
www.wimbledon.org

23 June-10 July **City of London Festival**
Various locations around the City
www.colf.org
A themed festival of mostly free music and art events.

July 2008

Ongoing Kew Summer Festival (see May); Watch This Space (see June); London Biennale Festival of Architecture (see June); The Courtauld Cézannes (see June); Jazz Plus (see June); Opera Holland Park (see June); Coin Street Festival (see June); Wimbledon Lawn Tennis Championships (see June); City of London Festival (see June)

mid July-mid Sept **Marble Hill House Concerts**

July **Greenwich & Docklands International Festival**
www.festival.org

July **The Chap Olympics**
Bedford Square, Bloomsbury
Events such as the Hop, Skip and G&T and the Pipe Smokers' Relay are fiercely contested every Thursday in July.

12-21 **Somerset House Summer Series**
Somerset House, p159
www.somerset-house.org.uk/music
A series of outdoor concerts.

20 (tbc) **Rise**
Finsbury Park
Anti-racist music festival.

26 July-1 Aug **Rushes Soho Shorts Festival**
Various venues in Soho
www.sohoshorts.com
Series of free screenings of short films and videos.

late July **World London Festival**
Southbank Centre, p71
www.southbank.co.uk
Fortnight of global sounds.

July-Aug **Dance Al Fresco**
Regent's Park
www.dancealfresco.org

mid July-mid Sept **BBC Sir Henry Wood Promenade Concerts**
Royal Albert Hall (p91)
& other venues
www.bbc.co.uk/proms

August 2008

Ongoing Kew Summer Festival (see May); The Courtauld Cézannes (see June); Opera Holland Park (see June); Coin Street Festival (see June); Marble

Hill House concerts (see July);
Rushes Soho Shorts Festival (see
July); Dance Al Fresco (see July);
BBC Sir Henry Wood Promenade
Concerts (see July)

2-3 (tbc) Innocent Summer Fête
Regent's Park
www.innocentvillagefete.com
Live music and posh food stalls.

7-26 (tbc) Portobello Film Festival
www.portobellofilmfestival.com

12 Time Out's 40th Birthday
www.timeout.com
A month of superb cultural activities,
focused around the 40th birthday of
London's best listings magazine.

24-25 Notting Hill Carnival
www.lnhc.org.uk
Europe's biggest street party.

25 Summer Bank Holiday

September 2008

Ongoing Kew Summer Festival
(see May); The Courtauld
Cézannes (see June); Marble
Hill House concerts (see July);
The Proms (see July)

7 Regent Street Festival
See above Sept 2007.

early Sept Tour of Britain
See above Sept 2007.

13 Great River Race
See above Sept 2007.

14 Brick Lane Festival
See above Sept 2007.

20-21 Mayor's Thames Festival
See above Sept 2007.

20-21 Open House London
See above Sept 2007.

24 Sept-5 Oct Raindance
See above Sept 2007.

27 (tbc) Great Gorilla Run
See above Sept 2007.

October 2008

**5 Pearly Kings & Queens
Harvest Festival**
See above Oct 2007.

16-19 Frieze Art Fair
See above Oct 2007.

**mid Oct-early Nov
London Film Festival**
See above Oct 2007.

late Oct Diwali
See above Nov 2007.

**from late Oct Shell Wildlife
Photographer of the Year**
See above Oct 2007.

November 2008

Ongoing London Film Festival (see
Oct); Shell Wildlife Photographer of
the Year (see Oct)

5 Bonfire Night

**7-9 (tbc) London to Brighton
Veteran Car Run**
See above Nov 2007.

8 Lord Mayor's Show
See above Nov 2007.

**9 Remembrance Sunday
Ceremony**
See above Nov 2007.

14-23 London Jazz Festival
See above Nov 2007.

**mid-late Nov State Opening
of Parliament**
See above Nov 2007.

Nov-Dec Christmas Tree & Lights
See above Nov 2007.

December 2008

Ongoing Shell Wildlife Photographer
of the Year (see Oct); Christmas
Tree & Lights (see Nov).

6 VIP Day
See above Dec 2007.

10-19 Spitalfields Festival
See above Dec 2007.

12-14 Bankside Frost Fair
See above Dec 2007.

25 Christmas Day

26 Boxing Day

31 New Year's Eve Celebrations
See above Dec 2007.

Itineraries

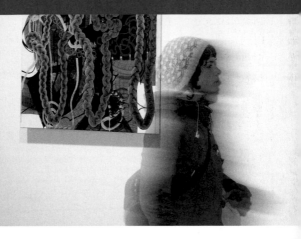

St Paul's

The Wren Route

St Paul's Cathedral is one City landmark with staying power: it's 300 years since Sir Christopher Wren's masterpiece was completed as the centrepiece of the post-Great Fire rebuilding of London. Like some 17th-century Richard Rogers or Norman Foster, Wren and his associates peppered the skyline with towers, and though many have disappeared through demolition or war, many can still be found.

Choose an appropriate weekday – most of the churches we're going to nose into are closed at weekends and, irritatingly, you'll have to make a hard decision between St Mary Aldermary (open Mon, Wed, Thur) and St Mary Abchurch (usually only open Tue) – and expect to start by 9am. We aren't going to hang around today.

We begin at unlovely Blackfriars tube – don't fret, things soon get better. Head uphill, away from the

river, on the left-hand side of New Bridge Street. At the Ludgate Circus crossroads look right up Ludgate Hill. You get a great impression of what St Paul's Cathedral must have looked like when it was built, rising above the huddle of rooftops and the spires of the lesser Wren churches – the black spire to the left of the dome belongs to one of them, **St Martin Ludgate**.

Hidden behind you is **St Bride's** (7427 0133, www.stbrides.com). Its steeple is the tallest of any Wren church and was supposedly the model for the tiered wedding cake. Head up Fleet Street and take the second left for the best front-on view. The church burnt out during the Blitz, so the interior is a reconstruction. But it's worth visiting the crypt to see the exhibition on the church's history – there's a facsimile of the *Evening*

News from 30 December 1940, with a graphic description of the huge devastation wreaked by one wartime raid.

Retrace your steps to Ludgate Circus and climb Ludgate Hill, braving the crowds on the cathedral steps. Pay a £9.50 fee and enter **St Paul's** (p152). What immediately impresses you is the great length of the cathedral – it may be baroque in style, but it is traditional in plan, a result of the compromises Wren had to make to gain approval for his design. Spend a couple of hours here: that should be sufficient to climb to the Whispering Gallery and, above it, the Stone Gallery for views across London. You should also visit the crypt: Wren's tomb is in the south aisle at the east end.

Emerging from the cathedral, turn right and pass through **Temple Bar**, another Wren creation. It originally stood at the western end of Fleet Street to mark the boundary between the City of London and Westminster, but was removed by the Victorians because it impeded traffic. It stood for many years on a country estate in Hertfordshire, returning in 2004 to serve as the entrance to the new Paternoster Square.

Grab a takeaway coffee from any of the outlets and cross the square, emerging on Newgate Street. Opposite is **Christ Church**, which was almost destroyed during World War II. The ruined nave is now a sunny rose garden; grab a seat and sip your coffee. The surviving tower is a spectacular private home, its ten storeys linked by lift.

Head east along Angel Street, across Aldersgate Street, to Gresham Street, where Wren churches are thick on the ground. First up is **St Anne & St Agnes**, with a leafy churchyard and regular classical recitals. Further along Gresham Street, catch a

glimpse of the tower of **St Alban, Wood Street**, like Christ Church now a private house. Continue past **St Lawrence Jewry** – the church of the Corporation of London – to Moorgate, crossing into Lothbury to enter **St Margaret Lothbury** (7606 8330, www.stml.org.uk). This has one of the loveliest interiors of any Wren church, with an impressive wood screen by the man himself.

Retrace your steps to Moorgate and turn left down Prince's Street to enter Bank tube. Take the Mansion House exit, following the path around to **St Stephen Walbrook** (39 Walbrook, 7606 3998, www.ststephenwalbrook.net), the most grandiose Wren church, a mass of creamy stone with a soaring dome, fabulously bulbous pulpit and a slightly incongruous modern altar by Henry Moore.

Turn left out of St Stephen Walbrook, left again into Cannon Street, passing Cannon Street station before ducking left into Abchurch Lane. **St Mary Abchurch** (7626 0306) is a real gem, with a shallow, painted dome and a beautiful carved reredos by Grinling Gibbons, shattered into 2,000 pieces by a wartime bomb but painstakingly pieced back together.

Return to Cannon Street, keeping on east until you reach the top end of London Bridge. Cross the street using the underpass, turning left off King William Street into Monument Street. The **Monument** (p152) is the world's tallest isolated stone column, built to commemorate the Great Fire. It was designed by Wren and his associate Robert Hooke. Pay the £2 entry fee and climb the 311 steps to enjoy some of the greatest views over the City and the Thames.

By now it's time for a late lunch, so take the second left off Monument Street into Pudding Lane, the seat of the Great Fire, where the appropriately named Fuego (1A Pudding Lane, 7929 3366, www.fuego.co.uk) serves tapas every weekday in smoke black and flame red surroundings. Fuel up quickly on albóndigas before striding back west along the right-hand side of Cannon Street to Bow Lane, which is topped and tailed by two churches from Wren's office: at the southern end, **St Mary Aldermary** (7248 4906, www.stmaryaldermary.co.uk) is obscure but beautiful, with flamboyant gothic vaulting; at the northern end, **St Mary-le-Bow** is famous for its bells, but it's a post-war reconstruction inside and frankly rather dull.

Retrace your steps down Bow Lane, this time turning right into Queen Victoria Street to reach Peter's Hill and the Millennium Bridge. Cross the river, turning left off the bridge for Shakespeare's Globe. Overshadowed by the theatre at **49 Bankside** is the house commonly – but incorrectly – supposed to be the one from which

Wren watched St Paul's rise across the river. Still, it's a good yarn, and the views of the cathedral are superb. Buy an ice-cream from one of the vans that congregate here; munch it while waiting for the Riverbus at Bankside Pier.

Take the Thames Clipper east to Masthouse Pier, from where it's a ten-minute walk along the river path to Island Gardens. Stock up on fluids from the kiosk, soak up the views of the **Old Royal Naval College** (8269 4747, www.oldroyal navalcollege.org.uk) then cross under the river by the Greenwich Foot Tunnel. Emerging from the tunnel, pass the *Cutty Sark* and turn left into College Approach. The College is straight ahead. It's one of the most extensive groups of baroque public buildings in England, surviving more or less as Wren planned it. Don't miss the Painted Hall, built to Wren's designs between 1696 and 1704; the name is apt, since most of the rich decoration is trompe l'oeil.

Continue through the college to the eastern gate, turn right into Park Row and enter Greenwich Park. Crowning the hilltop is the Royal Observatory (p186), where crowds wait their turn to stand astride the Prime Meridian Line. Push past to enter **Flamsteed's house**, the only bit of the complex designed by Wren. Built for the first Astronomer Royal, it's a dainty contrast to the Royal Naval College, the living quarters cosily domestic and only the Octagon room at the top hinting at Wren's baroque flair. You emerge through the 'Time & Greenwich' gallery. It has been a long day, and it's now time for a drink. Head back down the Avenue (the left side of the hill) to St Mary's Gate. Just beyond it on King William Walk is Greenwich Park Bar & Grill (no.1, 8853 7860, www.thegreenwichpark.com).

Monument p47

Royal Opera House p50

Stage to Screen

A fine morning is best for this wander from the theatrical West End to London's new cinema complex, and one bit of advance planning is required: pick up the phone and dial 7304 4000. This puts you through to the cultured voice of the Royal Opera House box office – you're going to book a tour backstage (£9, £7-£8 reductions), for the 10.30am timeslot. If you don't want to hold, you can book online (click 'Book tickets', followed by 'Backstage tours'), but if you're patient and stick with the phone, you'll be able to confirm the timetable and format of the tour (which changes daily) with a real person. Popular slots (a Saturday, say) can require a week's notice, but the tickets are sold the night before or even on the day, so long as there's still space.

Now we're set. Start at Leicester Square tube, at about 9.30am to avoid the commuters. Dive straight for Exit 1 (Charing Cross Road south and the National Gallery), head upstairs and turn left down the main road. Ignore St Martin's Court and instead take the next left, pedestrian Cecil Court, flanked by a chain Italian and a suit shop. At the far end, on the right, is **David Drummond at Pleasures of Past Times** (no.11, 7836 1142). This perfectly eccentric shop has crusty advice to mobile phone users stuck to the window and old playbills, books and theatre programmes within. Switch off your phone and have a quick riffle through the Victoriana.

At the end of Cecil Court, turn right past **Freed of London** (94 St Martin's Lane, 7240 0432, www.freedoflondon.com), supplier of shoes to the Royal Ballet. Further down St Martin's Lane you can see the bauble atop the Coliseum (p134), home to the English National Opera (ENO), and beyond it St Martin-in-the-Fields church (p74). On another day we might wander down that way for the National Portrait Gallery (p73) and its pictures of Shakespeare and Ian McKellen, but today just cross the road to May's Court and look back. Behind you is the late Victorian red-on-white façade of the **Duke of York's Theatre**; back in 1893, this was the first place in England to stage Ibsen's *The Master Builder*.

At the far end of May's Court, to the right, you might catch vans loading scenery from the Coliseum's back door or hear the warm-up warblings of a soprano, but turn left up Bedfordbury as far as the bookshop, then right. The other side of the crossroads you'll see a Paul bakery (29 Bedford Street, 7836 3304). Get a lunchtime snack – something light that you can stow in your bag, since later on we're going to be a little naughty.

Turn left down the hill out of the bakery and the first opening on your left is Inigo Court. At the end is a delicious cemetery garden in front of a rather plain red-brick church. Designed by the master architect Inigo Jones to be 'the handsomest barn in England' (his patron didn't want to spend much money on it), this is the Actors' Church, **St Paul's Covent Garden** (7836 5221, www.actorschurch.org). The interior is an airy rectangle, exactly half as wide as it is long. Gorgeous though it is, it's plaques we came for. Celebrity-hunters pay homage at memorials to Charlie Chaplin, Vivien Leigh and Noël Coward, but we really love the oddities: not just Boris Karloff, but Pantopuck the Puppetman

and Edna Best 'The Constant Nymph'. Morning prayers begin at 8.30am, so you should be fine to nose around by now.

From the front door, follow the path round the church to the left, past a fountain that turns into a camp open clam shell, poised as if for Botticelli's Venus to emerge. Head through the gate into **Covent Garden piazza**. You're too early for the buskers, but the grand portico is where George Bernard Shaw begins *Pygmalion*. Cut through the market and you come out with London's Transport Museum (p129) on your right. Go left, past an old-fashioned merry-go-round, behind which is the entrance to the **Royal Opera House** (p135). If all has gone to plan, your guide should be waiting at the cloakroom by the ticket desks. The tours, which last roughly 90 minutes, often include a real 'stolen moment' opportunity to watch the ballerinas in rehearsal.

Leave by the Bow Street exit and turn right. The Theatre Museum, at the junction, ceased operations in January 2007, so do a chicane off to the left to the **Theatre Royal Drury Lane** (p135). The oddly shaped, blocky theatre, which fronts on to Catherine Street, is very imposing, and has a rambunctious history, including assassination attempts on both George II and, decades later, his grandson George III. There's also a ghost, but only in the circle, so you're safe to nip in and enquire about same-day tickets – you never know your luck… and the 70-orc *Lord of the Rings* spectacular is likely still to be showing.

Left out of the Theatre Royal's foyer you can see the recently refurbished **Novello** (p135), which has for the last couple of years hosted the Royal Shakespeare Company's London seasons.

Opposite is the Duchess and, to your right as you hit the Strand, you'll see the Lyceum. This density of playhouses has led to the area being called 'Theatreland'.

Gingerly cross the Strand and head along the lefthand pavement towards Waterloo Bridge. It's time for lunch. On the left, just before the river, is the terrace entrance to **Somerset House** (p159). Ignore the shaded, waited tables and press on to the uncovered self-service tables: the distribution of trees leaves these with superior views. Buy a drink from the café indoors and – discreetly – scoff your pastries at a table overlooking the Thames. There's a better view to come, but you probably need the break – and this should be just before the lunchtime rush for tables.

Cross the bridge, keeping to the left. To the right are Big Ben, the London Eye and the Southbank Centre; to the left lie St Paul's, the Gherkin, Blackfriars Bridge and the grey, brutalist **National Theatre** (p71). That big concrete box nearest the bridge is the massive flytower which enables stagehands to 'fly' scenery on and off stage. Descend the stairs on the left to the lowest level, but turn left, away from the National – you're too late for day-tickets (queued for from 9.30am) and too early for stand-by (from 90 minutes before the show), so instead walk into the 'lightbox' entrance to the brand-new **BFI Southbank** (p69).

Check for a matinée (usually at 2.30pm or 3pm) and don't forget the 14 viewing stations of the Media-theque opposite the entrance. They're free to use: sit down, put on the headphones and call up whatever TV and film you like from the archive – perhaps 1896 footage of Blackfriars Bridge, the very one you admired as you crossed the river. Only then was the world silent, monochrome and every man was obliged to wear a top hat.

Novello Theatre

Victoria Miro

Arting Around

For a little district, London's East End has a big artistic reputation. Drawn here by cheap rents and big industrial spaces, the artists have populated hidden, widely spread and sometimes rather unappealing corners. But a couple of buses and a healthy dose of walking will enable you to flit between artist-run project spaces and ritzy showrooms – all of which are free to visit.

Set aside a Friday or Saturday, when all the galleries are open, and set off from **Old Street** station at around 10am. Take Exit 2 then follow the ramp to your left that leads to City Road. In a few minutes, you come to a petrol station and a branch of McDonald's. Look up as you turn right into Wharf Road, just past the golden arches, and you'll catch a glimpse of your

first stop: **Victoria Miro** gallery (16 Wharf Road, 7336 8109, www. victoria-miro.com), with its slab of curving, post-minimalist icing on top. This recent addition to the building isn't publicly accessible, but that still leaves you with two floors of elegant warehouse conversion to scoot around, taking in work by Miro's impressive international stable, which includes such artists as Peter Doig, Chris Ofili, Tal R and Grayson Perry. Next stop: head next door to **Parasol Unit** (14 Wharf Road, 7490 7373, www.parasol-unit.org). Run by Ziba de Weck, Parasol is a swanky, not-for-profit space that holds several first-rate exhibitions a year.

Leaving Parasol Unit, retrace your steps to Old Street station and turn left into Old Street itself,

VINEspace p54

keeping eyes peeled for interesting graffiti. (We've recently spotted stencils by both Blek the Rat and Banksy.) Immediately after the Holiday Inn Express take a sharp left into Coronet Street, then turn right into Hoxton Square.

Your first port of call here is **White Cube Hoxton Square** (no.48, 7930 5373, www.whitecube.com), Jay Jopling's smaller outpost following the 2006 launch of his Mason's Yard gallery in the West End, but nonetheless still a key destination for anyone interested in the Young British Artists (among them Tracey Emin, the Chapman brothers and Jopling's wife Sam Taylor-Wood). Be sure to visit the first-floor space, where artist projects are often to be found. Coming out of White Cube, follow the road round to the left of the square and grab a cup of coffee at Macondo (nos.8 & 9, 7729 1119, www.macondo.co.uk). If the

weather's good, park yourself in the square for a few minutes before heading back past White Cube.

Keep going, turning left into Hoxton Street. The new location of **STORE** (no.27, 7729 8171, www.storegallery.co.uk) is a few doors up on your left and shows rising stars like Bedwyr Williams and Ryan Gander. From STORE, turn right then (at the end of Hoxton Street) left. Here, outside Shoreditch Magistrate's Court, wait for the 55 (Leyton) bus. This will take you along Hackney Road.

The bus turns left into Cambridge Heath Road after about five minutes. Get off at the first stop after the canal and, turning slightly back on yourself, start heading along Andrew's Road. Passing gas holders and the Regent's Canal on your left, you'll come to **Regent Studios** (no.8), a mixed-use block set back from the road on your right. Walk through the yard to the building then take the lift or the stairs to the fifth floor. There you'll find **MOT** (Unit 54, 7923 9561, www.motinternational.org), a lively gallery and project space that affords spectacular views over the city. On your way back down, pop into the artist-run **Transition Gallery** (Unit 25a, 7254 4202, www.transitiongallery.co.uk) on the second floor to sample one of its themed group shows or pick up a copy of the latest *Arty* fanzine (www.artymagazine.com).

Coming out of Regent Studios continue along Andrew's Road. In a matter of seconds you'll reach **Broadway Market**; of several possible lunch stops, try to get a seat in Belgian beer specialist the Dove (nos.24-26, 7275 7617, www. belgianbars.com). Thus fortified, you'll be up for tackling the East End's main art thoroughfare.

Retrace your steps along Broadway Market and Andrew's Road. Back at the bus-stop, cross the canal and turn left into **Vyner Street**. Start at artist-run Alma Enterprises (no.1, 07769 686826, www.almaenterprises.com) and work your way along, pausing at Ibid Projects (no.21, 8983 4355, www.ibidprojects.com) and VINEspace (no.25A, 8981 1233, www.vinespace.net). Set back from the street, no.45 is home to three galleries: Fred (8981 2987, www. fred-london.com) and David Risley Gallery (8980 2202, www.david risleygallery.com) are on the ground floor, while One in the Other (8983 6240, www.oneintheother.com), accessed by a flight of stairs to the right of the main entrance, looks directly over the Regent's Canal.

Having made your way back along Vyner Street, turn left back on to Cambridge Heath Road. After about ten minutes, you'll cross Roman Road – keep going, with the public gardens on your left. When you reach the pedestrian crossing, use it. Located on the corner with Three Colts Lane, **Between Bridges** (223 Cambridge Heath Road, www.betweenbridges.net) is run by Turner Prize-winner Wolfgang Tillmans, and has recently established a reputation for championing overlooked figures.

From here turn right into Three Colts Lane, then right again into Herald Street. On the left is **Maureen Paley Gallery** (no.21, 7729 4112, www.maureenpaley. com). Moving to the East End long before it became so fashionable among artists, Paley is a true pioneer; she represents such heavyweights as Rebecca Warren, Gillian Wearing and Paul Noble.

Homage duly paid, veer slightly left out of the gallery to head along Witan Street, then cross Cambridge Heath Road and take the 254 (Aldgate) bus to your final stop: the **Whitechapel Art Gallery** (p176). East London's most important public space is currently undergoing an ambitious expansion into the historic next-door library building. The grand front entrance is closed for now, but if you head down Angel Alley along the left-hand side of the gallery you'll find the Laboratory, which is showing a busy programme of lens-based work.

The Laboratory closes at 6pm. If you still haven't had your fill, on a Friday night the gallery hosts out-there music, curated by *The Wire* magazine. If you don't fancy that, turn right out of Angel Alley and right again into Commercial Street. There you'll find two art world favourites: for food, get stuck into Fergus Henderson's **St John Bread & Wine** (p179); for a drink, it has to be the **Golden Heart** (p177), a pub whose landlady Sandra Esqulant is now almost as famous as her art-star regulars.

London by Area

Waterloo Bridge

The South Bank

LONDON BY AREA

It may be hard to believe, but the South Bank's pre-eminence in the city's cultural life is a very recent phenomenon – reaching back a decade, for sure, but not much more than that. Yes, this was where Shakespeare premièred his plays back in Elizabethan times, but that was precisely because the South Bank was so undesirable: playhouses belonged with prostitutes, gambling and cock-fighting outside the city proper, which kept its grandeurs safely north of the Thames. A tour of **Shakespeare's Globe** will give you some sense of how things must have been.

Things have changed. The massive refit of the **Southbank Centre**, due to reach completion in June 2007, looks to have finally imposed some kind of logic on what was an ill-disciplined cluster of national institutions, meaning that the broad riverside walkway that takes you from Tower Bridge to Westminster Bridge (and further, if you care to go) becomes an even greater attraction, stringing together sights, historic insights, tourist diversions and outdoor events against a progression of awe-inspiring views.

Then there are the buildings and bridges that were opened around the Millennium – **Tate Modern**, the **British Airways London Eye** and the Millennium and Hungerford Bridges – and have already become landmarks without which London would be unrecognisable. Revitalised **Borough Market**, foodie central, typifies the South Bank's appeal: visitors find it charming, but locals love it too.

Away from the river, there are further, sometimes even livelier cultural attractions – we welcome the return of the **Young Vic**, for example – in an increasingly inner-city setting, as well as the grand **Imperial War Museum**, isolated in a decidedly residential zone.

Sights & museums

Bramah Museum of Tea & Coffee

40 Southwark Street, SE1 1UN (7403 5650/www.bramahmuseum.co.uk). London Bridge tube/rail. **Open** 10am-6pm daily. **Admission** £4; £3.50 reductions. **Map** p59 D2 ❶

Edward Bramah, a former tea taster, set up this museum in the 1990s. The pots, caddies and coffee makers explain the role the beverages have played over time. Particularly popular are Bramah's regular tours, talks and the £7 afternoon cream teas. A pianist often tinkles away in the café in the early afternoon.

British Airways London Eye

Riverside Building, next to County Hall, Westminster Bridge Road, South Bank, SE1 7PB (0870 500 0600/ www.ba-londoneye.com). Westminster tube/Waterloo tube/rail. **Open** Oct-May 10am-8pm daily. *June-Sept* 10am-9pm daily. **Admission** £13.50; free-£10 reductions. **Map** p58 A3 ❷

It's hard to believe this giant wheel was originally intended to turn beside the Thames for only five years. It has proved so popular that no one wants it to come down, and should now keep spinning for another 20 years. The 450ft monster, whose 32 glass capsules each hold 25 people, commands superb views over the heart of London and beyond during each 30-minute 'flight'. You can book in advance (although you're taking a gamble with the weather), or just turn up and queue on the day. Night flights offer a more twinkly experience. There can be long queues in summer, and security is tight.

City Hall

Queen's Walk, South Bank, SE1 2AA (www.london.gov.uk). London Bridge tube/rail. **Open** 8am-8pm Mon-Fri; usually 10am-5pm Sat, Sun. **Map** p59 F2 ❸

Designed by Lord Foster, this eco-friendly rotund glass structure leans squiffily away from the river. Home to London's municipal government, the building has the Photomat (an huge aerial photo of the city you can walk across), a café, an information desk and the Scoop, an outdoor amphitheatre for lunch breaks and sunbathing.

Clink Prison Museum

1 Clink Street, SE1 9DG (7403 0900/ www.clink.co.uk). London Bridge tube/ rail. **Open** 10am-6pm Mon-Fri; 10am-9pm Sat, Sun. **Admission** £5; £3.50 reductions. **Map** p59 E2 ❹

This small, grisly exhibition looks behind the bars of the hellish prison owned by the Bishops of Winchester from the 12th century. On display are torture devices and the fetters whose clanking gave the prison its name.

Dalí Universe

County Hall Gallery, County Hall, Riverside Building, Queen's Walk, South Bank, SE1 7PB (7620 2720/ www.daliuniverse.com). Westminster tube/Waterloo tube/rail. **Open** 10am-6.30pm daily. **Admission** £11/£12; £6-£10 reductions. **Map** p58 A3 ❺

Trademark attractions such as the Mae West Lips sofa and *Spellbound* painting enhance the main exhibition, curated by long-term Dalí friend Benjamin Levi. There are sculptures, watercolours, etchings and lithographs, all exploring his favourite themes. Be sure to check out too the Bible scenes by the Catholic-turned-atheist-turned-Catholic again. The gallery also shows works by new artists.

Design Museum

Shad Thames, SE1 2YD (7403 6933/ www.designmuseum.org). Tower Hill tube/London Bridge tube/rail. **Open** 10am-5.45pm daily. **Admission** £7; free-£4 reductions. **Map** p59 F2 ❻

LONDON BY AREA

The South Bank

River Thames

Savoy Hotel

Savoy Pier

Cleopatra's Needle

Embankment Pier

VICTORIA EMBANKMENT

Hungerford Bridge

Festival Pier

British Airways London Eye **2**

Jubilee Gardens

London Aquarium **5** **13** Old County Hall

WESTMINSTER BRIDGE

St Thomas's Hospital

Florence Nightingale Museum **8**

St Thomas's Medical School

LAMBETH

Lambeth Palace Gardens

Lambeth Palace **15** Archbishop's Park

Museum of Garden History

King's College Institute **A**

Middle Temple **B** Inner Temple

Temple

TEMPLE AVE

Blackfriars **C**

Blackfriars Station

Blackfriars Millennium Pier

BLACKFRIARS BRIDGE

London Studios

Oxo Tower Wharf **26**

Bankside Gallery

Gabriel's Wharf

UPPER GROUND

RENNIE ST

STAMFORD STREET

PARIS GARDENS

COLOMBO ST

BURRELL ST

BEAR LANE

SOUTH

BFI Southbank **38**

National Theatre **41**

Queen Elizabeth Hall & Purcell Room

45

Hayward Gallery **10**

Royal Festival Hall **27** **29**

BFI London IMAX Cinema **37**

WATERLOO RD

UPPER GROUND

DUCHY ST

HATFIELDS

AQUINAS ST

THEED ST

WHITTLESEY ST

ROUPELL ST

BRAD STREET

CORNWALL RD

MEPHAM ST

Waterloo

EXTON ST

WOOTTON ST

Waterloo East Station

MEYMOTT

JOAN STREET

Waterloo **36**

Waterloo Station

YORK ROAD

BELVEDERE ROAD

CONCERT HALL APPROACH

CHICHELEY ST

SANDELL ST

WATERLOO ROAD

Young Vic Theatre **46**

THE CUT

Southwark **22**

SCORES ST

GAMBIA ST

Old Vic Theatre **42**

MITRE RD

UFFORD STREET

WEBBER

BLACKFRIARS ROAD

SURREY ROW

POCOCK STREET

WESTMINSTER BRIDGE ROAD

STATION RD

LEAKE STREET

LOWER MARSH

LWR MARSH

FRAZIER STREET

BAYLIS ROAD

CORAL ST

GRAY ST

CHAPLIN CL

VALENTINE PL

BARONS PL

WEBBER ROW

RUSHWORTH ST

WEBBER

SILEX ST

KING JA

LIBRARY ST

LANCASTER ST

Florence Nightingale Museum **8**

UPPER MARSH

ROYAL STREET

LAMBETH PALACE ROAD

WESTMINSTER BRIDGE ROAD

LOWER MARSH

LAMBETH ROAD

CARLISLE LANE

NEWNHAM TERRACE

CENTAUR ST

VIRGIL ST

HERCULES ROAD

COSSER ST

SIDFORD PL

OAKEY LANE

KING EDWARD ST

Lambeth North **Θ**

Imperial War Museum

Geraldine Mary Harmsworth Park **12**

MORLEY ST

GERRIDGE ST

PEARMAN STREET

ODDSON ST

GLADSTONE STREET

ST GEORGE'S CIRCUS

KEYWORTH STREET

BOROUGH

LONDON ROAD

GARDEN ROW

BORG

SO

Univ

London College of Print

St Thomas's Medical School

Lambeth Palace **15**

PRATT WK

JUXON STREET

SAIL STREET

LAMBETH WALK

WALNUT TREE WALK

FITZALAN STREET

LOLLARD STREET

KENNINGTON ROAD

LAMBETH ROAD

GEORGE'S ROAD

WEST SQUARE

AUSTRAL ST

BROOK DRIVE

WALCOT SQUARE

ST MARY'S GARDENS

HAYLES ROW

ELLIOT'S ROW

OSWIN STREET

PASTON ST

Leisure Centre

KENNINGTON

LAMBETH HIGH ST

OLD PARADISE ST

WHITGIFT ST

BLACK PRINCE RD

NEWPORT ST

RAVENTOL STREET

GIBSON RD

LAMBETH WALK

LOLLARD STREET

WINCOTT ST

GILBERT RD

DANTE ROAD

RENFREW RD

REEDWORTH STREET

KENNINGTON LANE

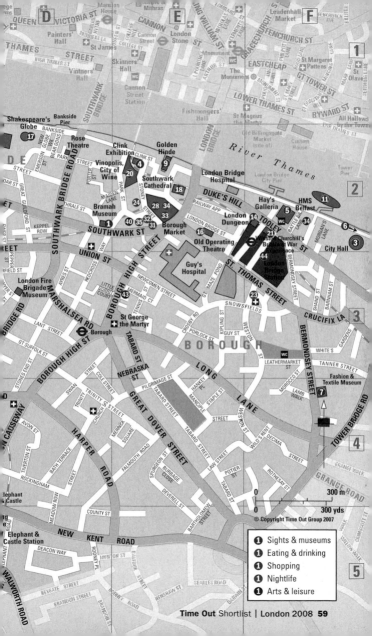

Exhibitions in this white 1930s-style building (a former warehouse) focus on modern and contemporary design. The Tank is a little outdoor gallery of rotating installations by leading contemporary designers, while the smart Blueprint Café has a balcony overlooking the Thames. The museum shop stocks mini design classics.
Event highlights 'Zaha Hadid: Design + Architecture' (until 29 Nov 2007).

Fashion & Textile Museum
83 Bermondsey Street, Bermondsey, SE1 3XF (7407 8664/www.ftmlondon. org). London Bridge tube/rail. **Open/ admission** check online for details. **Map** p59 F4 **7**
Flamboyant as its founder, fashion designer Zandra Rhodes, this pink and orange museum has 3,000 of her garments, along with her archive of paper designs, sketchbooks, silk screens and show videos. The exhibitions were being restructured as we went to press, with only pre-booked groups able to view the main collection, but full public access is expected to resume late in 2007.

Florence Nightingale Museum
St Thomas's Hospital, 2 Lambeth Palace Road, Borough, SE1 7EW (7620 0374/www.florence-nightingale.co.uk). Westminster tube/Waterloo tube/rail. **Open** 10am-5pm Mon-Fri; 10am-4.30pm Sat, Sun. **Admission** £5.80; free-£4.80 reductions. **Map** p58 A3 **8**
The nursing skills and campaigning zeal that made Florence Nightingale's Crimean War work the stuff of legend are honoured here with a chronological tour through her remarkable life.

Golden Hinde
St Mary Overie Dock, Cathedral Street, SE1 9DE (0870 011 8700/www.golden hinde.org). Monument tube/London Bridge tube/rail. **Open** 10am-6pm daily. **Admission** £5.50; £5 reductions. **Map** p59 E2 **9**
Weekends see this reconstruction of Sir Francis Drake's little 16th-century flagship swarming with children

Tate Modern p64

dressed up as pirates for birthday dos. The meticulously recreated ship is fascinating to explore. Thoroughly seaworthy, this replica has even reprised Drake's circumnavigatory voyage. As well as the pirate parties, the 'Living History Experiences' are a huge hit with kids.

Hayward Gallery
Belvedere Road, SE1 8XX (information 7921 0813/box office 0870 169 1000/ www.hayward.org.uk). Embankment tube/Waterloo tube/rail. **Open** *During exhibitions* 10am-6pm Mon, Thur, Sat, Sun; 10am-8pm Tue, Wed; 10am-9pm Fri. **Admission** £5; free-£2.50 reductions. **Map** p58 A2 **10**
In the Hayward's foyer extension and its mirrored, elliptical glass Waterloo Sunset Pavilion, designed in collaboration with light artist Dan Graham, casual visitors can watch cartoons on touch screens as they sip their Starbucks. Art lovers meanwhile enjoy the pavilion and the excellent exhibition programme.

LONDON BY AREA

HMS Belfast

Morgan's Lane, Tooley Street, SE1 2JH (7940 6300/www.iwm.org.uk). London Bridge tube/rail. **Open** *Mar-Oct* 10am-6pm daily. *Nov-Feb* 10am-5pm daily. **Admission** £8.50; free-£5.25 reductions. **Map** p59 F2 ⓫

This 11,500-ton battlecruiser is the last surviving big gun World War II ship in Europe. It makes an unlikely playground for children, who tear around its cramped complex of nine decks, boiler, engine rooms and gun turrets. The *Belfast* was built in 1938, provided cover for convoys to Russia and was instrumental in the Normandy Landings. She also supported UN forces in Korea before being decommissioned in 1965; a special exhibition looks at that 'forgotten war'.

Imperial War Museum

Lambeth Road, Lambeth, SE1 6HZ (7416 5320/www.iwm.org.uk). Lambeth North tube/Elephant & Castle tube/rail. **Open** 10am-6pm daily. **Admission** free. **Map** p58 B4 ⓬

In 1936, the central wing of the old Bethlehem Royal Hospital (Bedlam) became the Imperial War Museum. Its collection covers conflicts, especially those involving Britain and the Commonwealth, from World War I to the present day. The exhibits range from tanks, aircraft and big guns to photographs, letters, film and sound recordings and paintings.

Special areas include the smelly World War I Trench Experience, the teeth-chattering Blitz Experience, and the heartbreaking Holocaust Exhibition and Crimes Against Humanity (for over-16s only). Temporary exhibitions include Children's War, which runs until 2008.

Event highlights Camouflage (until 18 Nov 2007).

London Aquarium

County Hall, Riverside Building, Westminster Bridge Road, South Bank, SE1 7PB (7967 8000/tours 7967 8007/www.londonaquarium. co.uk). Westminster tube/Waterloo tube/rail. **Open** 10am-6pm daily. **Admission** £10.75-£11.75; free-£9.50 reductions. **Map** p58 A3 ⓭

The aquarium, one of Europe's largest, displays its inhabitants according to geographical origin, so there are tanks of fish from the coral reefs and the Indian Ocean, temperate freshwater fish from the rivers of Europe and North America, and crustaceans and rockpool plants from shorelines. Also here are tanks devoted to rays, jellyfish, sharks, piranhas, octopuses and even robotic fish.

London Dungeon

28-34 Tooley Street, SE1 2SZ (7403 7221/www.thedungeons.com). London Bridge tube/rail. **Open** *Sept-June* 10.30am-5.30pm daily. *July, Aug* 9.30am-7.30pm daily. **Admission** £16.95; £13.95 reductions. **Map** p59 F2 ⓮

A jokey celebration of torture, death and disease under the Victorian railway arches of London Bridge. Visitors are led through a dry-ice fog past gravestones and rotting corpses to experience nasty symptoms from the Great Plague exhibition: an actor-led medley of corpses, boils, vomiting, worm-filled skulls and rats. Other OTT revisions of horrible London history include the Great Fire and the Judgement Day Barge, where visitors play the part of prisoners.

Museum of Garden History

Lambeth Palace Road, Lambeth, SE1 7LB (7401 8865/www.museumgarden history.org). Waterloo tube/rail. **Open** 10.30am-5pm daily. **Admission** free. *Suggested donation* £3; £2.50 reductions. **Map** p58 A4 ⓯

John Tradescant, intrepid plant hunter and gardener to Charles I, is buried here at the world's first museum of horticulture. Topiary and box hedging, old roses, herbaceous perennials and bulbs give all-year interest, and a magnificent sarcophagus contains the remains of HMS *Bounty* captain William Bligh. Inside the museum are displays of ancient tools, exhibitions about horticulture, a shop and a vegetarian café.

High drama

Star power meets quality theatre on the South Bank.

When, in 2005, Kevin Spacey rode in to take over the Old Vic – a 'proper' theatre, with artistic pedigree – everyone was terribly impressed, but 2008 could be the year in which the starry world of celluloid finally gets to grip with grown-up, classic theatre.

First there's exciting news from the National Theatre (p71, pictured): Ralph Fiennes will play the title role in Sophocles' *Oedipus Rex* in the autumn of 2008. Nor is Fiennes the only film actor of international calibre on the programme. His *English Patient* co-star Juliette Binoche is hard at work developing an as-yet unnamed show with choreographer Akram Khan. While Binoche is well known, Khan is less familiar – only in his 30s, the Balham-born Bangladeshi has already built a formidable reputation applying techniques from Western modern dance to the South Asian classical style

known as Kathak. The prospect is appetising, but don't hold your breath – Gorillaz and Blur frontman Damon Albarn is said still to be 'developing' the musical about London announced last year.

It's reassuring that Nicholas Hytner, head of the National, is still managing to play what amounts to a pretty fancy three-card trick at the publicly funded theatre: producing headline-grabbing stars, keeping up standards and maintaining low prices (many seats cost as little as £10, almost unthinkable in London's more commercial West End theatres).

Remember that Spacey chap? Well, he hasn't exactly been cooling his heels. In fact, he has a pair of aces up his sleeve. The Old Vic (p71) has already confirmed Oscar-winning director Sam Mendes is to return to the London stage for the first time in five years. For three years from spring 2008, Mendes will put on two shows a year at the Old Vic. As part of the Bridge Project – which will employ equal numbers of British and American actors – Mendes first pairs *The Tempest* and *Hamlet*, then *The Winter's Tale* and Chekhov's *Cherry Orchard*. We'll also see him in more commercial vein in the West End if his Broadway production of David Hare's *The Vertical Hour* makes it over in 2008.

Even more intriguing is news of the first English-language stage adaptation of an Almodóvar film: *All About My Mother* is rumoured to be due at the Old Vic just as this guide hits the shelves.

Old Operating Theatre, Museum & Herb Garret

9A St Thomas's Street, SE1 9RY (7188 2679/www.thegarret.org.uk). London Bridge tube/rail. **Open** 10.30am-5pm Mon-Wed, Fri-Sun; 10.30am-7pm Thur. **Admission** £4.95; free-£3.95 reductions. No credit cards. **Map** p59 E2 ⑯

The tower that houses this salutary revelation of antique surgical practice used to be part of the chapel of St Thomas's Hospital, founded on this site in the 12th century. The centrepiece is a pre-anaesthetic Victorian operating theatre dating from 1822, but just as disturbing are the displays of operating equipment, strangulated hernias and jars of leeches.

Shakespeare's Globe

21 New Globe Walk, SE1 9DT (7902 1400/box office 7401 9919/www. shakespeares-globe.org). Mansion House or Southwark tube/London Bridge tube/rail. **Open** *Exhibition & tours* Oct-Apr 10am-5pm daily. May-Sept 9am-noon Mon-Sat; 9-11.30am Sun. **Admission** £9; £6.50-£7.50 reductions. **Map** p59 D2 ⑰

The original Globe theatre, where many of William Shakespeare's plays were first staged and which he co-owned, burned down in 1613 during a performance of *Henry VIII*. Nearly 400 years later, it was rebuilt not far from its original site using authentic construction methods and materials. In the UnderGlobe beneath the theatre is a fine exhibition (open year-round) on the history of the reconstruction, Bankside and its Elizabethan theatres. You can tour the Globe outside the May to September performance season; when the theatre is in use, the tour is around the site of the Rose Theatre (56 Park Street, 7593 0026, www.rosetheatre.org.uk) instead. Built by Philip Henslowe, the Rose was the first playhouse on Bankside.

Southwark Cathedral

London Bridge, SE1 9DA (7367 6700/ tours 7367 6734/www.dswark.org/ cathedral). London Bridge tube/rail. **Open** 8am-6pm daily. **Admission** free. *Audio tour* £2.50. **Map** p59 E2 ⑱

The oldest bits of this building, one of the few places south of the river that Dickens had a good word for, date back more than 800 years. The retrochoir was where the trials of several Protestant martyrs took place during the reign of Mary Tudor. After the Reformation, the church fell into disrepair; in 1905 it became a cathedral. An interactive museum, a refectory and a lovely garden are some of the millennial improvements. There are memorials to Shakespeare, John Harvard (benefactor of the US university) and Sam Wanamaker (the force behind Shakespeare's Globe), as well as stained-glass windows with images of Chaucer, who set off on his pilgrimage to Canterbury from a pub on Borough High Street.

Tate Modern

Bankside, SE1 9TG (7401 5120/7887 8888/www.tate.org.uk). Blackfriars tube/rail. **Open** 10am-6pm Mon-Thur, Sun; 10am-10pm Fri, Sat. *Tours* 11am, noon, 2pm, 3pm daily. **Admission** free. *Temporary exhibitions* prices vary. **Map** p59 D2 ⑲

A powerhouse of modern art, Tate Modern is awe-inspiring even before you see anything of the collection, thanks to its industrial architecture. It was built as Bankside Power Station and designed by Sir Giles Gilbert Scott, architect of Battersea Power Station and designer of the famous British red telephone box. Bankside stopped working in 1981 and opened as an art museum in 2000. The original cavernous turbine hall is used as the home of large-scale, temporary installations. The permanent collection draws from the Tate organisation's deep reservoir of modern art (international works from 1900 and on) and features heavy-hitters such as Matisse, Rothko, Giacometti and Pollock.

In 2006, the galleries enjoyed the first of what is likely to be a regular series of rehangings, with the artworks now grouped according to movement (Surrealism, Minimalism and so on). Almost half the pieces are new to the museum.

If you don't know where to start, take one of the guided tours. There are also various tour packages, some combined with Shakespeare's Globe and others including lunch or dinner (the café on Level 2 is highly recommended). The Tate-to-Tate boat service links with Tate Britain (p74) and runs every 20 minutes, stopping along the way at the London Eye (p57). Tickets are available from desks at the Tates, on board the boat, online or by phone (7887 8888).

Event highlights Doris Salcedo's first public commission in the UK is to fill the Turbine Hall for the Unilever Series (9 Oct 2007-24 Mar 2008).

Vinopolis, City of Wine

1 Bank End, SE1 9BU (0870 241 4040/www.vinopolis.co.uk). London Bridge tube/rail. **Open** *Jan-Nov* noon-9pm Mon, Fri, Sat; noon-6pm Tue-Thur, Sun. *Dec* noon-6pm daily. **Admission** £15-£25. **Map** p59 E2 ⓴

This glossy attraction is more for wine amateurs than committed oenophiles, but you do need to have some interest to get a kick out it. Participants are furnished with a wine glass and an audio guide. Exhibits are set out by country, with five opportunities to taste champagne or wine from different regions. Gin crashes the party courtesy of a Bombay Sapphire cocktail, and a whisky-tasting area, wine bar and microbrewery (the Wine and Brew Wharfs, p68) were recently added. The complex also contains a tourist information centre.

Winston Churchill's Britain at War Experience

64-66 Tooley Street, SE1 2TF (7403 3171/www.britainatwar.co.uk). London Bridge tube/rail. **Open** *Apr-Sept* 10am-6pm daily. *Oct-Mar* 10am-5pm daily. **Admission** £9.50; free-£5.75 reductions. **Map** p59 F2 ㉑

This old-fashioned exhibition recalls the privations endured by the British during World War II. Visitors descend

Tapas Brindisa p68

Borough Market p68

from street level in an ancient lift to a reconstructed tube station shelter that doubles as a movie theatre showing documentaries from the period. The experience continues with displays about London during the Blitz, including real bombs, rare documents, photos and reconstructed shopfronts. The displays on rationing, food production and Land Girls are fascinating, and the walk-through bombsite (you enter just after a bomb has dropped on the street) is disturbing.

Eating & drinking

One of the best places to eat in London is **Borough Market** (p68) – it's just a shame it isn't open all week. As we went to press, a great range of eateries was opening around the refurbished Southbank Centre – among them bakery **Le Pain Quotidien** (7486 6154, www.painquotidien. com), a Brit-foodie **Canteen** (0845 686 1122, www.canteen. co.uk), **Ping Pong** (p67) and **Skylon** (p67).

Anchor & Hope

36 The Cut, SE1 8LP (7928 9898).
Southwark or Waterloo tube/rail.
Open 5-11pm Mon; 11am-11pm Tue-Sat; noon-5pm Sun. **££**. **Gastropub**.
Map p58 B3 **22**
There are two problems: the A&H doesn't take bookings and it's always full. But persist: it is full because the food (seasonal British classics) is extremely good and the bar treats real ales and classic cocktails with appropriate respect. Come at 2pm or after 8.30pm and the crowds might have thinned.

Champor-Champor

62-64 Weston Street, Borough, SE1 3QJ, London Bridge (7403 4600/ www.champor-champor.com).
London Bridge tube/rail. **Open** 6.15-10.15pm Mon-Sat. **£££**. **Malaysian**.
Map p59 F3 **23**
Champor-Champor means 'mix and match' in Malay and the description applies both to the restaurant's decor – African masks, the papier mâché head of a crimson holy cow – and the modern interpretation of Malaysian cuisine: ostrich satay and crocodile nasi

goreng. Not all dishes work, but expect the place to be full – even midweek. Lunch is served by special arrangement only.

Market Porter

9 Stoney Street, SE1 9AA (7407 2495). London Bridge tube/rail.
Open 6-8.30am, 11am-11pm Mon-Fri; noon-11pm Sat; noon-10.30pm Sun.
Pub. Map p59 E2 ㉔

Alongside Borough Market, the Market Porter cheerfully serves ludicrously monikered beer to lovers of real ale all day long; the early opening time is a historical anomaly, allowing porters to satisfy their thirst. In the evenings, customers spill out on to the pavement.

Masters Super Fish

191 Waterloo Road, South Bank, SE1 8UX (7928 6924). Waterloo tube/rail.
Open noon-3pm, 5.30-10.30pm Mon; noon-3pm, 4.30-10.30pm Tue-Thur, Sat; noon-3pm, 4.30-11pm Fri. **Fish & chips**. Map p58 B/C3 ㉕

It ain't sophisticated, but the food's great. Takeaway or sit down, the menu offers everything from burgers to dressed Cromer crab, whitebait and calamares to own-made puddings.

Oxo Tower Restaurant, Bar & Brasserie

Eighth floor, Oxo Tower Wharf, Barge House Street, SE1 9PH (7803 3888/www.harveynichols.com). Blackfriars or Waterloo tube/rail. **Open** 11am-11pm Mon-Sat; noon-10.30pm Sun. **£££** Bar. **££££** Restaurant. **Modern European/bar**. Map p58 B1 ㉖

This landmark venue commands striking views across London – get a seat on the terrace if you want to make the most of it. Dinner times are very busy, but for lunch you can often book the same day. Food is of a high standard, although not especially ambitious. Brasserie Tamesa@oxo (7633 0088), down on the second floor, offers lovely river views.

Ping Pong

NEW *Festival Terrace, Southbank Centre, Belvedere Road, SE1 8XX (7960 4160/www.pingpongdim sum.com). Oxford Circus tube.*
Open noon-midnight Mon-Wed; noon-1am Thur-Sat; noon-10.30pm Sun.
£. Dim sum. Map p58 A2 ㉗

The latest installment of the 'designer dim sum' chain opened in April 2007. The food is hit and miss, but service is friendly and there are some theatrical touches such as jasmine tea served in a long glass with a budding flower inside.

Roast

Floral Hall, Borough Market, Stoney Street, SE1 1TL (7940 1300/www. roast-restaurant.com). London Bridge tube/rail. **Open** 7-9.30am, noon-2.30pm, 5.30-10.30pm Mon-Fri; 8-10.30am, 11.30am-3.30pm, 6-10.30pm Sat; 9-11am, noon-3.30pm Sun. **££££**.
British. Map p59 E2 ㉘

The location is terrific – a big, airy atrium of a room with views of Borough Market below and trains passing above. The food also deserves wholehearted enthusiasm (well-sourced meat and fish), and is accompanied by an intriguing range of drinks, many of them also British. Breakfast here is a treat.

Skylon

NEW *Southbank Centre, Belvedere Road, SE1 8XX (7654 7800/www.skyl onrestaurant.co.uk). Waterloo tube/rail.* **Open** Bar 11am-1am daily. Grill noon-11.45pm daily. Restaurant noon-2.30pm, 5.30-10.45pm daily. **£££. Modern European**. Map p58 A2 ㉙

We're excited about the new destination restaurant in the Royal Festival Hall. Floor-to-ceiling windows will make the most of its Thameside location, while the raised cocktail bar should keep things buzzing. For food, expect Brit-inflected modern European, supplemented with more relaxed fare from the grill.

Table

83 Southwark Street, Borough, SE1 0HX (7401 2760/www.thetablecafe. com). London Bridge tube/rail.
Open 8am-5.30pm Mon-Thur; 8am-11pm Fri. **£. Bar/café**.
Map p58 C2 ㉚

This gem of a café features raw concrete walls, chunky wooden tables and benches, an outdoor courtyard, an open kitchen and plate-glass windows. A long table displays sandwiches and a wonderful salad bar (ingredients come from Borough Market). Dishes like minute steak, chicken breast and tuna are ordered at a different counter. Evening hours should be extended to 8.30pm from June 2007 – we can't wait.

Tapas Brindisa
18-20 Southwark Street, SE1 1TJ (7357 8880/www.brindisa.com). London Bridge tube/rail. **Open** noon-11pm Mon-Thur; 9am-11am, noon-11pm Fri, Sat. **££. Spanish**. **Map** p59 E2 ③
The interior is basic, and you can't book ahead, but this is a class act. Quality imported Spanish ingredients – Brindisa also runs a deli in Borough Market (7407 1036) – make for superb food. The same attention to detail is applied to the drinks, with a sound selection of sherries and a wine list. Delightful service and a good selection of sherry and Spanish wine too.

Wine Wharf
Stoney Street, Borough Market, SE1 9AD (7940 8335/www.winewharf.com). London Bridge tube/rail. **Open** 11.30am-11pm Mon-Sat. **££. Wine bar**. **Map** p59 E2 ③
The wine list here is superb, with more than 100 by the glass, plenty of them under £5, balanced between the Old and New Worlds and managing to wave a flag for lesser-known regions such as Georgia. The food is less impressive; dishes seem designed mainly for soaking up alcohol. It shares a kitchen with the Brew Wharf microbrewery (7378 6601, www.brewwharf.com) next door; mod European restaurant Cantina Vinopolis is in the same complex.

Shopping

There are some great design and crafts shops in the Oxo Tower between Blackfriars and Waterloo Bridge, including Bodo Sperlein.

Bedales
5 Bedale Street, Bankside, SE1 9AL (7403 8853/www.bedalestreet. com). London Bridge tube/rail. **Open** 11.30am-8.30pm Mon-Thur; 11am-9.30pm Fri; 9am-5pm Sat. **Map** p59 E2 ③
Bedales sells wines from around the world, including kosher wines and even Luxembourg's best. Tastings cost £35-£50, with food.

Borough Market
8 Southwark Street, Borough, SE1 1TL (7407 1002/www.boroughmarket. org.uk). London Bridge tube/rail. **Open** 11am-5pm Thur; noon-6pm Fri; 9am-4pm Sat. **Map** p59 E2 ③
There's been a market here for two millennia, and even the Victorians thought it pretty swanky. Tucked under the atmospheric railway arches, it sells produce of such impeccable quality and sourcing that London's chefs love it. Meats encompass everything from Iberian acorn-fed ham to free-range chicken; add fruit and veg, organic cakes and breads, exotic teas, olive oil, dairy, fish and oysters, beers, ciders and wines and you've got the makings of a feast.

Paul Smith
13 Park Street, Borough, SE1 9AB (7403 1678). **Open** 10am-6pm Mon-Sat. **Map** p59 E2 ③
The front of this shop is an anarchic jumble of toys, kitsch novelties, art books and chocs from Rococo. Urban-casual clothes for men, women and kids (including selections from the Jeans and Pink collections) are stocked in the back room; cross the river to the Covent Garden store for Paul Smith's main lines.

Radio Days
87 Lower Marsh, Waterloo, SE1 7AB (7928 0800). Waterloo tube/rail. **Open** 10am-6pm Mon-Sat; 10am-7pm Fri. **Map** p58 B3 ③
This lovingly put-together vintage shop sells clothes and collectibles from the 1920s to 1970s. Look out for the glamorous cocktail accessories.

Arts & leisure

In season (May-Sept), check out the programme for **Shakespeare's Globe** (p64): the artistic director role has changed hands from Mark Rylance to Dominic Dromgoole, so there should be new writers alongside the venue's trademark historically authentic performances of the Bard.

BFI London IMAX Cinema

1 Charlie Chaplin Walk, South Bank, SE1 8XR (0870 787 2525/www.bfi. org.uk/imax). Waterloo tube/rail. **Map** p58 B2 **37**
The programming isn't all that exciting, but you'll catch occasional gems on the biggest screen in the country.

BFI Southbank

NEW *South Bank, SE1 8XT (information 7928 3535/bookings 7928 3232/ www.bfi.org.uk). Embankment tube/ Waterloo tube/rail.* **Map** p58 A2 **38**
As the National Film Theatre, this multiscreen cinema has long been a London institution, but it was in dire need of a revamp. The splendid new glass entrance faces the National Theatre building, there's a new café

and bar area, and the film and book-shop return. Even better, BFI Southbank incorporates the BFI Mediatheque: 14 state-of-the-art viewing stations at which visitors can access hundreds of hours of film and television from the BFI archive. A new gallery space presents screen-based works by contemporary artists.

Jerwood

171 Union Street, Bankside, SE1 0LN (7654 0171/www.jerwoodspace.co.uk). Borough or Southwark tube. No credit cards. **Map** p59 D3 **39**
The Jerwood combines theatre and dance spaces with a gallery and a great café. Exhibitions have been pretty erratic, but there are signs of a more cohesive approach, drawing together the Jerwood Foundation's various prizes.

Menier Chocolate Factory

51-53 Southwark Street, SE1 1TE (7907 7060/www.menierchocolate factory.com). London Bridge tube/rail. **Map** p59 E2 **40**
Housed, you'll have guessed, in a former chocolate factory, this is an attractive fringe venue with a restaurant attached.

BFI Southbank

LONDON BY AREA

Underground arts

Something's been going on in London's deserted buildings. In late 2006, there was the extraordinary China Power Station art exhibition in the massive dripping shell of Battersea Power Station. There were the bizarre ghost-voodoo theatricals of *Faust*, put on by Punchdrunk (www.punch drunk.org.uk) in an abandoned Wapping warehouse. Now, in the damp bowels of London Bridge station, an artists' and performers' collective has opened a members' bar.

Shunt (p71) isn't your normal members' bar. For a start everyone is welcome – non-members just rock up after 6pm, pay at the door to see whatever show is happening, then stay as late as they like in the bar. Then there's the space: vast, dark, musty arches, part church and part dungeon.

But the main difference is the programme. Every week a different member of the collective decides what will happen. That means some weeks you get to see something elaborate, but some weeks you'll see next to nothing. 'Fortunately,' as the website cheerily points out, 'the bar staff are more reliable.'

We nosed our way in from Tooley Street for Ray Lee's *Siren*, and it was captivating. Tripods of different heights were corralled into groups. At a given moment, their long arms were set in motion, spinning a red LED and small siren into strange echoes and traces that filled the cavernous dark.

Given the bleak setting, the bar is surprisingly lovely. Tucked through to the back of the main arches, there are plenty of mismatched chairs and tables with candles on, a little bar area aimably staffed and stocked with a decent range of booze, and sufficient interior arches to permit a degree of intimacy. Screens at the far end mean films can be projected as you drink, and the space is flexible enough to be put to any number of uses: cabaret, film fests, readings… you name it.
■ www.shunt.co.uk

National Theatre

South Bank, SE1 9PX (information 7452 3400/box office 7452 3000/www. nationaltheatre.org.uk). Embankment or Southwark tube/Waterloo tube/rail. **Map** p58 B2 **❹**

Under the aegis of Nicholas Hytner as artistic director, the National Theatre has blossomed, with the landmark success of such plays as Alan Bennett's *History Boys* showing that the venue can turn out quality drama at a profit – watch out for a collaboration between Akram Khan and Juliette Binoche (see box p63). The Travelex season, for which two-thirds of the seats are offered for £10, is set to continue for another year. In summer, the free outdoor performing arts stage is a great way to see booty-shaking bhangra or fire-swallowing dancers by the Thames.

Event highlights Stage adaptation of Michael Morpurgo's novel *War Horse* (Oct 2007-Feb 2008); Ralph Fiennes plays the lead in Sophocles' *Oedipus the King* (autumn 2008).

Old Vic

Waterloo Road, Waterloo, SE1 8NB (0870 060 6628/www.oldvictheatre.com). Waterloo tube/rail. **Map** p58 B3 **❷**

The combination of double-Oscar winner Kevin Spacey and top producer David Liddiment at this 200-year-old theatre, known in Victorian times as the 'Bucket of Blood' for its penchant for melodrama, continues to be a commercial success, if not a critical one. Expect a mix of high- and low-brow pieces.

Event highlights Sam Mendes directs *Hamlet* and *The Tempest* (May-June 2008; see box p63).

Roxy Bar & Screen

NEW *128-132 Borough High Street, Borough, SE1 1LB (7407 4057/www. roxybarandscreen.com). Borough tube.* **Open** noon-11pm Mon-Sat; noon-10.30pm Sun. **Map** p59 E3 **❸**

An intriguing new venture, the Roxy contains a back room housing a 12-foot screen, floor-to-ceiling red curtains and intimate, candlelit tables. You can pay

to watch 'live cinema' performances on Saturday's VJ nights, or settle in for a cocktail and free themed matinee.

Shunt

NEW *Joiner Street, Borough, SE1 (7378 7776/www.shunt.co.uk). London Bridge tube/rail.* **Open** 6-11pm Wed-Fri. **Map** p59 F3 **❹**

See box p70.

Southbank Centre

NEW *Belvedere Road, South Bank, SE1 8XX (box office 0870 380 0400/ recorded information 7921 0973/ www.rfh.org.uk). Waterloo tube/rail.* **Map** p58 A2 **❺**

Down on the South Bank, the 3,000-capacity Royal Festival Hall was finally scheduled to reopen in June 2007, just as this guide went to press, after a series of renovations said to have cost more than £110m. Some of the work was completed early on, such as the row of shops at pavement level on the river side of the buildings. But the real meat of the project is the acoustic refurbishment of the main hall itself, long criticised by both musicians and concert-goers. The RFH's resident ensembles – among them the London Philharmonic Orchestra, Philharmonia and London Sinfonietta – will finally return home after having to content themselves with the 900-capacity Queen Elizabeth Hall next door. Also within this building is the 360-capacity Purcell Room, for everything from chamber concerts to poetry readings, plus free foyer music.

Young Vic

NEW *66 The Cut, Waterloo, SE1 8LZ (7928 6363/www.youngvic.org). Waterloo tube/rail.* **Map** p58 C3 **❻**

The Young Vic returns! After a long-overdue makeover – built on a bomb-site in 1970, the theatre was intended to last only five years – it's back to nurturing young actors and directors. Two new theatres, the 160-seater Maria and 80-seater Clare, have been added to the former main stage, and the Cut Bar & Restaurant has an outdoor terrace.

Houses of Parliament

Westminster & St James's

Westminster

More imposing than atmospheric, Westminster is for many the heart of London – if not England. It has been the seat of power for almost 1,000 years, since the days of Edward the Confessor; in the 14th century the country's first Parliament met in **Westminster Abbey**. The area contains much of what the folks back home will expect you to see, including **Buckingham Palace**, the **Houses of Parliament** and **Nelson's Column**, along with major national cultural institutions.

Sights & museums

Banqueting House
Whitehall, SW1A 2ER (0870 751 5178/www.hrp.org.uk). Westminster tube/Charing Cross tube/rail. **Open** 10am-5pm Mon-Sat. **Admission** £4.50; free-£3.50 reductions. **Map** p75 C2 ❶

This Palladian building was designed by Inigo Jones in 1622. The austerity of the exterior belies the sumptuous Rubens ceiling inside; call to check the hall is open before you visit. Charles I was beheaded just outside in 1649.

Cabinet War Rooms & Churchill Museum
Clive Steps, King Charles Street, SW1A 2AQ (7930 6961/www.iwm.org.uk). St James's Park or Westminster tube. **Open** 9.30am-6pm daily. **Admission** £11; free-£8.50 reductions. **Map** p75 C2 ❷

This underground set of rooms was Churchill's bunker during World War II. Every book, chart and pin in the map room remains where it was in 1945, as does the microphone he used to broadcast to the nation. The adjoining Churchill Museum explores his life.

Houses of Parliament
Parliament Square, SW1A 0AA (Commons information 7219 4272/ Lords information 7219 3107/ tours information 0870 906 3773/

www.parliament.uk). Westminster tube.
Open in session only; phone for details.
Admission *Visitors' Gallery* free. *Tours*
£7; free-£5 reductions. **Map** p75 C3 ❸
Completed in 1860, this neo-Gothic
extravaganza was the creation of architect Charles Barry, who won the competition to replace the original Houses
of Parliament, which were destroyed
by fire in 1834. Barry was assisted on
the gorgeous interiors by Augustus
Pugin. The only remaining parts of the
original palace are the Jewel Tower and
Westminster Hall, one of the finest
medieval buildings in Europe. There's
a visitors' café, and you can watch MPs
and Lords in session from the galleries.
Parliament goes into recess in summer,
when there are tours of the main ceremonial rooms, including Westminster
Hall and the two Houses.

Jewel Tower

*Abingdon Street, SW1P 3JY (7222
2219/www.english-heritage.org.uk).
Westminster tube.* **Open** *Apr-Oct*
10am-5pm daily. *Nov-Mar* 10am-4pm
daily. **Admission** £2.70; free-£2
reductions. **Map** p75 C3 ❹
This old stone tower was built in 1365
to house Edward III's valuables. Along
with Westminster Hall, it is one of only
two surviving parts of the medieval
Palace of Westminster. Today, it contains an exhibition on Parliament's past.

National Gallery

*Trafalgar Square, WC2N 5DN
(7747 2885/www.nationalgallery.
org.uk). Leicester Square tube/Charing
Cross tube/rail.* **Open** 10am-6pm
Mon, Tue, Thur-Sun; 10am-9pm
Wed. *Tours* 11.30am, 2.30pm daily;
additionally 6pm, 6.30pm Wed;
12.30pm, 3.30pm Sat. **Admission**
free. *Special exhibitions* prices vary.
No credit cards. **Map** p75 C1 ❺
Founded in 1824, this is now one of the
greatest art collections in the world,
with more than 2,000 Western
European pieces, starting with 13th-
century religious works and approach-
ing modern times via da Vinci, Raphael,
Rubens, Rembrandt, Caravaggio,
Turner, Constable, Gainsborough,

Cézanne and Picasso. The big-ticket
items, however, are the Impressionist
paintings, including Monet's *Water
Lilies* series and Van Gogh's *Chair*.
Guided tours take in the major works.
There's also a fine café/restaurant in the
National Dining Rooms (p77).
Event highlights 'Pompeo Batoni
(1708-1787)' (20 Feb-18 May 2008);
Italy's painting revolution 1885-1910
(18 June-7 Sept 2008); Renaissance
portraits (from 15 Oct 2008).

National Portrait Gallery

*2 St Martin's Place, WC2H 0HE
(7306 0055/www.npg.org.uk). Leicester
Square tube/Charing Cross tube/rail.*
Open 10am-6pm Mon-Wed, Sat, Sun;
10am-9pm Thur, Fri. **Admission** free.
Special exhibitions prices vary. **Map**
p75 C1 ❻
Subjects of the portraits here range from
Tudor royalty to present-day celebs.
Highlights include the only known
contemporary portrait of Shakespeare.
The top-floor restaurant is lovely.
Event highlights 'Pop Art Portraits'
(11 Oct 2007-20 Jan 2008).

Routemaster buses

Stops B (Pall Mall) & F (the Strand).
Map p75 both C1 ❼
The iconic red Routemaster buses were
withdrawn from service in 2005, but
beautifully refurbished Routies run
Heritage Route 15 every 15 minutes
(9.30am-6.30pm). The Pall Mall stop
goes west to the Royal Albert Hall; the
Strand stop east via St Paul's to Tower
Hill. Buy tickets before you board.

St Margaret's Church

*Parliament Square, SW1P 3JX (7654
4840/www.westminster-abbey.org/
stmargarets). St James's Park or
Westminster tube.* **Open** 9.30am-3.45pm
Mon-Fri; 9.30am-1.45pm Sat; 2-5pm Sun.
Admission free. **Map** p75 C3 ❽
Originally founded in the 12th century,
this church houses some of the most
impressive pre-Reformation stained
glass in London. Later windows cele-
brate Sir Walter Raleigh, executed in Old
Palace Yard; and writer John Milton,
who married his second wife here.

Trafalgar Square

2pm, 3pm Mon-Fri; noon, 3pm Sat, Sun.
Admission free. *Special exhibitions*
prices vary. **Map** p75 C5 **⑩**

The original Tate contains London's
second great collection of historical art,
after the National Gallery. The displays
span five centuries of British art,
taking in Hogarth, the Blakes (William
and Peter), Gainsborough, Constable,
Reynolds, Bacon and more; Turner is
particularly well represented. There are
living artists too, with works by Howard
Hodgkin, Lucian Freud and David
Hockney. The shop is well stocked and
the restaurant is highly regarded. You
can also have the best of both art worlds,
thanks to the Tate-to-Tate boat service.
Event highlights '1807: Blake, Slavery
and the Radical Mind' (until 21 Oct
2007); Hockney on Turner watercolours (until 3 Feb 2008).

Trafalgar Square

Charing Cross tube/rail.
Map p75 C1 **⑪**
The centrepiece of London, Trafalgar
Square was conceived in the 1820s by
the Prince Regent, later George IV, who
commissioned John Nash to create a
grand square to pay homage to Britain's
naval power. The piazza has always
been a natural gathering point – more
so since it was semi-pedestrianised in
2003. The square's focal point is
Nelson's Column, a Corinthian pillar
topped by a statue of naval hero Horatio
Nelson. More interesting, the 'fourth
plinth' at the square's north-western
corner stood empty until it began to host
temporary contemporary sculptures: as
we go to press, the programme seems to
have ground to a bit of a halt – Thomas
Schütte's perspex acrylic *Hotel for the
Birds* was overdue; its replacement,
scheduled for September 2008, was yet
to be confirmed.

Westminster Abbey

*20 Dean's Yard, SW1P 3PA
(7222 5152/tours 7654 4900/
www.westminster-abbey.org).
St James's Park or Westminster
tube.* **Open** *Chapter House, Nave &
Royal Chapels* 9.30am-3.45pm Mon,
Tue, Thur, Fri; 9.30am-7pm Wed;

St Martin-in-the-Fields

*Trafalgar Square, WC2N 4JJ (7766
1100/Brass Rubbing Centre 7766 1122/
box office 7839 8362/www.stmartin
-in-the-fields.org). Leicester Square tube/
Charing Cross tube/rail.* **Open** *Church*
8am-6pm daily. *Brass Rubbing Centre*
10am-6pm Mon-Sat; noon-6pm Sun.
Admission free. **Map** p75 C1 **⑨**
A church has stood on this site since
the 13th century, 'in the fields' between
Westminster and the City; this one was
built in 1726 by James Gibbs. It is
perhaps best known for its evening
classical music concerts, but also
houses a good café, a small gallery and
the London Brass Rubbing Centre. A
£36m refurbishment was due for completion as we went to press. Improved
underground spaces will be entered
through a new glazed pavilion, and
concert facilities brought up to date.

Tate Britain

*Millbank, SW1P 4RG (7887 8000/
www.tate.org.uk). Pimlico tube.* **Open**
10am-5.50pm daily. *Tours* 11am, noon,

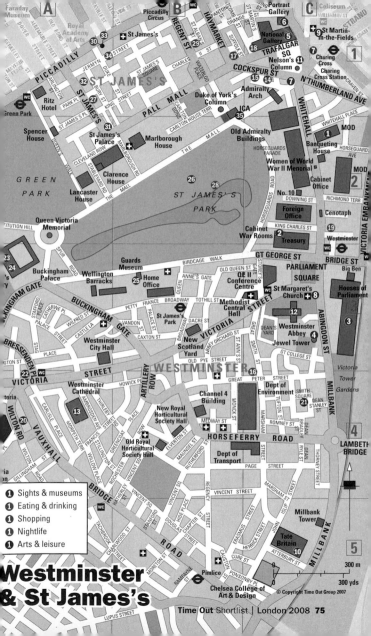

Westminster & St James's

- ❶ Sights & museums
- ❶ Eating & drinking
- ❶ Shopping
- ❶ Nightlife
- ❶ Arts & leisure

National Dining Rooms

9.30am-1.45pm Sat. *Abbey Museum* 10.30am-4pm Mon-Sat. *Cloisters* 8am-6pm Mon-Sat. *Garden* Apr-Sept 10am-6pm Tue-Thur. Oct-Mar 10am-4pm Tue-Thur. **Admission** £10, free-£6 reductions. **Map** p75 C3 ⑫

Westminster Abbey has been synonymous with British royalty since 1066, when Edward the Confessor built a church on the site just in time for his own funeral. Since then a 'who's who' of the monarchy has been buried here and, with two exceptions (Edwards V and VIII), every ruler since William the Conqueror has been crowned here. Of the original abbey, only the Pyx Chamber and the Norman undercroft remain. The Gothic nave and choir were rebuilt in the 13th century; the Henry VII Chapel, with its spectacular fan vaulting, was added in 1503-12, and Nicholas Hawksmoor's west towers in 1745. The interior is cluttered with monuments to statesmen, scientists and poets. The centrepiece of the octagonal Chapter House is its 13th-century tiled floor, while the Little Cloister garden offers respite from the crowds, especially during free lunchtime concerts.

Westminster Cathedral

42 Francis Street, SW1P 1QW (7798 9055/www.westminstercathedral.org.uk). Victoria tube/rail. **Open** 7am-7pm Mon-Fri, Sun; 8am-7pm Sat. **Admission** free. *Campanile* £3; £1.50 reductions. No credit cards. **Map** p75 A4 ⑬

Part wedding cake, part sweet stick, this neo-Byzantine confection is Britain's premier Catholic cathedral, built between 1895 and 1903. The inside has yet to be finished, but you can get a taste of what's planned from the magnificent columns and mosaics. Eric Gill's sculptures of the Stations of the Cross (1914-18) are world renowned. The view from the bell tower is superb.

Eating & drinking

Albannach

66 Trafalgar Square, WC2N 5DS (7930 0066/www.albannach.co.uk). Charing Cross tube/rail. **Open** noon-1am Mon-Wed; noon-3am Thur-Sat. **Bar**. **Map** p75 C1 ⑭

We rate both the main bar and the cocktail bar, Doon, at this upscale Scottish establishment. Decor is stylish, with dark oak and slate, stripy banquettes, tartan flourishes and chandeliers made from antlers. The main bar has one of the capital's best selections of Scottish whisky, and there's also a good range of cocktails. The first-floor dining room serves decent food.

Blackwood

NEW *21-24 Cockspur Street, SW1Y 5BN. Charing Cross tube/rail.* **Map** p75 C1 ⑮

See box opposite.

Cinnamon Club

Old Westminster Library, 30-32 Great Smith Street, SW1P 3BU (7222 2555/ www.cinnamonclub.com). St James's Park or Westminster tube. **Open** 7.30-9.30am, noon-2.30pm, 6-10.45pm Mon-Fri; 6-10.45pm Sat. **Main courses** £12-£26. **Indian**. **Map** p75 C3 ⑯

Housed in a spacious former Victorian library, the Cinnamon Club is a prime destination for politicians and power brokers. Executive chef Vivek Singh's menu isn't for timid palates – expect fiery flavours and robust masalas rather than delicate notes, along with innovation aplenty. Indian breakfasts too.

Mint Leaf

NEW *Suffolk Place, SW1Y 4HX (7930 9020/www.mintleafrestaurant.com). Piccadilly Circus tube/Charing Cross tube/rail.* **Open** *Bar* noon-midnight Mon-Wed; noon-1am Thur-Sat. *Restaurant* noon-3pm, 5.30-11pm Mon-Fri; 5.30-11pm Sat. **££. Indian & Pakistani.** Map p75 B1 ⑰
This trendy bar/restaurant has a gorgeous dark-wood interior, with several dining rooms lit with flickering lights. The food (hydrabadi lamb korma, lotus stem dumplings stuffed with dried figs) can be hit or miss – sometimes excellent, sometimes not – so be sure to begin with some of the brilliant cocktails at the bar.

National Dining Rooms

Sainsbury Wing, National Gallery, Trafalgar Square, WC2N 5DN (7747 2525/www.nationalgallery.co.uk). Charing Cross tube/rail. **Open** *Bakery* 10am-5.30pm Mon, Tue, Thur-Sun; 10am-8.30pm Wed. *Restaurant* noon-3.30pm Mon, Tue, Thur-Sun; 5-7.15pm Wed. **Main courses** £13.50-£18.50. **British.** Map p75 C1 ⑱
Three cheers for Oliver Peyton (who runs a growing number of eateries in attractions around town, including Inn the Park, p79). The National Dining Rooms serve fine British food, in a modern setting, at reasonable prices. Even the drinks list is interesting, with more than 20 teas, plus ales and ciders.

Red Lion

48 Parliament Street, Westminster, SW1A 2NH (7930 5826). Westminster tube. **Open** 11am-11pm Mon-Fri; 11am-9.30pm Sat; noon-8pm Sun. **Pub.** Map p75 C2 ⑲
The skinny main bar at this famous Westminster boozer (there's also a cellar bar and an upstairs grill room) has wooden alcoves full of chatter, a division bell and TVs screening BBC Parliament, all of them haughtily overseen by sideburned ministers in Empire-era portraits.

Cool food

Stuffy Westminster in the culinary spotlight.

When St Alban (p80) opened in early 2007 it was immediately the hottest table in town, with tales of celebrities heading to this land of stiff-necked parliamentarians in throngs. Let's hope the old boys are used to the attention, because more hot openings are on the way.

First out the blocks comes **Cha Cha No Hana** (p79), a high-end version of the low-end Japanese *izakaya* – in the original, a kind of snacks-and-saké pub. The excitement is due to the man behind it: Alan Yau, described by *Time Out*'s food editor Guy Dimond as 'the best restaurateur in London'. Already behind such winning ideas as the Busaba Eathai chain (p118) and sleekly superb Hakkasan (p144) and Yauatcha (p122), Yau should ensure Cha Cha No Hana is a perfect marriage of sleek decor and impeccably poised cooking. Perfection takes time: an initial, provisional opening date of February 2007 has slipped to the summer. Meanwhile, there's also talk of a new Busaba Eathai and a Sichuan-themed restaurant.

The other big news is Iqbal Wahhab's latest project. The man behind Borough Market's roaringly successful Roast (p67) and nearby Cinnamon Club (left) is to open **Blackwood** (left) right by Trafalgar Square. Expect upmarket surf-and-turf upstairs, a downstairs club with an Indian theme and, just maybe, a Christmas 2007 opening date.

Arts & leisure

St Martin-in-the-Fields (p74) hosts crowd-pleasing evening concerts, plus less predictable thrice-weekly lunchtime recitals.

Apollo Victoria

Wilton Road, SW1V 1LL (0870 400 0751/www.wickedthemusical.co.uk). Victoria tube/rail. **Map** p75 A4 ⓴
Smash-hit Broadway musical *Wicked* tells the untold back story of the Wicked Witch of the West and Glinda the Good Witch from *The Wizard of Oz*. Production subject to change.

St John's, Smith Square

Smith Square, SW1P 3HA (7222 1061/www.sjss.org.uk). Westminster tube. **Map** p75 C4 ㉑
This elegant 18th-century church hosts a more or less nightly programme of orchestral and chamber concerts, with occasional vibrant recitals on its magnificent Klais organ. There's a wonderfully secluded restaurant in the crypt, open even if there is no performance.

Victoria Palace Theatre

Victoria Street, SW1E 5EA (0870 895 5577/www.victoriapalacetheatre.co.uk). Victoria tube/rail. **Map** p75 A4 ㉒
Award-winning musical *Billy Elliot*, scored by Elton John, is the attraction here. Production subject to change.

St James's

St James's is one of central London's quietest and most exclusive areas. **Buckingham Palace** presides over the lovely lake in **St James's Park**, while **Jermyn Street** and a rejuvenated **Fortnum & Mason** encourage you to shop like gentry. There are several signs of a change of pace, though. Destination restaurants are opening (**St Alban**, **Cha Cha No Hana**), and the **ICA** keeps right on representing edgy contemporary art. Perhaps sleepy St James's is waking up after all.

Sights & museums

Buckingham Palace & Royal Mews

The Mall, SW1A 1AA (7766 7300/ Royal Mews 7766 7302/www.royal collection.org.uk). Green Park or St James's Park tube/Victoria tube/rail. **Open** *State Rooms* mid July-Sept 9.45am-5.30pm daily. *Queen's Gallery* 10am-5.30pm daily. *Royal Mews* Oct-July 11am-4pm daily. Aug, Sept 10am-5pm daily. **Admission** *Palace* £14; £8-£12.50 reductions. *Queen's Gallery* £7.50; £4-£6.50 reductions. *Royal Mews* £6.50; £4-£5.50 reductions. **Map** p75 A3 ㉓
Built in 1703, the palace started life as a grand house for the Duke of Buckingham, but George III liked it so much he bought it, in 1761, for his young bride Charlotte. His son, George IV, hired John Nash to convert it into a palace. Thus construction on the 600-room palace began in 1825. But the project was beset with disaster from the start. Nash was fired after George IV's death and the more reliable but unimaginative Edward Blore was hired to finish the job. Queen Victoria, the first

Inn the Park

royal to live here, called the place 'a disgrace to the country'. In August and September, while the Windsors are on their hols, the State Apartments are open to the public. The Queen's Gallery contains highlights of Elizabeth's decorative and fine art collection: Old Masters, Sèvres porcelain, ornately inlaid cabinets and the Diamond Diadem (familiar from millions of postage stamps).

Changing the Guard

(www.changing-the-guard.com).
Green Park tube/Victoria tube/rail.
Map p75 A3 **24**
The Changing of the Foot Guards happens here at 11.30am on alternate days, except in rain. The cavalry version is at 11am (10am Sun) on Horseguards Parade, just east of St James's Park.

Guards' Museum

Wellington Barracks, Birdcage Walk,
SW1E 6HQ (7414 3428/www.theguards
museum.com). St James's Park tube.
Open 10am-4pm daily. **Admission** £3;
free-£2 reductions. **Map** p75 B3 **25**
This small, immaculately maintained museum records the history of the

British Army's five Guards regiments. It contains uniforms, paintings, intriguing memorabilia and medals, including the first ever minted for the army.

St James's Park

Map p75 B2 **26**
Originally a royal deer park for St James's Palace, the park's pastoral landscape owes its influence to John Nash, who redesigned it in the early 19th century under the orders of George IV. The view of Buckingham Palace from the bridge over the lake is wonderful, especially at night. The lake is now a sanctuary for wildfowl, among them pelicans (fed at 3pm daily).

Eating & drinking

Cha Cha No Hana

NEW *23 St James's Street, SW1A 1HA.*
Green Park tube. **Map** p75 A1 **27**
See box p77.

Inn the Park

St James's Park, SW1A 2BJ
(7451 9999/www.innthepark.co.uk).
St James's Park tube. **Open** 8-11am,

n, 5-9.45pm Mon-Fri; 9-11am,
n, 5-9.45pm Sat, Sun. **££**.
café. Map p75 B2 ㉘

...is is one of the best-located restaurants in London. The modern wooden structure fits perfectly into a lakeside slot, and every table has a water view. Good for families, it's also a romantic night-time haunt. Food runs from breakfasts through sandwiches to full meals, with attention paid to British sourcing.

St Alban

NEW *4-12 Regent Street, SW1Y 4PE (7499 8558).* Piccadilly Circus tube.
Open noon-3pm, 5.30pm-midnight daily. **£££**. **Italian. Map** p75 B1 ㉙
St Alban is from Chris Corbin and Jeremy King, the duo who run the Wolseley (p111), and its booking rate is hot. The dining room is elegant, if a little plain, but the food is great. Expect heavenly dishes such as pappardelle with ragù, and sublime seafood. All very fine – just don't expect to drop in casually for dinner.

1707

NEW *Lower ground floor, Fortnum & Mason, 181 Piccadilly, W1A 1ER (7734 8040/www.fortnumandmason.co.uk).* Green Park or Piccadilly Circus tube
Open 10am-7.30pm Mon-Sat; noon-5pm Sun. **££**. **Wine bar. Map** p75 A1 ㉚
See box opposite.

Shopping

Berry Bros & Rudd

3 St James's Street, SW1A 1EG (7396 9600/www.bbr.com). Green Park tube.
Open 10am-6pm Mon-Fri; 10am-4pm Sat. **Map** p75 A2 ㉛
Britain's oldest wine merchant has been trading on the same premises since 1698 and its heritage is reflected in its panelled sales and tasting rooms. There are some 20,000 bottles in the cellars, and knowledgeable staff on hand to advise.

DR Harris & Co

29 St James's Street, SW1A 1HB (7930 3915/www.drharris.co.uk). Green Park or Piccadilly Circus tube.
Open 8.30am-6pm Mon-Fri; 9.30am-5pm Sat. **Map** p75 A1 ㉜

Boasting two royal warrants, DR Harris has been in business for two centuries, and on this site since 1963. A number of glass cabinets in the gorgeous interior display a wide range of products, including lovely own-brand lotions and potions.

Fortnum & Mason

NEW *181 Piccadilly, W1A 1ER (7734 8040/www.fortnumandmason.co.uk).* Green Park or Piccadilly Circus tube. **Open** 10am-6.30pm Mon-Sat; noon-6pm Sun (food hall only).
Map p75 A1 ㉝
Reaching its tercentenary in November 2007, London's oldest department store has been having a major makeover. See box opposite.

Jermyn Street

Green Park or Piccadilly Circus tube. **Map** p75 A1 ㉞
The material needs of the English gent are met by the anachronistic retailers and restaurants of Jermyn Street, such as old-fashioned shirt shop Harvie & Hudson (Nos.96-97) and classic British dining room Wiltons (No.55). Bates the Hatter (No.21A) has been providing classy headwear for more than 100 years, while Paxton & Whitfield (No.93) is (according to Winston Churchill) the only place from which a gentleman buys his cheese.

Arts & leisure

Institute of Contemporary Arts (ICA)

The Mall, SW1Y 5AH (7930 3647/ www.ica.org.uk). Piccadilly Circus tube/Charing Cross tube/rail.
Open *Galleries* noon-7.30pm daily.
Admission *Daily membership* £2-£3, £1.50-£2 reductions. **Map** p75 B1 ㉟
Founded in 1948, the ICA still revels in a remit that challenges traditional notions of art. Its cinema shows London's artiest films (and is the venue for the annual onedotzero digital film festival), its theatre stages performance art and quality gigs, and its exhibitions are always talking points. There's also a bar, café and small shop.

Happy birthday, Fortnum's!

Cynical, world-weary sorts that we are, it isn't often we get excited about a shop refurbishment. But when the shop is **Fortnum & Mason** (left), London's oldest department store, we take notice – and the signs are good.

Founded in 1707 by a former footman to Queen Anne, Fortnum's has been celebrating its tercentenary (in November 2007) with a rolling £24 million programme of refurbishments. First to reach completion was the fabled, over-the-top food hall on the lower ground floor. The marbled pillars and chandeliers are still in place, as are the jams, tea and fresh fish and game, but a new atrium pours in natural light from the ceiling.

Next came **1707** (left), the store's brilliant new wine bar. There was always a fantastic range of (mainly European) wines for sale, but nowhere for customers to try them. Designer David Collins has created a wine bar that mixes marble, mosaic tiles and wooden plank walls to unusual and quite beautiful effect: like a cross between a Finnish sauna and a Milanese shoe shop.

You can order any bottle from the cellar of several hundred displayed just outside, and drink for a flat-rate corkage charge of £10 (£5 for half-bottles), no matter how expensive the wine. If you find choosing from hundreds of wines daunting, there's a 20-strong bar list by the glass. And even the snack food is of utmost quality.

So when it comes to the four new in-store restaurants, opening between August and October 2007, we're expecting a lot. While the brasserie-style Fountain, seasonally focused Galley and fine-dining St James's all sound good, we're most looking forward to the Parlour, a modern take on a 1950s ice-cream parlour – back in 1955, Fortnum & Mason was one of the first places in London to serve a Knickerbocker Glory.

Nor is it all about food and drink. Three brand-new shopping floors cater for women (lingerie and perfumes in a boudoir setting), men (leather goods, games, stationery) and, well, cooks (cookware, dining sets). Even traditionalists should be happy: the courtly, tail-coated staff are set to remain.

LONDON BY AREA

Hyde Park

South Kensington & Chelsea

LONDON BY AREA

South Kensington & Knightsbridge

Knightsbridge is about be-seen-in restaurants and designer shops, but that doesn't mean it's particularly stylish: we're talking old-school money, which can at least make for great people-watching. South Kensington has a slightly lower stuffiness rating – and the majority of London's world-class museums. The **Natural History Museum**, **Science Museum** and **Victoria & Albert Museum** are clustered together, but such is the wealth of exhibits in each you'd be foolish to try to 'do' more than one of them in a single day. The enormous **Royal Albert Hall** and similarly overblown **Albert Memorial** pay homage to the man behind it all.

Sights & museums

Albert Memorial

Kensington Gardens, SW7 (tours 7495 0916). South Kensington tube. **Tours** 2pm, 3pm 1st Sun of mth. **Tickets** £4.50; £4 reductions. No credit cards. **Map** p84 B1 ❶

One of the Victorians' great sculptural achievements, the memorial centres on a gilded Prince Albert, attended by a white marble frieze of poets and painters. The 180ft spire is inlaid with semi-precious stones.

Apsley House

149 Piccadilly, W1J 7NT (7499 5676/ www.english-heritage.org.uk). Hyde Park Corner tube. **Open** 10am-4pm Tue-Sun. **Admission** £4.95; £2.50-£3.70 reductions. **Map** p85 E1 ❷

Built by Robert Adam in the 1770s, Apsley House was home to the Duke of Wellington for 35 years. Rooms hold interesting trinkets and paintings, including Goya's portrait of the Iron Duke after defeating the French in 1812.

Brompton Oratory

Thurloe Place, Brompton Road, SW7 2RP (7808 0900/www.brompton oratory.com). South Kensington tube. **Open** 6.30am-8pm daily. **Admission** free. **Map** p84 C3 ❸

The second-biggest Catholic church in the country (after Westminster Cathedral) was completed in 1884, but it feels older – partly because many of its marbles, mosaics and statuary pre-date the structure. The vast main space culminates in a magnificent Italian altarpiece. The 11am Solemn Mass on Sundays is sung in Latin.

Hyde Park & Kensington Gardens

(7298 2100/www.royalparks.gov.uk). **Map** p84 C1 ❹

At 1.5 miles long and about a mile wide, Hyde Park is the largest of London's Royal Parks. There's plenty of picnicking and outdoor activity here: in summer, rowing boats and pedaloes can be hired on the Serpentine (London's oldest boating lake), and year-round the park's perimeter is popular with roller-skaters, and bike- and horse-riders.

To the west is Kensington Gardens, home of the Diana, Princess of Wales Memorial Playground, and the ring-shaped Princess Diana Memorial Fountain (more of a babbling moat).

Hyde Park has long been a focal point for freedom of speech. The legalisation of public assembly in the park led to the establishment in 1872 of Speakers' Corner, an area in the north-east corner of the park where ranters sane and bonkers have the floor. Other points of interest include a bronze statue of Peter Pan, sculpted by Sir George Frampton in honour of JM Barrie.

Kensington Palace

Kensington Gardens, W8 4PX (7937 9561/booking line 0870 751 5180/www.hrp.org.uk). High Street Kensington or Queensway tube. **Open** Mar-Oct 10am-5pm daily. *Nov-Feb* 10am-4pm daily. **Admission** £11.50; £7.50-£9 reductions. **Map** p84 A1 ❺

The sections of this Wren-adapted Jacobean mansion open to the public mostly give the impression of intimacy, although the King's Apartments are pretty grand. The Royal Ceremonial Dress Collection contains lavish ensembles worn for state occasions and a collection of 14 dresses worn by Diana, Princess of Wales, the palace's most famous resident and – given the recent tenth anniversary of her death – the sole reason many will wish to visit. But do make time for tea in Queen Anne's Orangery (built 1704-5).

Natural History Museum

Cromwell Road, SW7 5BD (7942 5725/switchboard 7942 5000/www. nhm.ac.uk). South Kensington tube. **Open** 10am-5.50pm daily; **Admission** free. **Map** p84 B3 ❻

This cathedral to the Victorian mania for collecting and cataloguing is as impressive as the giant cast of a diplodocus skeleton in the main hall. If you've come with children, you may not see much more than the dinosaur gallery, with its animatronic T rex. But there's much more – 70 million plants, animals, fossils, rocks and minerals, to be exact. Some of the galleries are static and dry; others, like Creepy Crawlies, so beloved of children you can hardly not get near the exhibits. Entry to the Earth Galleries is portentous: you travel via an escalator, passing through a giant suspended globe and twinkling images of the star system. **Event highlights** Ice Station Antarctica (until 6 Apr 2008); Shell Wildlife Photographer of the Year (27 Oct 2007-Apr 2008); the Wildlife Garden, a living display of British lowland habitats (Apr-Oct each year, £1.50).

Science Museum

Exhibition Road, SW7 2DD (7942 4000/booking & information 0870 870 4868/www.sciencemuseum.org. uk). South Kensington tube. **Open** 10am-5.45pm daily. **Admission** free. **Map** p84 B3 ❼

LONDON BY AREA

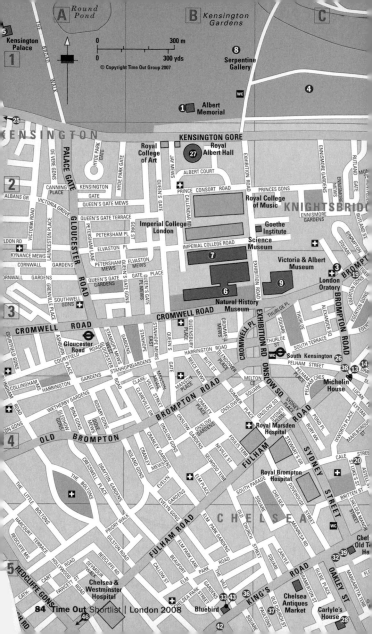

South Kensington & Chelsea

Shop, scoff and relax

Will foodies replace fashionistas on High Street Ken?

What's this? The striking art deco Barkers department store, opened in 1870 and long an outlet for fashion brands such as Karen Millen and Monsoon, has been refurbished and is to reopen in June 2007 as... a supermarket.

This is no ordinary supermarket: it's a swanky new outpost of the Texan organic food chain **Whole Foods Market**. Notwithstanding the new John Lewis food hall or the wonderfully refurbished Fortnum & Mason, Whole Foods Market is on an unprecedented scale – three floors and 80,000 square feet of scale.

Shoppers enter the Provisions Hall, where the smell of bread and pastries baked on the premises greets them. As well as carefully sourced olive oils, artisan cheese, wine and microbrewed beer, there's a wine bar and coffee shop. Beneath, the lower ground floor's Market Level sells fresh food – single-producer fish, meat, fruit and veg – and houses treatment rooms, health and beauty products, and green clothes. Upstairs, there are a dozen eateries offering tidbits from sushi and saké to oysters and champagne, from a crêpe to pizza. Where the hell will they fit the 'store artist' and DJ?
■ 63-97 Kensington High Street, W8 5SE (www.whole foodsmarket.co.uk)

The Science Museum demonstrates how science filters down through daily life, with displays on engines, cars, aeroplanes, ships, the home, medicine and computers. Landmark inventions such as Stephenson's Rocket, Whittle's turbojet engine, Arkwright's spinning machine and the Apollo 10 command module are celebrated in the Making the Modern World gallery. The Wellcome Wing has an IMAX cinema and the Who Am I? gallery, which explores human characteristics and discoveries in genetics, brain science and psychology. The new-look Energy Hall on the ground floor includes a hands-on gallery all about power and saving energy.

Event highlights Special events, including theatrical performances, science shows and hands-on workshops take place throughout the year.

Serpentine Gallery

Kensington Gardens (nr Albert Memorial), W2 3XA (7402 6075/ www.serpentinegallery.org). Lancaster Gate or South Kensington tube. **Open** 10am-6pm daily. **Admission** free. **Map** p84 B1 ❽

This light and airy gallery features a rolling programme of often challenging exhibitions, while the annual Serpentine Pavilion project commissions an internationally renowned architect to design and build a new pavilion.

Event highlights Each summer, the Serpentine commisions a major architect to build a temporary pavilion in its gardens. Previous master-builders include Rem Koolhaas, Oscar Niemeyer and Daniel Liebeskind.

Victoria & Albert Museum

Cromwell Road, SW7 2RL (7942 2000/ www.vam.ac.uk). South Kensington tube. **Open** 10am-5.45pm Mon, Tue, Thur-Sun; 10am-10pm Wed & last Fri of mth. **Admission** free. **Map** p84 C3 ❾

The 150-year-old V&A dazzles: its grand galleries contain about four million pieces of furniture, metalwork, ceramics, textiles, sculpture, paintings, posters, jewellery and glass from cultures across the world. The museum

Ladurée, at Harrods, p90

has the finest collection of Italian Renaissance sculpture outside Italy, while home-grown treasures include the Great Bed of Ware, Canova's *The Three Graces* and Henry VIII's writing desk. Also make time for the Fashion galleries, which run from the 18th century to the present day, and the Cast Courts, with their full-scale plaster casts such as Michaelangelo's David. The Jameel Gallery is dedicated to Islamic art. In February 2008, the Sackler Education Centre opens, with its new auditorium. Outside museum hours it functions as an arts centre.
Event highlights 'The Art of Lee Miller' (until 13 Jan 2008); 'The Golden Age of Couture – Paris and London 1947-1957' (22 Sept 2007-20 Jan 2008); 'China Design Now' (15 Mar-6 July 2008).

Wellington Arch

Hyde Park Corner, W1J 7JZ (7930 2726/www.english-heritage.org.uk). Hyde Park Corner tube. **Open** *Apr-Oct* 10am-5pm Wed-Sun. *Nov-Mar* 10am-4pm Wed-Sun. **Admission** £3; free-£2.30 reductions. **Map** p85 F1 ⑩

Built in the late 1820s to mark Britain's triumph over France, the arch has three floors of historical displays. There are views of the Houses of Parliament and Buckingham Palace from the balcony, though trees intervene in summer.

Eating & drinking

Those with a sweet tooth shouldn't miss Ladurée in Harrods (p90).

Amaya

Halkin Arcade, Motcomb Street, SW1X 8JT (7823 1166/www.realindianfood. com). Knightsbridge tube. **Open** 12.30-2.15pm, 6.30-11.15pm Mon-Fri; 12.30-2.30pm, 6.30-11.15pm Sat; 12.45-2.45pm, 6.30-10.15pm Sun. **£££**. **Indian**. **Map** p85 E2 ⑪

Amaya stands out for its innovative grazing menu of kebabs and birianis, and beautiful decor of rosewood panels, terracotta ornamentation and chandeliers. Our dining experiences have been mixed: some dishes so good they left us speechless, others far less so. There's a notable list of fabulous sugar-free desserts.

Awana

NEW *85 Sloane Avenue, SW3 3DX (7584 8880/www.awana.co.uk). South Kensington tube.* **Open** *Bar* noon-11.30pm Wed-Sun. *Restaurant* noon-3pm, 6-11pm Mon-Wed; noon-3pm, 6-11.30pm Thur-Sat; noon-3pm, 6-10.30pm Sun. **££. Malaysian.** Map p84 C4 **12**

Awana's sleek teak fit-out is reminiscent of a Malaysian plantation house. Stylised clouds drift across a deep-blue wall, in homage to the restaurant's name (Awana is Malay for 'in the clouds'). Food is of a consistently high standard: tuck in to juicy chicken satay and beautifully presented nasi goreng, or try the ten-course tasting menu. Service, too, is excellent.

Bibendum

Michelin House, 81 Fulham Road, SW3 6RD (7581 5817/www.bibendum.co.uk). South Kensington tube. **Open** noon-2.30pm, 6.30-11.30pm Mon-Fri; 12.30-3pm, 7-11.30pm Sat; 12.30-3pm, 7-10.30pm Sun. **£££. Modern European.** Map p84 C3 **13**

Set in the gorgeous art deco Michelin building, Bibendum is one of the classiest joints in town. Chef Matthew Harris gives clever spins on the pan-European dishes familiar from many a D&D London outlet, while the stunning wine list includes some reasonable options. Service is spot-on. Allow a fortnight if you want to book dinner.

Daphne's

112 Draycott Avenue, SW3 3AE (7589 4257/www.daphnes-restaurant.co.uk). South Kensington tube. **Open** noon-3pm, 5.30-11.30pm Mon-Fri; noon-3.30pm, 5.30-11.30pm Sat; 12.30-4pm, 5.30-10.30pm Sun. **£££. Italian.** Map p84 C3 **14**

Don't let the old-fashioned name and Brompton location fool you: Daphne's is a very impressive, up-to-date operation, run by the folks behind the Ivy. The dining room is an airy, simply decorated space complete with a glass ceiling, while, in true Italian style, the rustic cooking favours first-rate local (that is, British) ingredients.

La Noisette

NEW *164 Sloane Street, SW1X 9QB (7750 5000/www.gordonramsay.com). Knightsbridge or Sloane Square tube.* **Open** noon-2.30pm Mon-Fri; 6-11pm Mon-Sat. **££££. Modern European.** Map p85 E2 **15**

Head chef Bjorn van der Horst has already secured a Michelin star here. But while some dishes on the French-inspired, seasonal menu are traditional, his versions are anything but familiar. Staff are highly welcoming and the £21 three-course lunch (and early dinner) are great value.

Nag's Head

53 Kinnerton Street, SW1X 8ED (7235 1135). Hyde Park Corner or Knightsbridge tube. **Open** 11am-11pm Mon-Sat; noon-10.30pm Sun. **Pub.** No credit cards. Map p85 E2 **16**

In this eccentric pub, the floor of the main bar is a foot lower behind the counter, rendering staff in curious miniature; conversely, from the downstairs room, you can see bartenders' feet as they pour perfect pints. The interior is cluttered with relics, and mobile phones are banned.

Nahm

The Halkin, Halkin Street, SW1X 7DJ (7333 1234/www.nahm.como.bz). Hyde Park Corner tube. **Open** noon-2.30pm, 7-11pm Mon-Fri; 7-11pm Sat; 7-10pm Sun. **£££. Thai.** Map p85 E2 **17**

Nahm's Australian-born founder David Thompson is the world's most renowned Thai chef, and every dish from this menu of recreated Thai courtly cooking is faultless. Patient waiters steer you through a menu that strays far from the familiar. The sleek dining room has annoying acoustics, but then you are here for the food.

Pétrus

The Berkeley, Wilton Place, SW1X 7RL (7235 1200/www.petrus-restaurant. com). Knightsbridge or Hyde Park Corner tube. **Open** noon-2.30pm, 6-10.45pm Mon-Fri; 6-10.45pm Sat. **££££. Modern European.** Map p85 E2 **18**

Fifth Floor, at Harvey Nichols, p90

Stunning food, sumptuous decor and smooth, somewhat theatrical service, make this two Michelin-starred restaurant a fantastic venue for a celebration. The look is sophisticated, with purple velvet padding the walls, beautiful lights and an abundance of silverware. The kitchen is Marcus Wareing's domain, but the cuisine is firmly in the style of Gordon Ramsay, with carefully balanced menus showcasing luxurious ingredients. Finish with something from the matchless bonbon trolley.

Racine

239 Brompton Road, SW3 2EP (7584 4477). Knightsbridge or South Kensington tube/14, 74 bus. **Open** noon-3pm, 6-10.30pm Mon-Fri; noon-3.30pm, 6-10.30pm Sat; noon-3.30pm, 6-10pm Sun. **£££**. **French**. Map p84 C3 ⑲

Enter through curtains into one of London's most vibrant and consistently enjoyable restaurants. The food is a mix of modern and retro bistro classics, the staff focused and French. Racine's chef Henry Harris has sometimes been teased for creating a place that's too retro even for France; but judging by the variety of diners, this restaurant knows how to delight everyone.

Tom's Kitchen

27 Cale Street, SW3 3QP (7349 0202/www.tomskitchen.co.uk). South Kensington or Sloane Square tube. **Open** 7.30am-midnight Mon-Fri; 8am-midnight Sat, Sun. **££**. **Brasserie**. Map p84 C4 ⑳

'Tom' is Tom Aikens, one of the top chef/proprietors in the UK. He runs a haute cuisine restaurant in Chelsea, but this venue is an all-day brasserie with a menu that leans towards a rootsier style of Anglo-French cooking. It isn't a fancy place, but it's impressively focused. Head for the buzzing ground-floor brasserie, or pop in for breakfast or afternoon tea.

Townhouse

31 Beauchamp Place, SW3 1NU (7589 5080/www.lab-townhouse.com). Knightsbridge tube. **Open** 4pm-midnight Mon-Sat; 4-11.30pm Sun. **Pub**. Map p85 D3 ㉑

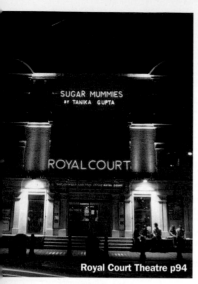
Royal Court Theatre p94

From the street the Townhouse is little more than a discreet sign and a doorway – and even that is hidden behind a meaty bouncer. Get past him and you'll find a sleek, narrow bar, with leather sofas in the tiny seating area at the back. The place is pleasantly chic, the bar staff are lovely and the cocktail list as big as a phonebook.

Zuma

5 Raphael Street, SW7 1DL (7584 1010/www.zumarestaurant.com). Knightsbridge tube. **Open** *Bar* noon-11pm Mon-Fri; 12.30-11pm Sat; noon-10pm Sun. *Restaurant* noon-2.15pm, 6-10.45pm Mon-Fri; 12.30-3.15pm, 6-10.45pm Sat; 12.30-2.45pm, 6-10.15pm Sun. **£££. Japanese. Map** p85 D2 ㉒
No longer new, Zuma has retained its glamorous sheen: *The Flintstones*-chic interior is a hoot and the food is as good as ever. New-style sushi and sashimi are just the ticket, and the saké list is amazing. Seats at the sushi bar, the grill or in the slickly designed main dining area still require booking a week or two in advance.

LONDON BY AREA

Shopping

The big shopping news in Kensington is the arrival of **Whole Foods Market** (see box p86).

Harrods

87-135 Brompton Road, SW1X 7XL (7730 1234/www.harrods. com). Knightsbridge tube. **Open** 10am-8pm Mon-Sat; noon-6pm Sun. **Map** p85 D2 ㉓
By turns tasteful and tacky, this is an exuberant cathedral to consumerism. The food halls are spectacular, while the meat and game room retains its original Edwardian tiling. The two Rooms of Luxury, plus the Egyptian Room, cover accessories by the likes of Louis Vuitton and Chloé. The main beauty hall includes a Lifestyle Beauty room showcasing Kiehl's and MAC. Across the street, Harrods 102 is a luxury convenience store, while Ladurée (Hans Road entrance) is an elegant café serving superlative macaroons.

Harvey Nichols

109-125 Knightsbridge, SW1X 7RJ (7235 5000/www.harveynichols.com). Knightsbridge tube. **Open** 10am-8pm Mon-Sat; noon-6pm Sun. *Café* 8am-10pm Mon-Sat; 8am-6pm Sun. *Restaurant* 10am-11pm Mon-Sat; 10am-6pm Sun. **Map** p85 D2 ㉔
Harvey Nicks is a stylish repository of upmarket brands. On the ground floor, the beauty hall has lots of exclusives, plus designer handbags and über-cool Fair Isle knits from Trovata. The third floor boasts one of the best denim ranges in London. The home department has a concession of Italian luxury brand Culti and there are pitstop beauty treatments courtesy of an Elemis SpaPod. The top storey houses a food hall, café and restaurant (Fifth Floor, 7235 5250) that knocks spots off every other department store eaterie.

Jaan

NEW *7 Thackeray Street, W8 5ET (7376 1006). Kensington High Street tube.* **Open** 11am-6pm Mon-Sat. **Map** p84 A1 ㉕

Bohemian boutique Jaan combines vintage pieces with unique artisan designs. Owner Jacqui Almond uses her 15 years of styling experience and frequent travels to unearth everything from vintage velvet boleros and silk evening gowns to hand-knitted gloves from the Andes.

Library

268 Brompton Road, SW3 2AS (7589 6569). South Kensington tube. **Open** 10am-6.30pm Mon, Tue, Thur-Sat; 10am-7pm Wed; 12.30-5.30pm Sun. **Map** p84 C3 **26**
Designer labels and literature may seem an unlikely combination, but this fantastic emporium convinces otherwise. For men, stock from seasoned greats like McQueen and Westwood hangs alongside that of newer stars like Kris Van Assche. There's a small selection of womenswear (cashmere, Balenciaga bags), and staff are helpful.

Arts & leisure

Royal Albert Hall

Kensington Gore, South Kensington, SW7 2AP (7589 3203/box office 7589 8212/www.royalalberthall.com). South Kensington tube/9, 10, 52 bus. **Map** p84 B2 **27**
Built as a memorial to Queen Victoria's husband, this 5,000-capacity rotunda is best known as the venue for the BBC Proms each summer, despite acoustics that don't do orchestras any favours. Occasional classical concerts are held throughout the year, alongside pop and rock gigs, boxing matches and opera.

Chelsea

When *Time* magazine declared in April 1966 that London was 'swinging', Chelsea's King's Road was the swingingest place of all. These days, kids tend to do better than adults in the shops along the King's Road, but **Daylesford Organic** and **Shop at Bluebird** provide more inviting retail opportunities. Chelsea proper

begins with Sloane Square, spoiled by traffic but redeemed by the **Royal Court Theatre**.

Sights & museums

Carlyle's House

24 Cheyne Row, SW3 5HL (7352 7087/www.nationaltrust.org.uk). Sloane Square tube/11, 19, 22, 49, 211, 319 bus. **Open** *Apr-Oct* 2-5pm Wed-Fri; 11am-5pm Sat, Sun. **Admission** £4.50; £2.30 reductions. **Map** p84 C5 **28**
Thomas Carlyle and his wife Jane moved to this four-storey house in 1834. After Carlyle's death the house was preserved as a museum, offering an intriguing snapshot of Victorian life, from the basement kitchen all the way up to Carlyle's attic office.

Chelsea Physic Garden

66 Royal Hospital Road (entrance on Swan Walk), SW3 4HS (7352 5646/ www.chelseaphysicgarden.co.uk). Sloane Square tube/11, 19, 239 bus. **Open** *Apr-Oct* noon-dusk Wed; noon-5pm Thur, Fri; noon-6pm Sun & bank hols. **Admission** £7; £4 reductions. *Tours* free. **Map** p85 D5 **29**
The garden was set up in 1673, but the key phase of development was in the 18th century. The beds are full of rare trees and healing herbs, dye plants and medicinal vegetables.

National Army Museum

Royal Hospital Road, SW3 4HT (7730 0717/www.national-army-museum. ac.uk). Sloane Square tube/11, 137, 239 bus. **Open** 10am-5.30pm daily. **Admission** free. **Map** p85 D5 **30**
Eccentric exhibits and displays make this museum far more entertaining than the modern exterior might suggest. The collection runs from Agincourt to National Service in the 1950s. Major Michael 'Bronco' Lane, conqueror of Mount Everest, kindly donated his frostbitten fingertips.

Saatchi Gallery

NEW *Duke of York's HQ, off King's Road, SW3 4RY (www.saatchi-gallery. co.uk). Sloane Square tube.* **Map** p85 E4 **31**

Charles Saatchi, the godfather of BritArt, has found an imposing new home for his collection. Due to open in November 2007, it will have 50,000 sq ft of space in which to display the works, and a café/bar.

Event highlights Inaugural exhibition 'Triumph of Painting' (from Nov 2007).

Eating & drinking

Apartment 195

195 King's Road, SW3 5ED (7351 5195/www.apartment195.co.uk). Sloane Square tube/11, 19, 22, 211 bus. **Open** 4-11pm Mon-Sat. **Bar**. **Map** p84 C5 ㉚

Despite buzzed-in access via a black door, this upmarket cocktail bar is very welcoming. You browse a flip-book menu of cocktails mixed by a corps of all-female bartenders.

Bluebird Dining Rooms

350 King's Road, entrance in Beaufort Street, SW3 5UU (7559 1129/www. conran.com). Sloane Square tube then 11, 19, 22, 49, 319 bus. **Open** 7-10.45pm Mon-Sat. **£££**. **British**. **Map** p84 B5 ㉝

A vision of 1930s masculine glamour down to its leather armchairs, this place always seems quiet. Perhaps people are deterred by having to pay £30 whether they eat three courses or two, yet the seasonal menu is an inventive roam around Britain. A shining example of ambitious British cooking.

Gordon Ramsay

68 Royal Hospital Road, SW3 4HP (7352 4441/www.gordonramsay.com). Sloane Square tube. **Open** noon-2pm, 6.30-11pm Mon-Fri. **££££**. **Modern European**. **Map** p85 D5 ㉞

Given how many side-projects Gordon Ramsay is involved in, it's just as well the staff here are able to keep things humming. Executive chef Mark Askew and restaurant director Jean-Claude Breton know all about sublime food and subliminal service. Booking a table is nigh-on impossible, but the reward for succeeding is amazing.

Shopping

Antiquarius

131-141 King's Road, SW3 5PH (7351 5353/www.antiquarius.co.uk). Sloane Square tube then 11, 19, 22, 319, 211 bus. **Open** 10am-6pm Mon-Sat. **Map** p85 D5 ㉟

Around 120 antiques dealers; everything from vintage trunks to original film art.

Austique

330 King's Road, SW3 5UR (7376 3663/www.austique.co.uk). Bus 11, 22. **Open** 10.30am-6.30pm Mon-Sat; noon-5pm Sun. **Map** p84 B5 ㊱

Austique stocks super-feminine clothes, lingerie and accessories. Find sexy cashmere sweaters and party dresses, as well as great denim from not-yet-ubiquitous names.

British Red Cross Shop

67 Old Church Street, SW3 5BS (7351 3206). Sloane Square tube then 11, 19, 22 bus. **Open** 10am-5pm Mon-Sat. **Map** p84 C5 ㊲

Buying from charity shops is all about location: the more affluent the area, the better the stock. This just happens to be the place where many designer neighbours, Manolo Blahnik and Catherine Walker among others, donate unwanted items.

Conran Shop

Michelin House, 81 Fulham Road, SW3 6RD (7589 7401/www. conran.com). South Kensington tube. **Open** 10am-6pm Mon, Tue, Fri; 10am-7pm Wed, Thur; 10am-6.30pm Sat; noon-6pm Sun. **Map** p84 C3 ㊳

Sir Terence Conran's elegant flagship store is packed with a beautifully arranged selection of design treats. A one-stop design destination, whatever your budget.

Daisy & Tom

181-183 King's Road, SW3 5EB (7352 5000/www.daisyandtom.com). Sloane Square tube then 11, 19, 22 bus/49 bus. **Open** 9.30am-6pm Mon, Tue, Thur, Fri; 10am-7pm Wed, Sat; noon-6pm Sun. **Map** p84 C5 ㊴

Rococo

Four times a day there's a call to the children to gather at the ground-floor carousel for a gentle spin. The toy selection is vast, while the clothing department carries its own label, plus Timberland, Catimini and more.

Daylesford Organic

NEW *44B Pimlico Road, SW1W 8LP (7881 8060/www.daylesfordorganic. com). Sloane Square tube.* **Open** 8am-8pm Mon-Sat; 11am-5pm Sun. **Deli.** **Map** p85 E4 ⓸

An impressive offshoot of Lady Bamford's Cotswolds-based farm shop, selling all sorts of goodies over three floors. Service in the café can be chaotic at busy times, but the food compensates – ultra-fresh salads, meaty pork pies and own-made chutneys.

Duke of York Square

King's Road, SW3 4LY. Sloane Square tube. **Map** p84 C5 ⓹

West London's first new public square for over a century is a former barracks transformed into a tastefully landscaped pedestrian area, with lovely fountains. A mix of listed and modern buildings houses high-end high-street clothes stores and various cafés.

Rococo

321 King's Road, Chelsea, SW3 5EP (7352 5857/www.rococochocolates. com). Sloane Square tube then 11, 19, 22 bus. **Open** 10am-6.30pm Mon-Sat; noon-5pm Sun. **Map** p84 B5 ⓷

The beautiful Rococo offers fruit and flower fondants, caramels and gingers. Chocolate bars come in flavours like orange and geranium, rosemary and lavender; truffles and chocolates are similarly exotic. Sugar-free, dairy-free and organic goodies are also sold.

Shop at Bluebird

350 King's Road, Chelsea, SW3 5UU (7351 3873/www.theshopatbluebird. com). Sloane Square tube then 11, 19, 22 bus. **Open** 10am-7pm Mon, Tue, Fri, Sat; 9am-7pm Wed, Thur; noon-6pm Sun. **Map** p84 B5 ⓸

Occupying the ground floor of the art deco Bluebird garage, this capacious space is a shifting showcase of clothes,

Tour-ific

The new way to tour London: go bespoke.

Forget sitting on an open-top bus while some ignoramus cracks jokes about a passing monument they know nothing about. Resist the MP3 tours your hotel provided. Launched in early 2007, two companies are offering walks tailored to young, fashion-conscious and trend-savvy travellers.

The themed itineraries run by **Urban Gentry** promise to take you to unknown, contemporary London. From the Sartorial Spy, which gives the inside scoop on cutting-edge men's fashion around Kensington, Mayfair and Notting Hill, to more familiar themes like the city's lively markets and cutting-edge galleries, Urban Gentry's informed young guides – moonlighting designers, hacks and artists – focus on trends and new locations, rather than history and traditions. Each tour (half-day, £159; full-day, £269) is for up to four people – the small size enables guides to adjust the itinerary according to the group's interests. There are also fully bespoke tours on offer.

Really London has a similar personalised approach: groups of two to six people take a day tour (£150) around the boutiques, markets and galleries of the East End, or a night tour (£160) focused on gigs, bars, clubs and eateries. For either tour, the guide first sits down with you for a chat – during which you can figure out what you want to do.

- www.reallylondon.co.uk
- www.urbangentry.com

lingerie, shoes, accessories, furniture, books and gadgets. Bluebird Epicerie (7559 1140), a deli and continental-style traiteur, recently opened here: some of the more unusual items include Corsican cured meats, fresh choucroute and Ketchoupade – a Basque 'ketchup'.

This Works

18 Cale Street, SW3 3QU (7584 1887/ www.thisworks.com). Sloane Square tube. **Open** 10am-6pm Mon-Sat. **Map** p85 D4 ㊹

A sleek, white haven for sleek, white own-brand lines: the Enjoy Really Rich Lotion, the bestselling Skin Deep Dry Leg Oil and the In the Zone Shower Oil are particular favourites.

Arts & leisure

Cadogan Hall

5 Sloane Terrace, SW1X 9DQ (7730 4500/www.cadoganhall.com). Sloane Square tube. **Map** p85 E3 ㊺

This former church was transformed into an auditorium in 2004. The Royal Philharmonic Orchestra is resident, but the hall hosts smaller ensembles too.

Chelsea Football Club

Stamford Bridge, Fulham Road, Chelsea, SW6 1HS (0870 300 1212/www.chelseafc.co.uk). Fulham Broadway tube. **Map** p84 A5 ㊻

The new standard-setters in the Premiership relinquished their title to Manchester United in 2007. If you want to see them in action, you can pretty much forget about getting Premiership tickets; cup games are more accessible and the stadium tours are fun, if basic.

Royal Court Theatre

Sloane Square, SW1W 8AS (7565 5000/www.royalcourttheatre.com). Sloane Square tube. **Map** p85 E4 ㊼

The emphasis here was always on new voices in British theatre – from John Osborne's *Look Back in Anger* in the inaugural year, 1956, to numerous more recent discoveries: Sarah Kane and Conor McPherson among them. And the current season shows signs of biting new vitality – we're gripped.

Ronnie Scott's p126

The West End

Marylebone

Oxford Street might be renowned as London's shopping street (it certainly bags a massive proportion of the till takings), but head north into Marylebone if boutiques are your thing. The mood changes swiftly: instead of Oxford Street's impassable pavement crowds and undistinguished chainstores (albeit with a few notables such as **John Lewis**, **Selfridges** and **Topshop**), there are quiet squares and a pretty high street that would sit quite happily in an affluent provincial town. In the past decade, the area dubbed 'Marylebone Village' and become increasingly fashionable and desirable, but it is still relaxed. Further north lie soothing **Regent's Park** and **London Zoo**, and the **Wallace Collection** is too frequently overlooked, but most of Marylebone's attractions will involve either shopping or scoffing.

Sights & museums

London Zoo

Regent's Park, NW1 4RY (7722 3333/www.zsl.org/london-zoo). Baker Street or Camden Town tube then 274, C2 bus. **Open** *Late Oct-mid Mar* 10am-4pm daily. *Mid Mar-late Oct* 10am-5.30pm daily. **Admission** £14.50; free-£12.70 reductions. **Map** p97 B1 ❶

Opened in 1828, this was the world's first scientific zoo, and today umbrella charity ZSL stresses its commitment to worldwide conservation. The zoo's habitats keep pace with the times – the elephants have been given room to roam at sister site Whipsnade Wild Animal Park in Bedfordshire, and the penguins have been moved from Lubetkin's famous modernist pool to a more suitable space. The new 1,500 square metre (16,000 square foot) walk-through squirrel monkey enclosure allows you to get close to the animals in an open environment, while the African Bird Safari, another new walk-through habitat, has replaced three small, outdated bird enclosures.

The Gorilla Kingdom opened in March 2007. It's a forest walk to see big apes and the creatures that share their world. It's advisable to follow the recommended route to avoid missing anything; check the daily programme of events to get a good view at feeding times. The old small mammals building should also have been transformed into the Clore Rainforest Lookout: uninterrupted views of monkeys, sloths, iguanas and birds.

Madame Tussauds
Marylebone Road, NW1 5LR (0870 400 3000/www.madame-tussauds. com). Baker Street tube. **Open** 9.30am-6pm daily; times vary during holiday periods. **Admission** 9.30am-5.30pm £24.99; £15.99-£20.99 reductions. 5.30-6pm £16; £11-£14 reductions. **Map** p97 A1 ❷

Tussauds compensates for its inherently static attractions with a flurry of attendant activity. As you enter, you're dazzled by fake paparazzi flashbulbs. Starry-eyed kids can take part in a 'Divas' routine with Britney, Beyoncé and Kylie. Figures are constantly being added to keep up with new stars, TV shows and movies – *Pirates of the Caribbean* is a recent addition. Other rooms contain public figures past and present, from Henry and his six wives to Blair and Bush. The Planetarium has been replaced by the Stardome, its 360° star show animated by Wallace and Gromit creators Aardman.

Regent's Park
Map p97 A1 ❸

With its varied landscape, from formal flowerbeds to extensive playing fields, Regent's Park (open 5am-dusk daily) is one of London's most treasured green spaces. As well as the famous zoo (p95), it has a boating lake with enchanting wildfowl, cafés and a lovely open air theatre (p103).

Wallace Collection
Hertford House, Manchester Square, W1U 3BN (7935 0687/www.wallace collection.org). Bond Street tube. **Open** 10am-5pm daily. **Admission** free. No credit cards. **Map** p97 A2 ❹

This handsome late 18th-century house – with freshly refurbished State Rooms – contains furniture, paintings, armour and objets d'art. There's room after room of Louis XIV and XV furnishings and Sèvres porcelain, and galleries of Titian, Velázquez, Gainsborough and Reynolds. There are regular temporary exhibitions. The Wallace (7563 9505), in the attractive glass-roofed courtyard, is the museum's new restaurant. Run by Oliver Peyton of the National Dining Rooms (p77) and Inn The Park (p79), it serves top-notch French food at top-notch prices.

Eating & drinking

Artesian
NEW *Langham Hotel, 1C Portland Place, W1B 1JA (7636 1000/www.artesian-bar.co.uk). Oxford Circus tube.* **Open** 7.30am-2am Mon-Fri; 8am-midnight Sat, Sun. **Cocktail bar. Map** p97 C2 ❺

Artesian has reopened after a makeover by David Collins, and while some of the new features sail close to being OTT, a subdued colour scheme makes the total effect soothing. Of the expertly made and beautifully presented cocktails, rum takes centre stage, with a 50-strong list. Expect to pay serious prices for both the drinks and the superior bar snacks.

Eat-Thai.net
22 St Christopher's Place, W1U 1NP (7486 0777/www.eatthai.net). Bond Street tube. **Open** noon-3pm, 6-10.30pm daily. **££. Thai. Map** p97 B3 ❻

This has to be one of our favourite Thai restaurants for sheer consistency. Chef Nipon Senkaewsai has produced a huge

Marylebone & Mayfair

REGENT'S PARK

A **B** **C** **1**

- Sights & museums
- Eating & drinking
- Shopping
- Nightlife
- Arts & leisure

numbered locations refer to the Marylebone and Mayfair sections on pp95-115

© Copyright Time Out Group 2007

300 m
300 yds

IMPERIAL
WAR MUSEUM
LONDON

offers a fascinating day out, with displays covering conflicts from the First World War to the present day.

Special exhibitions

Weapons of Mass Communication
Discover the influence of advertising
on propaganda and protest posters.
4 October 2007 - 30 March 2008

Ian Fleming and 007
Explore the life and work of
Ian Fleming and his most famous
creation, James Bond.
25 April 2008 - 1 March 2009

Free admission
Charges apply for some special exhibitions

⊖ Lambeth North, Waterloo, Elephant and Castle
020 7416 5320

IMPERIAL WAR
MUSEUM

menu of royal Thai classics, Esarn dishes from north-east Thailand and intriguing Thai-fusion creations. Service is prompt and presentation faultless.

FishWorks

89 Marylebone High Street, W1U 4QW (7935 9796/www.fishworks. co.uk). Baker Street tube. **Open** noon-2.30pm, 6-10.30pm Tue-Fri; noon-10.30pm Sat, Sun. **£££. Fish**. Map p97 B2 **7**
Each branch of this chain combines fishmonger and restaurant, and are all casual and relaxed. The menu offers 'classic' dishes as well as daily changing specials. Super-fresh ingredients, simply cooked.

Golden Hind

73 Marylebone Lane, W1U 2PN (7486 3644). Bond Street tube. **Open** noon-3pm, 6-10pm Mon-Fri; 6-10pm Mon-Sat. **£. Fish & chips**. Map p97 B3 **8**
The Golden Hind oozes character. Portion sizes are variable, as are the opening hours, but don't be put off – the food is excellent, and the atmosphere fun, young and friendly.

La Fromagerie

2-4 Moxon Street, W1U 4EW (7935 0341/www.lafromagerie.co.uk). Baker Street or Bond Street tube. **Open** 10.30am-7.30pm Mon; 8am-7.30pm Tue-Fri; 9am-7pm Sat; 10am-6pm Sun. **££. Deli**. Map p97 A2 **9**
The 'tasting café' in the back of this popular, rustic-style deli is a simple set-up: one communal wooden table and three small satellite tables. The daily cheese plate takes centre stage (the cheese room stocks over 100 varieties), but the exemplary ploughman's lunch and fish plate are as carefully sourced; superior cakes are served for tea.

Le Relais de Venise L'entrecôte

120 Marylebone Lane, W1U 2QG (7486 0878/www.relaisdevenise.com). Bond Street tube. **Open** noon-2.30pm, 6-10.45pm Mon-Fri; 12.30-3.30pm, 6.30-10.45pm Sat; 12.30-3.30pm, 6.30-10.30pm Sun. **££. French**. Map p97 B3 **10**

An outpost of the venerable Parisian brasserie, the Relais de Venise emphasises gastronomic simplicity with a fixed-price (£18) menu of salad and steak-frites. Its popularity can mean that service takes a back seat, but focus on the food – juicy meat, crunchy chips, superior cheese plates and desserts – and you won't go far wrong.

Locanda Locatelli

8 Seymour Street, W1H 7JZ (7935 9088/www.locandalocatelli.com). Marble Arch tube. **Open** noon-3pm, 6.45-11pm Mon-Thur; noon-3pm, 6.45-11.30pm Fri; noon-3.30pm, 6.45-11.30pm Sat; noon-3.30pm, 6.45-10pm Sun. **££££. Modern Italian**. Map p97 A3 **11**
The permanently darkened interior of wood veneer, convex mirrors and expansive tan leather lounges suggests louche Saturday nights rather than sunny Sunday lunchtimes; however, Sunday lunch is one of the easiest times to get a table at this notoriously popular venue. At £12 a bottle, the pleasant house white might be the only bargain that's on offer, but the food here is undeniably delicious.

Moose

NEW *31 Duke Street, W1U 1LG (7224 3452).* Bond Street tube. **Open** 4pm-2am Mon-Thur; 4pm-3am Fri, Sat. **Bar**. Map p97 B3 **12**
Cosy, reasonably priced and with decor that's simultaneously eccentric and inviting, this bar is a rarity in the West End. There are two spaces: a small ground-floor bar and a much larger downstairs bar with DJs. The decorative motif is that of a ski lodge in the Canadian Rockies. The extensive cocktail list is well priced, with prices as low as £3.75 during happy hour. Food (pies, finger-food) is served until 10pm.

Prince Regent

71 Marylebone High Street, W1U 5JN (7467 3811). Baker Street tube. **Open** noon-11pm Mon-Sat; noon-10.30pm Sun. **££. Gastropub**. Map p97 B1 **13**
Giant pink fluffy umbrellas add a sprinkle of flamboyance to this well-thought-out pub. The food is a touch

Mint

short of bona fide gastro, but everything else makes the grade: dark wood, seating, extensive blackboard wine list and an impressive selection of wheat beers. Often very busy.

Providores & Tapa Room

109 Marylebone High Street, W1U 4RX (7935 6175/www.theprovidores.co.uk). Baker Street or Bond Street tube. **Open** *Providores* noon-2.45pm, 6-10.30pm Mon-Sat; noon-2.45pm, 6-10pm Sun. *Tapa Room* 9-10.30pm Mon-Fri; 10am-10.30pm Sat; 10am-10pm Sun. **£££.** **International.** Map p97 B2 ⑭

The buzzy street-level Tapa Room is frequently packed to capacity, the crowds attracted by the exquisite global tapas and breakfasts. Upstairs, the restaurant is small and refined, offering dishes that are a rarefied fusion of mainly Asian and Middle Eastern ingredients. The cooking is exceptional, as reflected in the prices.

Rhodes W1

Cumberland, Great Cumberland Place, W1A 4RF (7479 3838/www.gary rhodes.co.uk). Marble Arch tube.

Open 11am-11pm Mon-Sat; 11am-10.30pm Sun. **£££.** **British.** Map p97 A3 ⑮

The Cumberland's dining room is resolutely modern, and while the look of the place won't be to everyone's taste, the cooking probably is. Certainly everything we tried left us wanting more and, unlike many upmarket British restaurants, there's no dress code or stiff atmosphere.

Shopping

Alfies Antique Market

13-25 Church Street, NW8 8DT (7723 6066/www.alfiesantiques.com). Edgware Road tube/Marylebone tube/ rail. **Open** 10am-6pm Tue-Sat. Map p97 A1 ⑯

Although antiques are slowly being replaced by shiny (and pricey) 20th-century furniture and lighting, there are still plenty of treasures at Alfies. The Girl Can't Help It is a particular highlight, stocking 1940s dresses and corsets, 1950s bikinis and divine shoes; Biba Lives covers classy clothes from the 1930s to 1960s.

Daunt Books

83-84 Marylebone High Street, W1U 4QW (7224 2295/www.dauntbooks. co.uk). Baker Street tube. **Open** 9am-7.30pm Mon-Sat; 11am-6pm Sun. **Map** p97 A2 ⑰

Our favourite place in town for travel guides and literature, Daunt also sells a well-selected array of general fiction and non-fiction. The shop itself is gorgeous, with a galleried area illuminated by a vast fan light.

Fresh

92 Marylebone High Street, W1U 4RD (7486 4100/www.fresh.com). Baker Street tube. **Open** 10am-7pm Mon-Wed, Fri, Sat; 10am-8pm Thur; noon-5pm Sun. **Map** p97 A2 ⑱

Made with ingredients such as soy, milk, rice and sugar, these exquisitely packaged (but pricey) American skin-, body- and haircare products smell good enough to eat. The budget-conscious take note: the cost of a mini-treatment is redeemable against products.

John Lewis

278-306 Oxford Street, W1A 1EX (7629 7711/www.johnlewis.co.uk). Bond Street or Oxford Circus tube. **Open** 9.30am-7pm Mon-Wed, Fri, Sat; 9.30am-8pm Thur; noon-6pm Sun. **Map** p97 B3 ⑲

Renowned for solid reliability and the courtesy of its staff, John Lewis also deserves a medal for its breadth of stock. A major £60 million renovation, which should have been completed by the time you read this, includes the removal of the old escalators to open up the floorspace, and the addition of a swanky new restaurant, brasserie and food hall.

Kabiri

37 Marylebone High Street, W1U 4QE (7224 1808/www.kabiri.co.uk). Baker Street tube. **Open** 10am-6.30pm Mon-Sat; noon-5pm Sun. **Map** p97 B2 ⑳

This small shop showcases an incredible variety of contemporary jewellery by over 50 designers, many of them locally based. Established names are juxtaposed with talent fresh out of art college.

Mallon & Taub

35D Marylebone High Street, W1U 4QB (7935 8200/www.mallonand taub.com). Baker Street tube. **Open** 10am-6.30pm Mon-Wed, Fri, Sat; 10am-7pm Thur; noon-6pm Sun. **Map** p97 B2 ㉑

This simple, airy and award-winning independent stocks original, funky, sculptural and cutting-edge specs and sunglasses, as well as immensely practical designs. Service is excellent.

Margaret Howell

34 Wigmore Street, W1U 2RS (7009 9009/www.margarethowell. co.uk). Bond Street tube. **Open** 10am-6pm Mon-Wed, Fri, Sat; 10am-7pm Thur. **Map** p97 B2 ㉒

Howell's timeless British aesthetic – deftly tailored trousers and jackets, neat knitwear and crisp white shirts – has become a wardrobe staple for those who appreciate impeccably made clothes in sturdy fabrics. There are also denim and workwear-inspired clothes on offer.

Marimekko

16-17 St Christopher's Place, W1U 1NZ (7486 6454/www.marimekko. co.uk). **Open** 10am-6.30pm Mon-Wed, Fri, Sat; 10am-7pm Thur; noon-5pm Sun. **Map** p97 B3 ㉓

Founded in 1951 by Finn Armi Raita, Marimekko took an experimental approach to textile design from the start, inviting young graphic designers to apply bold graphics and bright colours to a variety of fabrics. As well as the textiles and clothes, you can now buy bags and tableware.

Mint

70 Wigmore Street, W1U 2SF (7224 4406/www.mintshop.co.uk). Bond Street tube. **Open** 10.30am-6.30pm Mon-Wed, Fri, Sat; 10.30am-7.30pm Thur. **Map** p97 B3 ㉔

Mint is a compact two-level space full of globally sourced pieces from established designers and recent graduates. One-off items might include illustrated plates or sleek-with-a-twist Italian brushed-steel cutlery.

Mulberry

*41-42 New Bond Street, W1S 2RY
(7491 3900/www.mulberry.com).
Bond Street tube.* **Open** 10am-6pm
Mon-Wed, Fri, Sat; 10am-7pm Thur.
Map p97 C3 **㉕**

Best known for its bags, Mulberry
manages to maintain a strong sense of
tradition while still being very much of
the moment, largely thanks to design
director Stuart Vevers. Clothes include
lots of buttery leathers and cottons that
are soft as handkerchiefs.

Reiss

*Kent House, 14-17 Market Place,
W1H 7AJ (7637 9112/www.reiss.
co.uk). Oxford Circus tube.* **Open**
10am-6.30pm Mon-Wed, Fri, Sat;
10am-7.30pm Thur; noon-6pm Sun.
Map p97 C3 **㉖**

Perennially popular, Reiss proves that
if you do something consistently well,
you reap the rewards. In terms of style
and value, the chain sits somewhere
between high street and high-end,
delivering quality fashion for 25- to 35-
year-olds. Womenswear has a designer air, looking youthful yet classy,
while the menswear runs from suits to
chunky knitwear.

Selfridges

*400 Oxford Street, W1A 1AB (0870
837 7377/www.selfridges.com). Bond
Street or Marble Arch tube.* **Open**
9.30am-8pm Mon-Sat; noon-6pm Sun.
Map p97 A3 **㉗**

Selfridges' innovative displays, concession boutiques and themed events
bring a sense of theatre to shopping.
The designer accessory department is
home to covetable bags, while Spirit,
which houses a Topshop outpost
among its high-street concessions,
has recently upped its fashion cred
with hip diffusion lines. Menswear
covers everything from high-street
staples to 'Superbrands'. The second
floor's nine mini-boutiques of hot
international labels for women have
almost been eclipsed by the elegant
new designer room, showcasing such
labels as Missoni, Jonathan Saunders
and Roland Mouret.

Topshop

*214 Oxford Street, W1N 9DF (0845
121 4519/www.topshop.com). Oxford
Circus tube.* **Open** 9am-8pm Mon-Wed,
Fri, Sat; 9am-9pm Thur; noon-6pm Sun.
Map p97 C3 **㉘**

There aren't many shops that can keep
everyone from teenies to 40-year-old
fashion editors happy, but Topshop
does so with seeming ease – the frenzy
surrounding the arrival of Kate Moss's
long-awaited line in April 2007 even
made mainstream news. The renovated London flagship now accommodates
an even bigger shoe department, a dedicated denim section and a brilliant
maternity shop. Following in the strides
of its older sister's success, Topman
(www.topman.com) has acquired cult
status leaps ahead of its high-street
rivals. For affordable, directional casualwear, there is no competition.

Weardowney Get-Up
Boutique

*9 Ashbridge Street, NW8 8DH
(7258 3087/www.weardowney.com).
Marylebone tube/rail.* **Open** 10am-4pm
Mon-Sat. **Map** p97 A1 **㉙**

An idiosyncratic complex in a converted pub, Amy Wear and Gail
Downey's boutique sells almost anything so long as it's knitted: vintage-
inspired wrap dresses and shrugs,
frilly knickers and, for men, oversized
stripy wool boxers. Goods are displayed in weathered wardrobes, and
knitting and hand-sewing courses are
held under the watchful eye of the resident cat Pantoufle. A charmed world.

Nightlife

Social

*5 Little Portland Street, W1W 7JD
(7636 4992/www.thesocial.com).
Oxford Circus tube.* **Open** noon-
midnight Mon-Fri; 1pm-midnight Sat.
Map p97 C2 **㉚**

An unnoticeable, opaque front hides
this daytime diner and DJ bar of
supreme quality. It's popular with
music industry workers and other
trendies who, after drinks upstairs,

Topshop

descend to the basement rocked by DJs six nights a week. Monthly Hip Hop Karaoke is a giggle.

Arts & leisure

Open Air Theatre

Regent's Park, NW1 4NR (7935 5756/ box office 0870 060 1811/www.open airtheatre.org). Baker Street tube. **Map** p97 B1 ③①

The verdant setting of this alfresco theatre lends itself perfectly to summery Shakespeare romps and music performances; the season runs June to September. Book well ahead and take an extra layer for chills in Act 3.

Wigmore Hall

36 Wigmore Street, W1U 2BP (7935 2141/www.wigmore-hall.org.uk). Bond Street tube. **Map** p97 B2 ③②

With its perfect acoustics, art nouveau decor and excellent basement restaurant, it is one of the world's top concert venues for chamber music and song. The Monday lunchtime recitals and Sunday morning coffee concerts are great value.

Mayfair

South of Oxford Street, Mayfair was conceived as an elegant residential suburb, arranged around squares with service mews tucked behind them. Other than the fact the city has advanced and surrounded the district, that's how things remain. International toffs are still in residence, as are the rarefied shops, restaurants, hotel bars and galleries they frequent (Cork Street is regarded as the heart of London's commercial artworld). If you're shopping you might feel out of place without a platinum card, but if you have one – there's no better place to push your limit. The quieter streets are fascinating to wander for their architecture and atmosphere, and the voyeuristic pleasures of spying on how the other half lives. This being England, the wealth isn't ostentatious – but a tiny mews home, once stables, would cost several racehorses these days.

Superchef

A trio of French masters have set up in London.

Gordon Ramsay opening a restaurant in New York might have been big news in Blighty, and homegrown restaurateurs such as Alan Yau, Tom Aiken or the duo Chris Corbin and Jeremy King are capable of making a huge splash, but when when it comes to fine dining, many believe the French still can't be beat. These days, if you want to test this thesis, you don't even have to go to France.

The first of these superchefs to reach beyond France was Pierre Gagnaire, who opened the famously expensive – we're talking à la carte at around £150 a head – **Sketch** (p111) in 2003. In 2005, Glade even brought Gagnaire's food within reach of ordinary diners.

But 2007 is set to be the year of French immigration. Joël Robuchon has already followed his restaurants in Tokyo, New York and Las Vegas with another top-class **L'Atelier** (p130), this time opening cheekily close to celeb-magnet restaurant the Ivy. Touché. And hot on his heels comes the biggest news of all: the daddy of all superchefs, the man with more Michelin stars in France than exist in the whole of Ramsay's native Scotland, is to open here. Alain Ducasse has completed a deal that will result in him opening a small restaurant in the Dorchester hotel. As we go to press, details of **Ducasse at the Dorchester** (53 Park Lane, W1K 1QA, 7629 8888 ext 691) are few – but expect nothing less than the very finest dining.
■ www.thedorchester.com

Sights & museums

Faraday Museum

NEW *Royal Institution, 21 Albemarle Street, W1S 4BS (7409 2992/www.rigb.org). Green Park tube.* **Open** 10am-5pm Mon-Fri. **Admission** phone for details. **Map** p97 C4 ❸❸

Due to reopen in spring 2008 after major refurbishment, the expanded museum will now reflect the history of the Royal Institution, while keeping in place the re-created lab in which Michael Faraday discovered the laws of electromagnetics.

Handel House Museum

25 Brook Street (entrance at rear in Lancashire Court), W1K 4HB (7495 1685/www.handelhouse.org). Bond Street tube. **Open** 10am-6pm Tue, Wed, Fri, Sat; 10am-8pm Thur; noon-6pm Sun. **Admission** £5; free-£4.50 reductions. **Map** p97 B3 ❸❹

George Frideric Handel lived in this Mayfair house for 36 years, until his death in 1759. The house has been beautifully restored with original and re-created furnishings, paintings and a welter of scores (in the same room as photos of Jimi Hendrix, who lived here rather more recently). Recitals are held every Thursday.

Royal Academy of Arts

Burlington House, Piccadilly, W1J 0BD (7300 8000/www.royalacademy.org.uk). Green Park or Piccadilly Circus tube. **Open** 10am-6pm Mon-Thur, Sat, Sun; 10am-10pm Fri. **Admission** varies. **Map** p97 C4 ❸❺

Britain's first art school was founded in 1768 and moved to the extravagantly Palladian Burlington House a century later. It's best known for its galleries, which stage populist temporary exhibitions. Those in the John Madejski Fine Rooms are drawn from the RA's holdings – ranging from Constable to Hockney – and are free. The popular Summer Exhibition draws on works entered by the public. **Event highlights** 'A Passion for British Art, 1700-1850: Paul Mellon's Legacy' (20 Oct 2007-27 Jan 2008).

LONDON BY AREA

Gaucho p108

Eating & drinking

Benares

12A Berkeley Square House, Berkeley Square, W1J 6BS (7629 8886/www. benaresrestaurant.com). Green Park tube. **Indian & Pakistani**. **Open** noon-2.30pm, 5.30-10.30pm Mon-Fri; 5.30-10.30pm Sat; noon-2.30pm, 6-10pm Sun. **££££**. Map p97 C4 ③⑥

Swathed in glossy black granite, Benares sighs with sumptuousness. Chef/patron Atul Kochhar was the first Indian chef to be awarded a Michelin star and his creative cooking style combines modern influences and classic Indian favourites. Service can be inconsistent.

Bentley's Oyster Bar

NEW *11-15 Swallow Street, W1B 4DG (7734 4756). Piccadilly Circus tube. Oyster Bar* noon-midnight Mon-Sat; noon-10pm Sun. *Restaurant* noon-3pm, 6-11pm Mon-Sat; noon-3pm, 6-10pm Sun. **£££**. **Fish**. Map p97 C4 ③⑦

Chef Richard Corrigan has done an immaculate job of breathing new life into this oyster bar. At centre stage on the ground floor is a swanky, marble-topped bar with studded leather chairs; smaller tables with banquette seating line the walls. Mains include seafood and a range of classics, each with a modern twist. The more formal dining room on the first floor has a lengthier (and pricier) grill menu. The drinks list has plenty of wines by the glass and good range of chilled sherries.

Chisou

4 Princes Street, W1B 2LE (7629 3931). Oxford Circus tube. **Open** noon-2.30pm, 6-10.15pm Mon-Sat. **£££**. **Japanese**. Map p97 C3 ③⑧

During the day, Chisou – with its rice-paper lamps, Japanese screens and cushioned banquettes – is fast, efficient and businesslike. At night, groups linger over a bottle, picking from the daily list of out-there specials, including pan-fried spicy burdock, and monkfish liver with ponzu. More familiar are the likes of black cod with miso, fresh sushi and oysters.

Donovan Bar

Brown's Hotel, Albemarle Street, W1S 4BP (7493 6020). Green Park tube. **Open** 11am-1am Mon-Sat; 11am-10.30pm Sun. **Bar**. Map p97 C4 ③⑨

Its design inspired by the Helmut Newton Bar in Berlin, this bar incorporates a Bill Amberg leather counter. Against the backdrop of a stained-glass window are set black leather chairs and checked fabric banquettes, and the walls are hung with Terence Donovan's iconic photographs. Sip from the wide selection of champagnes by the glass, or settle down with a Box Brownie (raspberry purée, raspberry vodka and fizz).

Dorchester Bar

NEW *53 Park Lane, W1K 1QA (7317 6336/www.dorchester.com). Hyde Park Corner tube.* **Open** noon-1am Mon-Thur; noon-2am Fri, Sat; noon-midnight Sun. **Bar**. Map p97 A4 ④⓪

The new-look bar at the Dorchester is back with a vengeance. Elaborate, with plush purple and gold swirly banquettes and red glass spikes fringing the room, it feels a little Eurotrashy, but fun and luxurious. A sense of grand tradition is conveyed through the impressive drinks list, which includes a flight of vermouths intended for showcasing the hotel's selection, said to be the largest in the UK.

Galvin at Windows

NEW *28th floor, London Hilton, Park Lane, W1K 1BE (7208 4021). Green Park or Hyde Park Corner tube.* **Open** *Bar* noon-1am Mon-Thur; noon-3am Fri; 5.30-3am Sat; noon-10.30pm Sun. *Restaurant* 7-10.30am, noon-2.30pm, 6-10.30pm Mon-Fri; 7-10.30am, 6-10.30pm Sat; 7-10.30am, noon-3pm Sun. **Admission** *Bar* £7 after 11pm. **££££**. **French**. Map p97 B5 ④①

We really prefer brasserie-style Galvin Bistrot de Luxe (66 Baker Street, 7935 4007), but the sumptuous views over Hyde Park from the 28th floor of the Hilton get this place included. The food is excellent – quality modern French in full special-occasion mode, with service to match – but you're paying for the location. The bar is stylish, if pricey.

LONDON BY AREA

Gaucho Piccadilly

25 Swallow Street, W1B 4QR (7734 4040/www.gaucho-grill.com). Piccadilly Circus tube. **Open** noon-1am Wed-Sat; noon-midnight Sun-Tue. **£££**.
Argentinian. Map p97 C4 **42**

This revamped flagship of the steakhouse chain stretches over four floors. The steaks – rump, sirloin, fillet, ribeye and churrasco de lomo (a fillet cut open and turned out to soak up the marinade) – are fabulously flavoursome and tender. Enjoy with thin chips, spicy sweetcorn and cheese bread.

Gordon Ramsay at Claridge's

Claridge's, 55 Brook Street, W1K 4HR (7499 0099/www.gordonramsay.com). Bond Street tube. **Open** noon-2.45pm, 5.45-11pm Mon-Fri; noon-3pm, 5.45-11pm Sat; noon-3pm, 6-11pm Sun. **££££**. **Modern European**. Map p97 B3 **43**

The setting is impressively vintage-luxe, but the restaurant is buzzy and more relaxed than the other Gordon Ramsay (p92). The menu is exciting without resorting to whimsy. Dress up and enjoy an exceptional restaurant experience, but only if you arrive around midday on a Monday to Thursday are you likely to secure a precious table; otherwise, a tedious telephone booking system awaits.

Guinea

30 Bruton Place, W1J 6NL (7499 1210/www.theguinea.co.uk). Bond Street or Green Park tube. **Open** 11am-11pm Mon-Fri; 6-11pm Sat.
Pub. Map p97 B4 **44**

In contrast to the English sophistication of the Restaurant & Grill that lurks at the back, the pub part of the operation is fairly rough and ready, with slightly unruly customers kept in check by stern, elegant women who operate the bar with efficiency.

Haiku

NEW *15 New Burlington Place, W1S 2HX (7494 4777). Oxford Circus tube.* **Open** noon-3pm, 6-11pm Mon-Sat.
£££. **Asian**. Map p97 C3 **45**

The London outpost of Haiku is a clone of the Cape Town original. It's a real stunner of a place: dark wood, low lighting, screens and three levels provide atmosphere, helped along by well-chosen chill-out music and beautiful tableware. The menu covers sushi, sashimi, dim sum, grilled dishes, curries and wok-fried dishes; everything we sampled was excellent. Staff are charming and attentive.

Maze

10-13 Grosvenor Square, W1K 6JP (7107 0000/www.gordonramsay.com). Bond Street tube. **Open** noon-midnight daily. **£££**. **Modern European**. Map p97 B3 **46**

Maze has repackaged Ramsay in a bid to tempt younger diners into fine dining and to keep pace with the trend towards smaller portions of more daring combinations. Head chef Jason Atherton brings Asian-French know-how, but the food is pure Ramsay – haute cuisine courses rather than punchy bursts of tapas. The expensively reared protein is prepared and cooked to perfection, and the presentation is finely tuned.

Mews of Mayfair

NEW *10-11 Lancashire Court, W1S 1EY (7518 9388/www.mewsofmayfair. com). Bond Street or Oxford Circus tube.* **Open** *Restaurant* noon-3pm, 6-11.30pm Mon-Sat; noon-7pm Sun. *Bar* 11am-11pm daily. *Lounge* 5pm-2am Mon-Sat. **£££**. **British**. Map p97 B3 **47**

Mews of Mayfair's gorgeously feminine interior is a showstopper. The ground-floor bar is decked with chandeliers and mirrors, while the first-floor restaurant is all creamy white with glittering coloured butterflies on the walls and pretty floral porcelain. Mains range from dainty (seabass in a bonito dressing) to hearty (venison wellington), and while the restaurant is just one facet of this multi-storey operation (there's also a cocktail lounge and private dining facilities), if chef David Selex maintains the standard we've enjoyed here, it will become a worthy venue in its own right.

Postcard Teas p111

Nagomi

NEW *4 Blenheim Street, W1S 1LB (7165 9506). Oxford Circus tube.* **Open** noon-2.30pm, 6-10.30pm Mon-Fri; 6-10.30pm Sat. **££. Japanese. Map** p97 B3 ㊽

There's no real equivalent of a British pub in Japan, but an izakaya is close; a relaxed bar where the lager, shochu (Japanese vodka), saké and whisky flow, with snacks to mop up the drink. Nagomi is surely the smartest izakaya-style diner in London. There are fried dishes aplenty, plus grilled fish and meats, mostly of a high standard.

Nobu

First floor, The Metropolitan, 19 Old Park Lane, W1K 1LB (7447 4747/ www.noburestaurants.com). Hyde Park Corner tube. **Open** noon-2.15pm, 6-10.15pm Mon-Thur; noon-2.15pm, 6-11pm Fri; 12.30-2.30pm, 6-11pm Sat; 12.30-2.30pm, 6-9.30pm Sun. **££££. Japanese. Map** p97 B5 ㊾

The Nobu chain extends from the US to Tokyo, with three Nobus in London alone. Here at the Met, you still get great Hyde Park views and a substantial waiting list, but Nobu Matsuhisa's signature dishes – rock shrimp tempura with spicy sauce, new-style sashimi, black cod with miso – no longer hold the same wow factor.

Postcard Teas

9 Dering Street, W1S 1AG (7629 3654/www.postcardteas.com). Bond Street or Oxford Circus tube. **Open** 10.30am-6.30pm Tue-Sat. **£. Tearoom. Map** p97 B3 ㊿

This exquisite tearoom and shop sells a score of brews, which can be sampled at a shared table with stools. The teas cost a mere £1.50 per pot and cover the full range of black teas, green teas and oolongs – owner Timothy d'Offay has has visited many of the growers. There are well-matched nibbles too, such as chocolate cake and medjool dates.

Red Lion

1 Waverton Street, W1J 5QN (7499 1307). Green Park tube. **Open** 11.30am-11pm Mon-Fri; 6-11pm Sat; 6-10.30pm Sun. **Pub. Map** p97 B4 (51)

Hidden in the back streets, this Red Lion (there are hundreds in London) has an intimate, front-room feel with its miniature tables and toby jugs. The landlord is always hospitable, pulling pints with a cheeky wink. There's honest, unpretentious pub food too – think pies and roast meat.

Sketch

9 Conduit Street, W1S 2XZ (0870 777 4488/www.sketch.uk.com). Oxford Circus tube. **Open** *Lecture Room* noon-2.30pm, 7-10.30pm Tue-Fri; 7-10.30pm Sat. *Gallery* 7-11pm Mon-Sat. *Glade* noon-3.30pm Mon-Sat. **£££** Gallery/ Glade. **££££** Lecture Room. **Modern European. Map** p97 B4 (52)

Greeters at the entrance lead you down to the Gallery (Louis XIV meets IMAX theatre) or up to the legendarily expensive Lecture Room ('Pierre Gagnaire's fine dining experience'). Food is designed to challenge culinary preconceptions, with technically brilliant nibbles giving way to exotic tasting menus. A pâtisserie, the Parlour, resides on the ground floor and, in 2005, the quirky Glade opened. Here, a large starter or small main (also under the supervision of Gagnaire) costs a comparatively proletarian £9. Specify which venue you want when booking, and expect a time limit.

Wolseley

160 Piccadilly, W1J 9EB (7499 6996/ www.thewolseley.com). Green Park tube. **Open** 7am-midnight Mon-Fri; 9am-midnight Sat; 9am-11pm Sun. **£££. Modern European. Map** p97 C5 (53)

One of the city's loveliest-looking restaurants, the Wolseley has a high, multi-domed ceiling, a sleek black and cream colour scheme, and loads of old-fashioned charm. The inspiration is grand Viennese café, so wiener schnitzel and soufflé suisse sit beside steak tartare, omelettes and a superlative mix of English cakes and French pâtisserie. Teatime is a relaxed hour to experience the place; a lunchtime booking is likely to have a 90-minute time limit, even though walk-ins are still welcomed.

Shopping

Angela Hale

5 Royal Arcade, 28 Old Bond Street, W1S 4SE (7495 1920/www.angela-hale.co.uk). Green Park tube. **Open** 10am-6pm Mon-Sat. **Map** p97 C4 **54**

The destination for those in search of retro glamour. Edwardian styles are a recurring influence on the handmade costume jewellery, which is based on hypoallergenic bronze and prettified with Swarovski crystals.

Browns

24-27 South Molton Street, W1K 5RD (7514 0000/www.brownsfashion.com). Bond Street tube. **Open** 10am-6.30pm Mon-Wed, Fri, Sat; 10am-7pm Thur. **Map** p97 B3 **55**

Joan Burstein's venerable store has reigned supreme for over 35 years. Among the 100-odd designers represented are Chloé, Dries Van Noten and Balenciaga, with an entire floor for Jil Sander. On the same street, Browns Focus (nos.38-39) is younger and edgier, and Browns Labels for Less (no.50) sells leftovers from the previous season.

b store

24A Savile Row, W1S 3PR (7734 6846/www.bstorelondon.com). Oxford Circus tube. **Open** 10.30am-6.30pm Mon-Fri; 10am-6pm Sat. **Map** p97 C4 **56**

To preview the UK's hottest up-and-coming designers, this is the place. New names include Alex Foxton, Ehud Joseph and Carola Euler. b store continues to champion Peter Jensen's offbeat mens- and womenswear, and Bernhard Willhelm's eye-catching designs. A range of footwear from Eley Kishimoto and b store's own Buddhahood label are further draws, as are the Judy Blame accessories.

Burlington Arcade

W1 (www.burlington-arcade.co.uk). Green Park tube. **Open** 9am-6pm Mon-Sat. **Map** p97 C4 **57**

Opened in 1819, Burlington may be the most famous and traditional of London's arcades, but an ambitious renovation programme (due to be completed in spring 2008) aims to bring in a younger, hipper clientele. Old favourites will remain, however, among them Penfriend (no.34, 7499 6337, www.penfriend.co.uk), which stocks a fantastic choice of fountain pens, and Penhaligon's (nos.16/17), which has been selling distinguished scents and bath goodies since 1870. For luxury gifts, try Pickett (nos.32/33 & 41). Of course, no arcade should be without a cashmere shop, and Berk (nos.6 & 46/49) is one of the best. Sweet-toothed shoppers note: a branch of the wonderful macaroon shop Ladurée should have opened here by the time you read this.

Dover Street Market

17-18 Dover Street, W1S 4LT (7518 0680/www.doverstreetmarket.com). Green Park tube. **Open** 11am-6pm Mon-Wed, Fri, Sat; 11am-7pm Thur. **Map** p97 C4 **58**

Comme des Garçons designer Rei Kawakubo's six-storey space combines the edgy energy of an indoor market with rarefied labels. The high-profile concessions are designed by the designers themselves, making the whole place intriguingly theatrical.

Electrum Gallery

21 South Molton Street, W1K 5QZ (7629 6325). Bond Street tube. **Open** 10am-6pm Mon-Fri; 10am-5pm Sat. **Map** p97 B3 **59**

This establishment is at the forefront of fresh, exciting jewellery design. Some of its newest arrivals are straight out of the Royal College of Art, but there are also established names among the 100 designers.

Grays Antique Market & Grays in the Mews

58 Davies Street, W1K 5LP & 1-7 Davies Mews, W1K 5AB (7629 7034/www.graysantiques.com). Bond Street tube. **Open** 10am-6pm Mon-Fri. **Map** p97 B3 **61**

Stalls in this smart covered market sell everything from jewellery to rare books. More than 200 dealers.

Donovan Bar p107

Marc Jacobs

NEW *24-25 Mount Street, W1K 2RR (7399 1690/www.marcjacobs. com). Bond Street tube.* **Open** 11am-7pm Mon-Sat; noon-6pm Sun. **Map** p97 B4 62

In February 2007, to coincide with London Fashion Week, New York-based über-designer Jacobs opened his first store in the capital. The swanky, specially designed space, featuring antique marble fireplaces and parquet flooring, stocks diffusion line Marc by Marc Jacobs, as well as the ready-to-wear collection, accessories and shoes.

PPQ

NEW *47 Conduit Street, W1S 2YP (7494 9789). Oxford Circus tube.* **Open** 10am-6pm Mon-Wed, Fri, Sat; 10am-7pm Thur. **Map** p97 C4 63

Hip London label PPQ has opened its first store. Expect plenty of luxe casualwear, maybe swing dresses in primary colours or belted wrap coats, as well as slim jeans and knits for men.

Rupert Sanderson

32 Bruton Place, W1J 6NP (0870 750 9181/www.rupertsanderson.co.uk). Bond Street or Green Park tube. **Open** 10am-6pm Mon-Fri; 11am-6pm Sat. **Map** p97 C4 64

Focused on craftsmanship rather than passing trends, Rupert Sanderson works with artisan shoemakers in his Bologna factory to ensure every element of his designs is spot-on. The result is understated, graceful and essentially English shoes – displayed in a quietly tasteful mews shop.

Savile Row

Map p97 C4 65

Running south off Conduit Street, this is the spiritual home of bespoke British tailoring. At no.15, Henry Poole & Co has cut suits for clients including Charles Dickens and Winston Churchill, while Ede & Ravenscroft (8 Burlington Gardens) is London's oldest tailor. The young whippersnappers have been cutting in of late, though: try the denim at Evisu (no.9) or check out b store (p112).

Nightlife

Hedges & Butler

NEW *3 New Burlington Mews, W1B 4QB (7434 2232/www.hedgesandbutler. co.uk). Oxford Circus tube.* **Open** varies with event. **Map** p97 C4 66

Counter me in

No booking? No matter – counter-dining is all the rage.

Booking one of London's hot tables takes planning – about a month's advance warning should do the trick for a sensible slot at Gordon Ramsay's new gastropub, for example. How does that work if you're on a short holiday?

New Soho tapas joint **Barrafina** (p118, pictured) is one of an increasing number of London restaurants with the answer. The place is small, but dining is at the L-shaped, marble-topped counter that runs around the periphery of the room, with 23 high stools for customers. Given the place's popularity, this means you're going to have to queue at peak times, but everyone's in the same boat: turn up, take your chance.

Counter-dining isn't just about convenience: at Barrafina it's also part of the fun. From your perch you can sip a glass of fino or manzanilla, the dry sherries that traditionally accompany tapas; chat to the cheery, engaging staff, and watch the steel hotplate in action as dishes are prepared. Order razor clams, for example, and you can watch the live

bivalves squirm on the hot steel plancha – disquieting perhaps, but an indispensable experience in the search for authentic tapas.

There's not a lot of artifice involved in the dish preparation, but the tip-top ingredients don't require it. Probably the most complex dish Barrafina serves is tortilla. Again the counter comes into its own as you watch the Spanish-style omelette cooked to order in front of you in a tiny pan.

Counter-dining is also a god-send for single travellers: eating alone at a table rarely feels comfortable, but at the bar you can be less self-conscious. Most bar staff enjoy chatting and the repartee is often be a founding principle of the whole setup.

Barrafina isn't the only place to have recognised how sociable, relaxed and versatile the counter can be. Try seafood specialists **Bentley's** (p107) and **J Sheekey** (p130), **Roka**'s (p145) splendid Japanese robata grill, Gordon Ramsay's **Maze** (p108) or the always terrific **Moro** (p163).

A private members' club since 1667, Hedges & Butler has recently become better known as the atmospheric host of intriguing cabaret. See box p134.

Pigalle Club

NEW *215-217 Piccadilly, W1J 9HN (7287 3834). Piccadilly Circus tube.* **Open** 7pm-4am Mon-Sat. **Map** p97 C4 ⑰

Vince Power may have sold his stake in the Mean Fiddler, the company he founded in 1982, but he's not ready to retire just yet. The Pigalle is chalk to the cheese of his previous venues: located right by Piccadilly Circus, it's an old-fashioned supper club where the prices demand – or, at least, imply – a certain measure of sophistication. Acts are usually jazzy, with occasional big-name singers thrown in. See box p134.

Arts & leisure

Curzon Mayfair

38 Curzon Street, W1J 7TY (7495 0500/www.curzoncinemas.com). Green Park or Hyde Park Corner tube. **Map** p97 B5 ⑱

A superb cinema programming shorts, rarities, double bills and mini-festivals of new films from around the world.

Soho

The only 'sights' listed for Soho are really locations – **Leicester Square** and **Gerrard Street**, the centre of London's Chinatown. It isn't that the district's unfriendly to tourists – far from it: this bit of London doesn't give a stuff where you're from or, more importantly, what you plan to do. It still feels a little anarchic and non-conformist, with jazz (**Ronnie Scott's** and the **Black Gardenia**), prostitution and serious boozing. The best approach is to have a wander among the skinny streets – start with Old Compton Street, the main artery, and Soho Square, full of sunbathing bodies in summer, but be sure to take a hike down **Berwick Street**.

Sights & museums

Gerrard Street

Map p116 C3 ❶

The city's original Chinatown was around Limehouse in east London, but bomb damage during World War II forced the community to head west. The ersatz oriental gates, stone lions and pagoda-topped phone boxes round Gerrard Street suggest some kind of Chinese theme park, but this is a close-knit residential and working enclave. The area is crammed with restaurants, grocery stores and shops selling tea and cheap tickets to Beijing.

Leicester Square

Map p116 C3 ❷

Leicester Square is reasonably pleasant by day, but by night it's a hellhole of inebriates out on a big night 'up west'. It's hard to believe that in the 17th century the square was one of London's most exclusive addresses. Later, William Hogarth and Joshua Reynolds had studios here; both are commemorated by busts in the gardens in the heart of the square, although it's the statue of Charlie Chaplin that gets all the attention.

Eating & drinking

Great people-watching and 24-hour opening make **Bar Italia** (7437 4520), on Frith Street at Old Compton Street, essential Soho – but we prefer the eccentric atmosphere of **Maison Bertaux** (p120) and **Pâtisserie Valerie** (p122).

Alastair Little

49 Frith Street, W1D 4SG (7734 5183). Leicester Square or Tottenham Court Road tube. **Open** noon-3pm, 6-11.30pm Mon-Fri; 6-11.30pm Sat. **£££**. **Modern European**. **Map** p116 C2 ❸

This unassuming little restaurant was at the forefront of the cooking revolution that introduced modern European food to Britain. Little himself has departed, but a meal here will still involve highest-quality seasonal ingredients that are cooked simply but with aplomb.

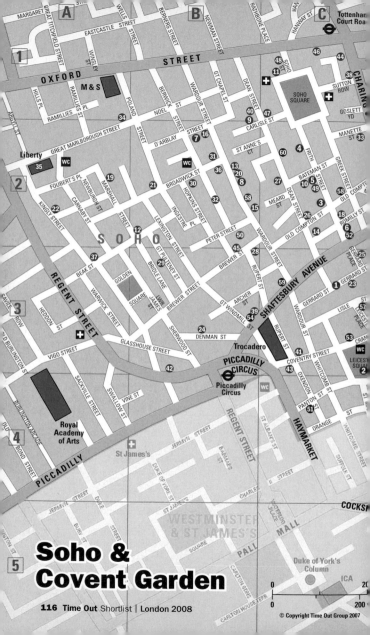

Soho &
Covent Garden

© Copyright Time Out Group 2007

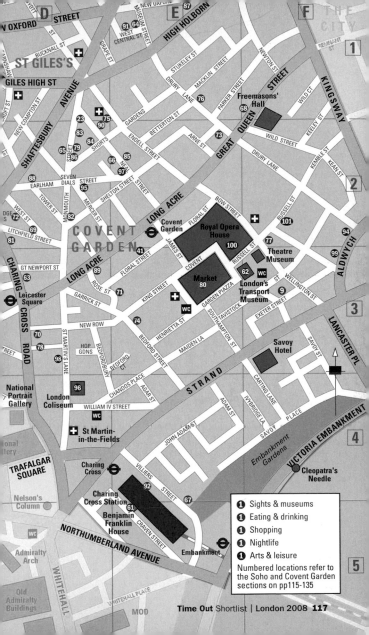

Bar Shu

Arbutus

NEW *63-64 Frith Street, W1D 3JW (7734 4545/www.arbutusrestaurant. co.uk). Tottenham Court Road tube.* **Open** noon-2.30pm, 5-11pm Mon-Sat; 12.30-3.30pm, 6.30-9.30pm Sun. **££.** **Modern European.** Map p116 C2 ❹

For the prices alone, *Time Out*'s Best Restaurant of 2006 deserves to succeed. The set lunch/pre-theatre menu (£13.50 two courses, £15.50 three courses) is a steal for cooking of this imagination and flair, and the wine prices are almost shockingly diner-friendly. Book ahead.

Barrafina

NEW *4 Frith Street, W1D 4SL (7813 8016). Leicester Square or Tottenham Court Road tube.* **Open** noon-midnight Mon-Sat. **££.** **Tapas.** Map p116 C2 ❺ See box p114.

Bar Shu

NEW *28 Frith Street, W1D 5LF (7287 6688). Leicester Square tube.* **Open** noon-11pm daily. **££.** **Chinese.** Map p116 C2 ❻

This isn't London's first Sichuan restaurant, but it is one of the most authentic. The smart three-floor site is an appealing mix of dark stone, carved wood, blue lighting and bold graphics. Service can be chaotic, but it's a must-visit.

Breakfast Club

NEW *33 D'Arblay Street, W1F 8EU (7434 2571). Oxford Circus or Tottenham Court Road tube.* **Open** 8am-6pm Mon-Fri; 9.30am-5pm Sat. **£.** **Café.** Map p116 B2 ❼

This friendly caff does breakfasts that aren't the usual fry-up: cereal, toast, even toasted Nutella sarnies. The attractive split-level room offers respite from busy Soho, the coffee is decent, and there are iMacs with free net access. A good place for lunch too.

Busaba Eathai

106-110 Wardour Street, W1F 0TR (7255 8686). Oxford Circus, Tottenham Court Road or Leicester Square tube. **Open** noon-11pm Mon-Thur; noon-11.30pm Fri, Sat; noon-10pm Sun. **££.** **Thai.** Map p116 B2 ❽

Style is paramount at this mini-chain, with chunky, dark wood tables bathed in pools of light from huge lanterns. Food arrives in a trice and is consumed as quickly, while theatrical waiters buzz around the place. Dishes are often subtle and inspired: pick of the bunch is the kwaiteow pad thai, with smoked chicken and basil.

Candy Bar

4 Carlisle Street, W1D 3BJ (7494 4041/ www.thecandybar.co.uk). Tottenham Court Road tube. **Open** 5-11.30pm Mon-Thur; 5pm-2am Fri, Sat; 5-11pm Sun. **Bar**. Map p116 B1 ❾
This well-known lesbian bar attracts a mixed clientele, from students to lipstick lesbians. Drinks aren't the cheapest, but there's a late licence at weekends, and erotic dancers in the basement bar.

Dog & Duck

18 Bateman Street, W1D 3AJ (7494 0697). Tottenham Court Road tube. **Open** noon-11pm Mon-Thur; noon-midnight Fri, Sat; noon-10.30pm Sun. **Pub**. Map p116 C2 ❿
Built in 1734, the Dog & Duck is as trad as can be, although the carved wood and glazed tiles date to the fin-de-siècle. Past guests include Orwell, after whom the upstairs wine bar is named. Downstairs in the bar and cosy back room, ale rules.

Edge

11 Soho Square, W1D 3QE (7439 1313/ www.edge.uk.com). Tottenham Court Road tube. **Open** noon-1am Mon-Sat; noon-11.30pm Sun. **Bar**. Map p116 C1 ⓫
Following its revamp, this busy polysexual venue is one of the best bars in town: spread over four floors, it has an alfresco bar for cocktails and a top-floor club space with its own *Saturday Night Fever* dancefloor.

Fernandez & Wells

NEW *73 Beak Street, W1F 9SR (7287 2814). Oxford Circus tube.* **Open** 8am-6pm Mon-Fri; 9am-6pm Sat. **Coffee bar**. Map p116 B2 ⓬
Round the corner from its forebear – a sandwich bar on Lexington Street – this espresso bar serves great coffee and nibbles to punters perched on a handful of high stools. That's it, but that's all it needs.

Floridita

100 Wardour Street, W1F 0TN (7314 4000/www.floriditalondon.com). Tottenham Court Road tube. **Open** 5.30pm-2am Mon-Wed; 5.30pm-3am Thur-Sat. **Bar**. Map p116 B2 ⓭
Floridita recreates the glitz and gluttony of pre-Castro Cuba, concocting faithful Daiquiris in an expansive, sparkling basement space. Various Cuban musicians and dancers provide entertainment after midnight, and there's an extensive cigar menu and fabulous bar snacks.

French House

49 Dean Street, W1D 5BG (7437 2799). Leicester Square or Piccadilly Circus tube. **Open** noon-11pm Mon-Sat; noon-10.30pm Sun. **Pub**. Map p116 C2 ⓮
The French House began between the wars; De Gaulle and his Free French had their office upstairs. The post-war era saw legendary boozers Brendan Behan, Dylan Thomas and Francis Bacon let rip. Today, with a restaurant upstairs, French House lager on tap and John Claridge's black-and-white photographs, it's all a bit more civilised.

Hummus Bros

88 Wardour Street, W1F 0TJ (7734 1311/www.hbros.co.uk). Oxford Circus or Tottenham Court Road tube. **Open** 11am-10pm Mon-Wed; 11am-11pm Thur, Fri; noon-11pm Sat. **£**. **Middle Eastern**. Map p116 B2 ⓯
At this chain of small, stylish fast-food cafés, houmous is the main event. It's served in bowls, topped with Levantine-inspired extras, such as chicken in tomato sauce, or roasted veg; you then scoop it up with warm pitta bread. No forks, no fuss. Great side dishes too.

Imli

167-169 Wardour Street, W1F 8WR (7287 4243/www.imli.co.uk). Tottenham Court Road tube. **Open** noon-11pm daily. **££**. **Indian & Pakistani**. Map p116 B2 ⓰
Popular with young office types, Imli is a spacious venue blending contemporary fittings with Indian antiques

and vibrant splashes of colour. The food is tapas-style bites for sharing; Punjabi-style samosas are a good start, while makhani dahl is a creamy dream. The curries are adequate, but could do with bolder spicing.

Imperial China

White Bear Yard, 25A Lisle Street, WC2H 7BA (7734 3388/www.imperial-china.co.uk). Leicester Square tube. **Open** noon-11.30pm Mon-Sat; 11.30am-10.30pm Sun. **££. Chinese. Map** p116 C3 **17**

Menus here are now fully translated, so even non-speakers of Chinese can try rarities such as baked lobster with salted duck egg yolk. Be adventurous also with the dim sum list: some items marked 'not recommended' aren't too challenging. Smarter than most of the other Chinatown eateries, but service can be shambolic.

Maison Bertaux

28 Greek Street, W1D 5DQ (7437 6007). Leicester Square tube. **Open** 8.30am-11pm daily. **£. Café.** No credit cards. **Map** p116 C2 **13**

Opened in 1871, Maison Bertaux's charms have remained unchanged for decades, with eccentric staff straight out of *Monsieur Hulot's Holiday*. With no espresso machine, the choice is café crème or pots of tea, plus fruit tarts and variations on cream and choux pastry.

Masala Zone

9 Marshall Street, W1F 7ER (7287 9966/www.realindianfood.com). Oxford Circus tube. **Open** 12.30am-3.30am, 5pm-11pm Mon-Fri; 12.30-11pm Sat; 12.30pm-3.30pm; 5.30-10.30pm Sun. **£. Indian. Map** p116 A2 **19**

Mini-chain Masala Zone serves cheery and affordable grub to trendy office wallahs who have more taste than spare cash. In addition to standard tikkas, samosas and bhajias there's a wide range of regional dishes.

Meza

100 Wardour Street, W1F 0TN (7314 4002/www.danddlondon.com). Leicester Square or Tottenham Court Road tube. **Open** noon-2.30pm, 5pm-2am Mon-Thur; noon-2.30pm, 5pm-3am Fri, Sat. **£. Spanish. Map** p116 B2 **20**

Hummus Bros p119

Meza is in the same building as Cuban-themed bar Floridita (p119), occupying a space as big and sleek as you'd expect from a D&D London restaurant. Waiters are charming and professional, and the tapas simply and stylishly prepared. The sherry selection will please connoisseurs.

Milk & Honey
(7292 9949/0700 655 469/www.mlk hny.com). Oxford Circus tube. **Open** *Non-members* 6-11pm Mon-Fri; 7-11pm Sat. **Bar**. **Map** p116 B2 ㉑
The London incarnation of New York's legendary referral-only destination is a triumph. It isn't just the 40-odd cocktails (although they are exquisite and fairly priced), it's the pretension-free service too. A limited number of non-members is allowed before 11pm, generally at the start of the week – phone ahead.

Mother Mash
NEW *26 Ganton Street, W1F 7QZ (7494 9644/www.mothermash.co.uk). Oxford Circus tube.* **Open** 8.30am-10pm Mon-Fri; noon-10pm Sat; noon-5pm Sun. **£££**. **Café**. **Map** p116 A2 ㉒

A modernised and much better version of London's traditional pie 'n' mash shops. Choose from several types of mash, pies, sausages and gravy, or try one of the main-course salads. Old-school puddings round things off. Breakfast options range from butties to the full English.

New Mayflower
68-70 Shaftesbury Avenue, W1D 6LY (7734 9207). Leicester Square or Piccadilly Circus tube. **Open** daily. **££**. **Chinese**. **Map** p116 C3 ㉓
Not even a booking can ensure you slip past the perpetual queue just inside, but it is fast-moving, and once you've sat down service is eager and attentive. The Cantonese cooking here is excellent, the three menus – English, Chinese and specials – feature lots of surprises.

New Piccadilly
8 Denman Street, W1D 7HQ (7437 8530). Piccadilly Circus tube. **Open** noon-8.30pm daily. **£**. **Café**. No credit cards. **Map** p116 B3 ㉔
This cathedral among caffs revels in Festival of Britain glory. You don't

LONDON BY AREA

really come to a place like this for the food, although the kitchen serves decent risottos and canelloni. Tea is served in proper Pyrex cups underneath wall-to-wall yellow Formica. Cravated proprietor Lorenzo Marioni is fast passing into Soho legend.

New World

1 Gerrard Place, W1D 5PA (7734 0396). Leicester Square tube. **Open** *11am-11.45pm Mon-Sat; 11am-11pm Sun. Dim sum served 11am-6pm daily.* **££. Chinese.** **Map** p116 C3 ㉕

One of the very few London dim sum restaurants with service from trolleys. Turn up when the doors first open to guarantee you get the freshest food (and be prepared to queue for at least half an hour at weekends). The dining is over three floors, with the ground floor the liveliest.

Pâtisserie Valerie

44 Old Compton Street, W1D 4TY (7437 3466/www.patisserie-valerie. co.uk). Leicester Square, Piccadilly Circus or Tottenham Court Road tube. **Open** *7.30am-8.30pm Mon, Tue; 7.30am-9pm Wed-Fri; 8am-9pm Sat; 9.30am-7pm Sun.* **£. Café.** **Map** p116 C2 ㉖

These days there are much better cake shops in London, but we keep returning here for the quirkily gloomy atmosphere downstairs and the views of Soho streetlife from the bright and breezy first floor. Decor is 1920s Parisian café.

Red Fort

77 Dean Street, W1D 3SH (7437 2115/www.redfort.co.uk). Leicester Square or Tottenham Court Road tube. **Open** *noon-2.15pm, 5.45-11pm Mon-Fri; 5.45-11pm Sat; 5.30-10pm Sun.* **£££. Indian.** **Map** p116 C2 ㉗

Providing rich pickings for smart young media types, the classy Red Fort is a calming place, decorated with a sleek water feature and antique artefacts. Its largely north Indian cooking is legendary for its blends of spices. Booking advisable.

Shadow Lounge

5 Brewer Street, W1F 0RF (7287 7988/www.theshadowlounge.co.uk). Piccadilly Circus tube. **Open** *10pm-3am Mon-Wed; 9pm-3am Thur-Sat.* **Bar. Map** p116 B3 ㉘

The original gay lounge bar and members' club is still popular with celebs and gay wannabes alike. Expect funky, comfy decor, professional cocktail waiters and friendly door staff.

Sun & Thirteen Cantons

21 Great Pulteney Street, W1F 9NG (7734 0934). Oxford Circus or Piccadilly Circus tube. **Open** *noon-11pm Mon-Fri; 6-11pm Sat.* **Pub/bar. Map** p116 B3 ㉙

A pleasant mix of corner pub and clubby bar, this once-traditional tavern is a smart alternative to either. Etched glass and dark wood make a pleasing backdrop to the main bar, adjoined by an understatedly stylish dining area. The clientele is an appealing jumble.

Yauatcha

15 Broadwick Street, W1F 0DL (7494 8888). Leicester Square, Oxford Circus or Tottenham Court Road tube. **Open** *Tea house noon-11pm Mon-Fri; 11.45am-11pm Sat; 11.45am-10.30pm Sun. Restaurant noon-midnight Mon-Sat; noon-10.30pm Sun.* **£££. Chinese. Map** p116 B2 ㉚

Within Lord Rogers' glassy Ingeni building, designer Christian Liagre has created a ground-floor tea room (for exquisite East-meets-West cakes and 150 varieties of tea) and a buzzing basement restaurant where lights twinkle from a black ceiling, a fish tank runs the length of the bar, and staff flit among the tables and banquettes. Innovative dim sum is served till late.

Shopping

Agent Provocateur

6 Broadwick Street, W1V 1FH (7439 0229/www.agentprovocateur.com). Oxford Circus or Tottenham Court Road tube. **Open** *11am-7pm Mon-Wed, Fri, Sat; 11am-8pm Thur; noon-5pm Sun.* **Map** p116 B2 ㉛

A leader in the luxury lingerie market, with everything from transparent slips of near-nothingness to sculptured bras, from full-on corsets to half-cup peepholes. Brand staples include decadent, pure silk PJs and the lacy Love range.

Berwick Street

Map p116 B2 **32**

This street retains something of the lively scuzziness that drew people to Soho before it sucked in the media firms and starting shooting upmarket. There's the fruit and veg stall at salt-of-the-earth Berwick Market, the dispirited survivors of what was a thriving outpost of record shops, plus fine tailors Eddie Kerr (no.52) and Tony Lutwyche (no.83).

Foyles

113-119 Charing Cross Road, WC2H 0EB (7437 5660/www.foyles.co.uk). Tottenham Court Road tube. **Open** 9.30am-9pm Mon-Sat; noon-6pm Sun. **Map** p116 C2 **33**

Independently owned and open since 1906, Foyles is London's best-known bookshop, revered for the sheer volume of its stock, which is spread over five floors. Ray's Jazz (7440 3205), selling CDs and a few books, and the attached café are on the first floor.

Harold Moores Records

2 Great Marlborough Street, W1F 7HQ (7437 1576/www.hmrecords.co.uk). Oxford Circus tube. **Open** 10am-6.30pm Mon-Sat; noon-6pm Sun. **Map** p116 A1 **34**

The astonishing basement vinyl collection has perhaps 90,000 records, extending into all reaches of classical music.

Liberty

Regent Street, W1B 5AH (7734 1234/www.liberty.co.uk). Oxford Circus tube. **Open** 10am-7pm Mon-Wed, Fri, Sat; 10am-8pm Thur; noon-6pm Sun. **Map** p116 A2 **35**

Housed in a 1920s mock Tudor structure, Liberty may not be London's most dynamic department store, but it is its most attractive. The gift room is in the middle of a soaring, galleried atrium,

with the company's characteristic prints adorning everything from lingerie to handbags. The fourth-floor furniture department dazzles. For menswear, women's shoes and cosmetics, head to nearby Regent House on Regent Street.

Sounds of the Universe

7 Broadwick Street, W1F 0DA (7734 3430/www.soundsoftheuniverse.com). Tottenham Court Road tube. **Open** 11.30am-7pm Mon-Fri; noon-6.30pm Sat. **Map** p116 B2 **36**

Easily navigable, Sounds is a browser's paradise. There's quality and quantity in house, broken beat and US garage, and lots of jazz, on both vinyl and CD. Downstairs, the second-hand vinyl is strong on African music.

Twinkled

Unit 1.5, Kingly Court, Carnaby Street, W1B 5PW (7734 1978/www.twinkled. net). Oxford Circus tube. **Open** 11am-7pm Mon-Wed, Sat; 11am-8pm Thur, Fri; noon-6pm Sun. **Map** p116 A3 **37**

Combining vintage clothes and furniture, this is the place to come for Stepford Wives teasets and moulds for petits fours. Expect a wide range of dresses from the 1930s to the '80s, and airline-logo bags.

Nightlife

Astoria

157 Charing Cross Road, WC2H 0EL (8963 0940/box office 0870 060 3777/www.meanfiddler.com). Tottenham Court Road tube. **Map** p116 C1 **38**

Rumours that this historic old 2,000-capacity alt-rock sweatbox may close in 2008 have been greeted with nostalgia-tinged outrage (see box p145). The sound system is atrocious, decor is shabby, sight lines are poor and the room is habitually packed to the point where breathing is difficult. Four nights a week (Mon, Thur-Sat) it becomes G.A.Y., London's largest gay venue, whose congregation of disco-bunnies forgive the place's shortcomings for a roster of pop and star PAs.

Bar Rumba

*36 Shaftesbury Avenue, W1D 7EP
(7287 6933/www.barrumba.co.uk).
Piccadilly Circus tube.* **Open** 9pm-
3.30am Mon; 6pm-3am Tue; 7pm-3am
Wed; 6pm-3.30am Thur, Fri; 9pm-5am
Sat; 8pm-2am Sun. **Map** p116 B3 **③**
This basement space is a favourite
haunt for proper music bods, despite
its West End location. The superstar
junglist line-up of Movement reigns on
Thursdays, while Fridays' Get Down
is full-on hip hop.

Black Gardenia

NEW *93 Dean Street, W1D 3SZ
(7240 8848/www.wcukdev.co.uk/
ryan/cellardoor/backend). Tottenham
Court Road tube.* **Open** 4pm-1am
daily. *Shows* 9.30pm, 11pm. **Map**
p116 B1 **④**
Forget the corporate jazz clubs, our
favourite Soho jazz session is at that
this funky, intimate dive. Sunday sees
an organ trio, fronted by hard-blowing
saxman Brandon Allen, play classic
hard bop in a Blue Note style. Other
nights see cabaret or a chantoose drop
by from one of the nearby West End
stage shows. Punters adhere to a sharp
vintage dress code.

Café de Paris

*4 Coventry Street, W1D 6BL (7734
7700/www.cafedeparis.com). Piccadilly
Circus tube.* **Open** phone for details.
Map p116 C3 **④**
The two floors of opulence at Café de
Paris – all drapes and decadent chandeliers – might seem an odd setting for
house nights and new bands, but they
really come into their own for dressed-
up Bond theme nights and Kitsch
Lounge Riot's excellent parties.

Café Royal

*68 Regent Street, W1B 5EL (7437
9090). Piccadilly Circus tube.* **Open**
phone for details. **Map** p116 B3 **④**
Described by Cecil Beaton as the most
beautiful room in London, the opulent
Grill Room is popular with dashing
young things who dress like it's the
1920s. Try Rakehell's Revels on
Tuesday or a supper-club event.

Comedy Store

*1A Oxendon Street, SW1Y 4EE
(Ticketmaster 0870 060 2340/www.
thecomedystore.co.uk). Leicester Square
or Piccadilly Circus tube.* **Open** *Shows*
8pm Tue-Thur, Sun; 8pm & midnight
Fri, Sat. **Map** p116 C3 **④**
The legendary Comedy Store was
where the 1980s alternative comedy
boom took hold and it's still the place
every comic wants to play, with the best
bills on the circuit. Go on Tuesdays for
the topical 'Cutting Edge' shows, or on
Wednesdays for top improv outfit the
Comedy Store Players.

Ghetto

*5-6 Falconberg Court (behind the
Astoria), W1D 3AB (7287 3726/
www.ghetto-london.co.uk). Tottenham
Court Road tube.* **Open** 10.30pm-3am
Mon-Wed; 10.30pm-4am Thur, Fri;
10.30pm-5am Sat; 10.30pm-3am Sun.
No credit cards. **Map** p116 C1 **④**
This gritty indie club offers Nag Nag
Nag for electro fans on Wednesday
and Mis-Shapes for cool lesbians on
Thursdays, while the Cock puts the
spunk back into gay Soho every Friday

Ronnie Scott's p126

night. Saturdays are the long-running trash night Wig Out, while the disingenuously named Detox happens every Sunday.

Madame Jo Jo's

8 Brewer Street, W1F 0SE (7734 3040/www.madamejojos.com). Leicester Square or Piccadilly Circus tube. **Open** 10pm-3am Tue-Sat. **Map** p116 B2 ⑮
Calling itself the heart of Soho's darkness, Jo Jo's is a beacon for those seeking to escape the All Bar Ones of this world. The indie kids glam up at White Heat every Tuesday, and apply the eyeliner and glitter for Glitz on Thursday. Electrogogo and Keb Darge's legendary soul and funkfest take care of Friday.

Metro

19-23 Oxford Street, W1D 2DN (7437 0964/www.blowupmetro.com). Tottenham Court Road tube. **Open** 11pm-3am Tue-Thur; 11pm-4am Fri, Sat. No credit cards. **Map** p116 C1 ⑯
With the waning of the garage-rock boom, this shambolic dive is no longer *the* place to play, but still gets enjoyably messy; expect to be drenched with beer and sweat by the time you leave.

Pizza Express Jazz Club

10 Dean Street, W1D 3RW (restaurant 7437 9595/jazz club 7439 8722/www. pizzaexpress.co.uk). Tottenham Court Road tube. **Open** *Restaurant* 11.30am-midnight daily. *Club* 7.45pm-midnight daily. **Map** p116 C1 ⑰
Like the pizzas dished up by the busy kitchen (the upstairs restaurant is jazz-free), the acts in this small basement range from the appetising to the bland, and are perhaps priced a little higher than their qualities merit. Still, the room is agreeably intimate and the sound is well up to snuff.

Punk

NEW *14 Soho Street, W1D 3DN (7734 4004/www.fabbars.com). Tottenham Court Road tube.* **Open** 5pm-3am Tue-Fri; 9pm-3am Sat. **Admission** £3-£10. **Map** p116 C1 ⑱
Basement space for nearly 300 bodies, bespoke Mapplethorpe-type flower prints and Rock Galpin furniture suit this venue's mix of surreal cabaret nights, up-and-coming drag types and Guilty Pleasures (songs you shouldn't like but do) knees-ups. The freaky-

LONDON BY AREA

dressing club kids seem to approve, swarming here for nights like Tesco Disco and Domestic (Goddess).

Ronnie Scott's

NEW *47 Frith Street, W1D 4HT (7439 0747/www.ronniescotts.co.uk). Leicester Square or Tottenham Court Road tube.* **Open** 6pm-3am Mon-Sat; 6pm-midnight Sun. **Map** p116 C2 ㊾

Over four decades, this famous hangout has hosted an A-to-Z of jazz greats. Scott died in 1995 and business partner Pete King sold the venue in 2005. A subtle yet character-altering refurb, completed in late 2006, means the lights are a little brighter, the food and drinks revamped, and the prices higher. Yet the place retains its mystique and the programming has room for old favourites like Georgie Fame and George Melly alongside the increasingly commercial acts.

Soho Revue Bar

11-12 Walker's Court, off Brewer Street, W1F 0ED (7734 0377). Leicester Square or Piccadilly Circus tube. **Open** 5pm-4am Tue-Sat. **Map** p116 B2 ㊿

Soho's grooviest club has two grand rooms that host the terrific monthly retro-rock rolling grindfest Lady Luck, but its the Sunday cabaret that really catches the eye – pole-dancing clowns, drag queens and burlesque beauties.

Arts & leisure

The concentration of playhouses that makes up London's theatrical 'West End' runs between Soho and Covent Garden (p134). The **tkts** booth (p219) has cheap tickets.

Comedy Theatre

6 Panton Street, SW1Y 4DN (0870 040 0046). Piccadilly Circus tube. **Map** p116 C4 (51)

Matthew Warchus's stylish revival of *Boeing-Boeing*, adapted from Marc Camoletti's 1961 play, revolves around Bernard, an architect who is three-timing a trio of air hostesses. The plotline may stretch credibility at times, but that's easy to ignore when the aeroplane is piloted by a crack cast on tip-top form. Production subject to change.

Curzon Soho

99 Shaftesbury Avenue, W1D 5DY (information 7292 1686/bookings 7734 2255/www.curzoncinemas.com). Leicester Square tube. **Map** p116 C2 (52)

The Curzon provides a reliably excellent line-up of indie, foreign and art-house fare, serves exquisite cakes and pastries in the lobby café, and has the best bar on Shaftesbury Avenue (downstairs and open to anyone). This is arguably London's best cinema.

Empire

4-6 Leicester Square, WC2H 7NA (0871 471 4714/www.empirecinemas.co.uk.) Leicester Square tube. **Map** p116 C3 (53)

Programming of the lowest common denominator, though the immense main auditorium is impressive.

Lyric Theatre

Shaftesbury Avenue, W1V 7DH (0870 040 0046). Piccadilly Circus tube. **Map** p116 B3 (54)

Cabaret continues to pull in the crowds. Rufus Norris's radical reworking can be heavy-handed, but mostly it's inventive, cheekily outrageous and thought-provoking. Production subject to change.

Odeon Leicester Square

Leicester Square, WC2H 7LQ (0871 224 4007/www.odeon.co.uk). Leicester Square tube. **Map** p116 C3 (55)

Lots of premières are held at this big art deco cinema, which has the UK's largest screen, a much-admired 1937 organ – and possibly the UK's highest ticket prices. Hosts London Film Festival gala events.

Palace Theatre

Cambridge Theatre, W1D 5AY (0870 895 5579/www.montypythonsspamalot.com). Leicester Square tube. **Map** p116 C2 (56)

The Tony Award-winning *Spamalot* is a slight but entertaining take on *Monty*

Gordon's p129

Python and the Holy Grail, with a hapless King Arthur and lovelorn Lady of the Lake. Production subject to change.

Prince Charles
7 Leicester Place, Leicester Square, WC2H 7BY (0870 811 2559/www. princecharlescinema.com). Leicester Square tube. **Map** p116 C3 ⑤⑦
The best value in town for cinema releases that have finished their first run. Singalong screenings (www.sing alonga.net/uk) help make this a cherished institution – as does the £4.50 ticket price for normal screenings.

Prince Edward Theatre
Old Compton Street, W1D 4HS (0870 850 9191). Leicester Square tube. **Map** p116 C2 ⑤⑧
Chimney sweeps and spoonfuls of magic in a satisfyingly dark *Mary Poppins*, directed by Sir Richard Eyre. Production subject to change.

Queen's Theatre
Shaftesbury Avenue, W1D 6BA (7494 5040/www.lesmis.com). Leicester Square or Piccadilly Circus tube. **Map** p116 C3 ⑤⑨

The RSC's version of *Les Misérables* has spent more than two decades on the London stage. It's still raking in the crowds with Victor Hugo's vision of the destitute in revolutionary Paris. Production subject to change.

Soho Theatre
21 Dean Street, W1D 3NE (7478 0100/ box office 0870 429 6883/www.soho theatre.com). Tottenham Court Road tube. **Map** p116 C2 ⑥⓪
Its cool blue neon lights, front-of-house café and occasional late-night performances have a Soho vibe that's echoed in the production style. The brilliant comedy shows are a highlight.

Covent Garden

Covent Garden Market is looked on as a little touristy by locals, but the Piazza is a handsome galleried space with lots of outdoor restaurant seating, some decent shops and no traffic. Most of the street entertainment (quality-vetted but, yes, living

LONDON BY AREA

London's Transport Museum

When it closed for major refurbishments in September 2005, the whole point of visiting Covent Garden seemed to have been removed: **London's Transport Museum** (right) is one of the few attractions in the area that pulls in as many locals as it does tourists. And – £21 million later – it's due to reopen in November 2007.

The museum redesign sounds impressive. The horse-drawn bus and trams have been placed on a new floor, surrounded by the rest of the historical displays in logical chronological sequence. The extra space means a wider range of topics can be covered – 'the complete door-to-door journey', as the museum puts it – giving river transport, bicycles and even walking their fair share of the spotlight, alongside the uniforms, models and photographs. We suspect the clamber-on vehicles will, however, remain the stars of the show.

Structural improvements to the Grade II-listed museum building – a draughty covered flower market in Victorian times – have allowed fragile artefacts to be displayed for the first time, among them artwork and drawings that help bring new focus to bear on the wonderful design work that is such an appealing aspect of London's transport history.

Families are well catered for too. The new Tube simulators should go down a treat, and with the exhibits made more interactive throughout and a brand-new play area, parents should be safe from being pestered by bored kids.

The new two-storey museum shop (pictured) is already in business – and the swanky redesign makes it even better than we remember. The brilliant deco posters, for example, are stored in shelves colour-coded by Underground lines, an elegantly practical approach. You'll still be able to buy the suave espresso mugs with motifs from Harry Beck's classic Tube map, but quirky new products like a shopping trolley in the shape of the London Underground roundel freshen things up a bit.

■ www.ltmuseum.co.uk

statues make it through) takes place under the portico of St Paul's (the Actors' Church). Good boutique shopping can be found to the north of the tube station – another area that is largely pedestrianised. Aside from the theatres and a couple of opera houses, Covent Garden only has one major sight: the brand spanking new **London's Transport Museum**.

Sights & museums

Benjamin Franklin House
36 Craven Street, WC2N 5NF (7839 2006/www.benjaminfranklinhouse.org). *Charing Cross tube/rail.* **Open** pre-book tour by phone or online. **Admission** £8. Map p117 E5 ❻①
The restored house where Franklin lived from 1757 to 1775 is an academic centre rather than a conventional museum, but it can be explored on pre-booked tours, lasting a short but intense 45 minutes and led by an actress playing Franklin's landlady.

London's Transport Museum
NEW *39 Wellington Street, WC2E 7BB (7565 7299/www.ltmuseum.co.uk).* *Covent Garden tube.* **Open/admission** phone for details. Map p117 F3 ❻②
See box left.

Eating & drinking

Abeno Too
17-18 Great Newport Street, WC2H 7JE (7379 1160/www.abeno.co.uk). *Leicester Square tube.* **Open** noon-11pm Mon-Sat; noon-10.30pm Sun. **£. Japanese**. Map p117 D3 ❻③
Its discreet exterior makes it easy to miss, but this modest place is always packed. Furnishings are simple, staff are polite and efficient, and the food is delicious. The original Abeno is near the British Museum (p136).

AKA
18 West Central Street, WC1A 1JJ (7836 0110/www.akalondon.com).

Holborn or Tottenham Court Road tube. **Open** 10pm-3am Tue; 6pm-3am Thur; 6pm-4am Fri; 7pm-5am Sat; 10pm-4am Sun. **Bar**. Map p117 E1 ❻④
Joined physically and musically to the End (p133) next door, this popular pre-club hangout attracts top international DJs to entertain punters loosened up by good food and cocktails. The venue is incorporated into the End's club nights on Saturdays; prepare to queue.

Canela
Thomas Neal Building, 33 Earlham Street, WC2H 9LS (7240 6926/www.canelacafe.com). *Covent Garden tube.* **Open** 9.30am-10pm Mon-Sat; 10am-8pm Sun. **£. Café**. Map p117 D2 ❻⑤
Canela's high-ceilinged room with lots of natural light is an attractive showcase for a compelling mix of Portuguese and Brazilian snacks and baked dishes. The cakes are a high point.

Food for Thought
31 Neal Street, WC2H 9PR (7836 9072). *Covent Garden tube.* **Open** noon-8.30pm Mon-Sat; noon-5pm Sun. **£. Vegetarian**. No credit cards. Map p117 E2 ❻⑥
A compact subterranean café, Food for Thought is furnished with chunky wooden furniture and a small service counter crammed with friendly staff. Loyal customers munch old-school veggie and vegan food.

Gordon's
47 Villiers Street, WC2N 6NE (7930 1408/www.gordonswinebar.com). *Embankment tube/Charing Cross tube/rail.* **Open** 11am-11pm Mon-Sat; noon-10pm Sun. **Wine bar**. Map p117 E4 ❻⑦
A candelit warren of a cellar wine bar – the oldest in London, established in 1890 – where schooners of sherry are still dispensed from the barrels behind the bar. Wonderfully atmospheric.

Great Queen Street
NEW *32 Great Queen Street, WC2B 5AA (7242 0622).* *Covent Garden or Holborn tube.* **Open** 5-11pm Mon; 11am-midnight Tue-Sat. **££. Brasserie**. Map p117 F1 ❻⑧

This new brasserie is run by the team who brought London St John, the Eagle and the Anchor & Hope, three of the city's best eateries, so the signs are good. The feel is bohemian, the dishes use seasonal British produce to effects both simple (radishes and butter) and inventive (bottled rabbit and caponata). Come during the afternoon to graze on bar snacks and explore the extremely well-chosen wine list. Charming service.

Ivy

1 West Street, WC2H 9NQ (7836 4751/www. caprice-holdings.co.uk). Leicester Square tube. **Open** noon-3pm, 5.30pm-midnight Mon-Sat; noon-3.30pm, 5.30pm-midnight Sun. **£££**
Modern European. Map p117 D2 ⑥⑨
Behind its old-fashioned latticed windows and the well-worn legend of impossible-to-book tables groaning with celebs, the Ivy is an elegant and vivacious restaurant, serving excellent modern European classics. Book weeks ahead if you want dinner, but you can sometimes nab a same-day table for lunch.

J Sheekey

28-32 St Martin's Court, WC2N 4AL (7240 2565/www.caprice-holdings. co.uk). Leicester Square tube. **Open** noon-3pm, 5.30pm-midnight Mon-Sat; noon-3.30pm, 6pm-midnight Sun. **£££**
Fish. Map p117 D3 ⑦⓪
Sheekey's continues to earn its renown as London's star fish restaurant. You can choose between the immaculate restaurant rooms or a stool at the handsome bar to peruse a plain-speaking menu, egalitarian enough to sit caviar beside jellied eels. Service strikes the perfect balance of formality and friendliness. Book well in advance.

Lamb & Flag

33 Rose Street, WC2E 9EB (7497 9504). Covent Garden tube. **Open** 11am-11pm Mon-Sat; noon-10.30pm Sun. **Pub**. Map p117 E3 ⑦①
The Lamb & Flag is by far the best pub in the Covent Garden area, so most evenings you'll be hard pushed to get

anywhere near its 350-year-old (or more) interior. The location is picture-perfect, at the head of a cobbled lane. Elderly musicians play rousing trad jazz on a Sunday evening.

L'Atelier de Joël Robuchon

NEW *13-15 West Street, WC2H 9NQ (7010 8600). Leicester Square tube.* **Open** noon-3pm, 5.30pm-midnight Mon-Sat; 12.30-10.30pm Sun. **££££**.
French. Map p117 D2 ⑦②
The most celebrated chef in France has finally come to London. The design is stunning, the food is imaginative and flavoursome, and it's a lot more fun than stuffier haute cuisine restaurants. The biggest drawback – aside from the pricing – is that it's very difficult to get in. After 7pm, bookings are only taken for the first-floor dining room, La Cuisine (it's worth noting that the menu in both dining areas is broadly similar). You even have to reserve seats for the bijou second-floor cocktail bar.

Orla Kiely p133

Lowlander

36 Drury Lane, WC2B 5RR (7379 7446/www.lowlander.com). Covent Garden or Holborn tube. **Open** noon-11pm Mon-Sat; noon-10.30pm Sun. **Bar**. **Map** p117 E2 ⑦

The bar counter is a vision: no fewer than 15 tall, gleaming chrome beer taps line up behind a twinkling array of upturned beer glasses of all shapes and sizes. Not had enough? Then try one of the 40 bottled beers. Too much? Steady yourself with some moules-frites.

Paul

29 Bedford Street, WC2E 9ED (7836 3304/www.paul.fr). Covent Garden tube. **Open** 7.30am-8pm Mon-Fri; 9am-8pm Sat; 9am-7.30pm Sun. **£**. **Bakery/café**. **Map** p117 E3 ⑦

This stylish French chain, with more than a dozen branches in London, focuses on high-quality, attractive pâtisserie, sweet and savoury tarts and artisan breads. The smart, black decor may seem exclusive, but staff are welcoming.

Rock & Sole Plaice

47 Endell Street, Covent Garden, WC2H 9AJ (7836 3785). Covent Garden tube. **Open** 11.30am-11pm Mon-Sat; noon-10pm Sun. **Fish & chips**. **Map** p117 D1 ⑦

There has been a chippie on this site since 1871. The chips are hand-cut, wide and lightly fried, the fried fish moist and crisp, the portions huge. In clement weather the outside seats get thronged – and waiting staff shoo off takeaway customers who are hoping to rest their legs.

Tamarai

NEW *167 Drury Lane, WC2B 5PG (7831 9399/www.tamarai.co.uk). Holborn tube.* **Open** *Restaurant* noon-3pm, 5.30-11.30pm Mon-Sat. *Bar* noon-2am Mon-Thur; noon-3am Fri, Sat. **£££**. **Asian**. **Map** p117 E1 ⑦

This vast former club has been kitted out in black, with pulsing lights, a claustrophobically low ceiling and cost-conscious finish. The cocktail and wine list is the best we've seen in a long time, which is just as well since the restaurant (book ahead) food is basically just expensive bar snacks.

Shopping

Cadenhead's Covent Garden Whisky Shop

3 Russell Street, WC2B 5JD (7379 4640/www.coventgardenwhiskyshop. co.uk). Covent Garden tube. **Open** 11am-6.30pm Mon, Sat; 11am-7pm Tue-Fri; noon-4.30pm Sun. **Map** p117 F2 ⓥ
There are four casks of pure malt whisky in store, plus one of rum, from which three bottle sizes (20cl, 35cl and 70cl) are dispensed. There are also around 800 pre-bottled single malts.

Cecil Court

(www.cecilcourt.co.uk). Leicester Square tube. **Map** p117 D3 ⓨ
Often overlooked, Cecil Court offers concentrated second-hand browsing opportunities in a picturesque pedestrian cut-through with nearly a dozen bookshops. Most are for collectors, but others sell cheaper paperbacks.

Coco de Mer

23 Monmouth Street, WC2H 9DD (7836 8882/www.coco-de-mer.co.uk). Covent Garden tube. **Open** 11am-7pm Mon-Wed, Fri, Sat; 11am-8pm Thur; noon-6pm Sun. **Map** p117 D2 ⓩ
Sam Roddick's erotic emporium is a glamorous introduction to kinkiness. The Victorian boudoir aesthetic maintains a sense of refined old-fashioned naughtiness – albeit with a modern commitment to ethical products.

Covent Garden Market

(7836 9136/www.coventgarden market.co.uk). Covent Garden tube. **Map** p117 E3 ⓰
The original market appeared on this site in 1640, selling fruit and veg; today Inigo Jones's Piazza remains an attractive space and Charles Fowler's market hall gets lovelier with age. Visitors flock here for a combination of retail therapy (both twee shops and upmarket chains), outdoor restaurant and café seating, street artists and classical renditions in the lower courtyard. The Apple Market, in the North Hall, has arts and crafts stalls (Tue-Sat) and antiques (Mon).

G Smith & Sons

74 Charing Cross Road, WC2H 0BG (7836 7422). Leicester Square tube. **Open** 9am-6pm Mon-Fri; 9.30am-5.30pm Sat. **Map** p117 D2 ⓛ
Tobacco, pipe and cigar buffs travel miles to visit this unique shop, virtually unchanged since its 1869 founding. There's also a natty line in lighters, cutters, ashtrays, pipes and snuff.

Koh Samui

65-67 Monmouth Street, WC2H 9DG (7240 4280/www.kohsamui.co.uk). Covent Garden tube. **Open** 10.30am-6.30pm Mon-Wed, Fri, Sat; 10.30am-7pm Thur; noon-5.30pm Sun. **Map** p117 D2 ⓜ
A well-established name in any serious London shopper's black book. Alongside a mix of heavyweight labels like Marc Jacobs and Chloé are hand-picked vintage finds and pieces by new designers. Beautiful jewellery and accessories round out the stock.

Monmouth Coffee House

27 Monmouth Street, WC2H 9EU (7379 3516/www.monmouthcoffee. co.uk). Covent Garden tube. **Open** 8am-6.30pm Mon-Sat. **Map** p117 D2 ⓝ
An atmospheric coffee merchant that sources beans directly from single farms, co-operatives and estates and roasts them on the premises. There's a small café area – and terrific smells.

Neal's Yard Dairy

17 Shorts Gardens, WC2H 9UP (7240 5700/www.nealsyarddairy. co.uk). Covent Garden tube. **Open** 11am-6.30pm Mon-Thur; 10am-6.30pm Fri, Sat. **Map** p117 D2 ⓞ
This long-established shop began a quarter of a century ago making its own cheese. Now it buys in a huge range of artisan cheeses from across the British Isles, maturing them in the cellar; there are over 50 seasonal varieties sold at any given time. Be sure to have a taste – it's all part of the fun.

Office

*57 Neal Street, WC2H 9PP (7379 1896/
www.office.co.uk). Covent Garden tube.*
Open 10am-8pm Mon-Fri; 10am-7pm
Sat; 11am-6pm Sun. **Map** p117 E2 ❽
Office has yet to take its finger off the
fashion pulse, offering catwalk
designs at high-street prices. The
chain's retro focus shows no signs of
abating, with high-heeled T-bars next
to Mary Janes.

Orla Kiely

*31 Monmouth Street, WC2H 9DD (7240
4022/www.orlakiely.com). Covent Garden
tube.* **Open** 10.30am-7pm Mon-Sat; noon-
5pm Sun. **Map** p117 D2 ❽
This flagship houses the designer's full
range of clothing and accessories. Bags
come in all materials, from her famous
graphic prints to richly hued leather.
Scarves, hats, wellies and luggage too.

Planet of the Grapes

NEW *90 New Oxford Street, WC1A
1BA (7405 4912/www.planetofthe
grapes.co.uk). Holborn tube.* **Open**
10am-8pm Mon-Sat. **Map** p117 E1 ❽
This new independent off-licence has a
great range of wine, a wonderfully
straightforward attitude and prices
that challenge (and sometimes beat)
the supermarkets. There's an on-site
tasting cellar too.

Santos & Mowen

*10 Earlham Street, WC2H 9LN (7836
4365/www.santosandmowen.com).
Covent Garden or Leicester Square
tube.* **Open** 11am-7pm Mon-Sat.
Map p117 D2 ❽
Mainly stocking DSquared and Dolce
& Gabbana alongside comparable
niche brands, S&M has a well-edited
selection. There's something for everyone, from leather trousers to monochrome T-shirts.

Stanfords

*12-14 Long Acre, WC2E 9LP
(7836 1321/www.stanfords.co.uk).
Covent Garden or Leicester Square
tube.* **Open** 9am-7.30pm Mon, Wed,
Fri; 9.30am-7.30pm Tue; 9am-8pm
Thur; 10am-7pm Sat; noon-6pm Sun.
Map p117 D3 ❽

Three floors of travel guides, travel
literature, maps, language guides,
atlases, globes and magazines. There's
a Trailfinders concession and a select
range of equipment. The basement
houses the complete range of British
Ordnance Survey maps.

Terra Plana

*64 Neal Street, WC2H 9PA (7379
5959/www.terraplana.com). Covent
Garden tube.* **Open** 10am-8pm Mon-
Sat; noon-6pm Sun. **Map** p117 D2 ❾
Terra Plana produces eco-friendly
shoes that are stitched rather than
glued. Check out the stylish lace-up
Aveiro kitten-heels, made with nubuck
leather and sustainable wood.

Nightlife

End

*18 West Central Street, WC1A 1JJ
(7419 9199/www.endclub.com).
Holborn or Tottenham Court Road
tube.* **Open** 10pm-3am Mon, Wed;
phone for details Tue, Sun; 10pm-4am
Thur; 10pm-5am Fri; 10pm-7am Sat.
Map p117 E1 ❾
The End continues to get queues
around the block. Erol Alkan is steer-
ing new night Durrr; there's also Ben
Watt's excellent Buzzin' Fly, acid men-
talists Bugged Out!, owner Mr C's minimal tech house session Superfreq,
notorious after-party Jaded and
Discotec, London's classiest 'midweek-
end' gay party. Attracts an international, super-friendly crowd.

Heaven

*The Arches, Villiers Street, WC2N 6NG
(7930 2020/www.heaven-london.com).
Embankment tube/Charing Cross
tube/rail.* **Open** 10.30pm-late Mon,
Wed, Fri, Sat. **Admission** £1-£15.
Map p117 E4 ❾
London's most famous gay club is still
a firm favourite with tourists. The best
nights are Popcorn and Fruit Machine
– both upbeat early-week fun – but
attempts to revitalise Saturdays have
done little to prevent muscle boys
migrating south over the Thames to
the Vauxhall Gay Village.

LONDON BY AREA

Variety clubs

Hot on the patent leather heels of London's vintage music and burlesque scenes comes the variety show. A year ago, nights offering a mix of stand-ups, magicians, burlesque starlets, crooners, even hula-hooping striptease were few. Now there's such a wide, well, variety they're spawning sub-scenes.

At one end of the spectrum is the supper club. The natural progression from posing in your original 1920s threads and long strings of pearls, the recently opened **Pigalle Club** (p115) is something straight out of 1940s New York, while **Volupté** (p167) has proven so successful that they offer two sittings most evenings just to meet demand.

Hedges & Butler (p113) is one of a growing breed of Mayfair and West End members' clubs that is opening its doors to promoters willing to do something truly avant-garde. Popular here is Loss – a night of exquisite misery, with onion-chopping to help along the tears. At the other end of the spectrum, **Royal Vauxhall Tavern** (p188) hosts a spit-and-sawdust cabaret spectacular each Thursday, with hairy gay blokes doing burlesque and bearded drag queens offering side-show entertainment.

Bethnal Green Working Men's Club (p182) is still pushing the variety-club envelope: a recent addition to its roster is Lucha Britannia, a Mexican wrestling show. Men in gimp masks throw each other around, while between bouts the entertainment takes in German spoken-word performers and all-you-can-eat contests.

12 Bar Club

22-23 Denmark Place, WC2H 8NL (office 7240 2120/box office 7240 2622/www.12barclub.com). Tottenham Court Road tube. **Open** *Café* 9am-9pm Mon-Sat. *Gigs* 7.30pm; nights vary. **Map** p117 D1 ③

Atmospheric with its candle-lit tables, this much-cherished hole-in-the-wall books a real grab-bag of stuff. Its tiny size dictates a predominance of singer-songwriters, but occasionally full bands also appear.

Arts & leisure

The concentration of playhouses that makes up London's theatrical 'West End' extends from Covent Garden into Soho, see p126.

Aldwych Theatre

Aldwych, WC2B 4DF (0870 040 0046/www.aldwychtheatre.com). Charing Cross/Embankment tube. **Map** p117 F2 ④

Big-budget films adapted for the stage tend to prove gawdy affairs, but supercharged *Dirty Dancing* is proving to be the exception to the rule, with record advance bookings and rave reviews. Production subject to change.

Cambridge Theatre

Earlham Street, WC2H 9HU (0870 890 1102/www.cambridgetheatre. co.uk). Covent Garden or Leicester Square tube. **Map** p117 D2 ⑤

The jailbird roles are passed at regular intervals from one blonde TV star to the next, but *Chicago* is still razzle-dazzling with its superslick show-dancing. Production subject to change.

Coliseum

St Martin's Lane, WC2N 4BR (box office 7632 8300/www.eno.org). Leicester Square tube/Charing Cross tube/rail. **Map** p117 D4 ⑥

Home to the English National Opera (ENO), the Coliseum was built in 1904 by Frank Matcham and restored to its former glory in 2004. Now all it needs is a similarly impressive programme. Fingers crossed that this will happen under Music Director Edward Gardner, due to come on board in May 2007. Unlike at the Royal Opera House, all works are performed in English.

Donmar Warehouse

41 Earlham Street, WC2H 9LX (0870 060 6624/www.donmarwarehouse.com). Covent Garden or Leicester Square tube. **Map** p117 E2 **97**

Less a warehouse than an intimate chamber, the 250-seat Donmar is a favourite crossover spot for actors who are more often associated with screen roles. Michael Grandage is keeping the venue on a fresh, intelligent path as he approaches his fifth anniversary as artistic director.

Event highlights Ewan MacGregor plays Iago in *Othello* (29 Nov 2007-23 Feb 2008).

Noël Coward Theatre

St Martin's Lane, WC2N 4BW (0870 040 0046). Leicester Square tube. **Map** p117 D3 **98**

The current smash hit here is Muppet-fest *Avenue Q*, a sing-along story of the residents of a down-at-heel New York street in which the cuddly characters exist side-by-side with humans. Songs include 'The Internet is for Porn', but the cynicism is only ever skin (or fur) deep. Production subject to change.

Novello Theatre

Aldwych, WC2B 4CD (0870 950 0940/ www.delfontmackintosh.co.uk/www.rsc. org.uk). Temple tube/Charing Cross tube/rail. **Map** p117 F3 **99**

While the RSC ploughs on with its project to perform Shakespeare's Complete Works in a year at Stratford-upon-Avon, its London residency at Sir Cameron Mackintosh's newly renovated Novello Theatre (formerly the Strand Theatre) continues at a less frenetic pace. The 2007 season saw two appearances by Patrick Stewart, in *Antony & Cleopatra* and *The Tempest*.

Royal Opera House

Royal Opera House, WC2E 9DD (7304 4000/www.royaloperahouse.org.uk). Covent Garden tube. **Map** p117 E2 **100**

Founded in 1732 and rebuilt three times, 'Covent Garden' is one of the world's greatest opera houses. It's home to the Royal Opera and Royal Ballet companies; facilities and programming are tip-top all round. Parts of the building open to the public include the handsome glass-roofed Floral Hall (which hosts afternoon tea dances twice a month), the Crush Bar and the Amphitheatre Café Bar, overlooking the Piazza. Among productions scheduled for the 2007 season are three complete performances of Wagner's Ring cycle.

Theatre Royal Drury Lane

Catherine Street, WC2B 5JF (0870 890 1109/www.lotr.com). Covent Garden tube. **Map** p117 F2 **101**

The musical version of *The Lord of the Rings* hit the stage here in May 2007. It's a monster, with a budget of £12.5 million, an amazing high-tech stage and a 70-strong cast that has orcs rampaging around the aisles. Production subject to change.

Bloomsbury

Bloomsbury's gracious squares can feel a little sterile – something the Farrell architectural practice is looking to address steadily in a pedestrianisation scheme. Not even the area's literary heritage, counting not only Virginia Woolf's literary set among its former residents, but Dickens, Poe and Yeats, does much for the district. Still the academic centre of London, endowed with hospitals, museums (the **British Museum** prime among them) and libraries (the **British Library**), Bloomsbury's main raison d'être is idle browsing: perhaps for books on Marchmont Street or Woburn Walk, or among the eateries and shops of Lamb's Conduit Street. The **Wellcome Collection** promises to be a fine addition to the area, and the church of **St George's Bloomsbury** has been wonderfully renovated.

Cartoon Museum

Sights & museums

In November 2007 the Eurostar terminal is to open in the grand Victorian red-brick **St Pancras** station building, making King's Cross London's gateway to Europe. The terminal will contain a Foyles bookshop (p123) and a gastropub, and new venues will doubtless be springing up through 2008.

British Library

96 Euston Road, NW1 2DB (7412 7332/www.bl.uk). Euston Square tube/Euston or King's Cross tube/rail. **Open** *9.30am-6pm Mon, Wed-Fri; 9.30am-8pm Tue; 9.30am-5pm Sat; 11am-5pm Sun.* **Admission** *free.* **Map** p139 D1 ❶
Unveiled in 1997, the new British Library went over budget by £350m and was 15 years behind schedule. When it finally opened, architecture critics ripped it to shreds. But don't judge a book by its cover: this is still one of the greatest libraries in the world, with 150 million items. In the John Ritblat Gallery, the library's main treasures are displayed: the Magna Carta, the Lindisfarne Gospels and original manuscripts from Chaucer. There's fun stuff too: Beatles lyric sheets, first editions of *The Jungle Books* and archive recordings of everyone from James Joyce to Bob Geldof. The library is also famous for its 80,000-strong stamp collection.

British Museum

Great Russell Street, WC1B 3DG (7636 1555/recorded information 7323 8783/www.thebritishmuseum. ac.uk). Russell Square or Tottenham Court Road tube. **Open** *10am-5.30pm Mon-Wed, Sat, Sun; 10am-8.30pm Thur, Fri. Great Court 9am-6pm Mon-Wed, Sun; 9am-11pm Thur-Sat.* **Admission** *free. Temporary exhibitions prices vary. Highlights tours £8; £5 reductions. Eye opener tours free.* **Map** p139 D4 ❷
Officially London's most popular tourist attraction, the museum is a neoclassical marvel built in 1847 by Robert

Smirke, one of the pioneers of the Greek Revival style. Also impressive is Lord Foster's glass-roofed Great Court, the largest covered space in London, which opened in 2000. This £100 million landmark surrounds the domed Reading Room, where Marx, Lenin, Thackeray, Dickens, Hardy and Yeats once worked. Star exhibits include ancient Egyptian artefacts – the Rosetta Stone and statuary on the ground floor, and mummies upstairs – and Greek antiquities including the marble friezes from the Parthenon known as the Elgin Marbles. The Celts gallery has the Lindow Man, preserved in peat since 300 BC. The Wellcome Gallery holds an Easter Island statue and regalia from Captain Cook's travels.

The King's Library, opened in 2004, is the finest neo-classical space in London, and home to a permanent exhibition, 'Enlightenment: Discovering the World in the 18th Century', a 5,000-piece collection devoted to the formative period of the museum. Its remit covers physics, archaeology and the natural world, and it contains objects as diverse as 18th-century Indonesian puppets and a beautiful orrery.

You won't be able to see everything in a day, so buy a guide and pick out the showstoppers – or just revisit. **Event highlights** 'The First Emperor of China' (13 Sept 2007-7 Apr 2008).

Cartoon Museum

35 Little Russell Street, WC1N 2HH (7580 8155/www.cartoonmuseum.org). Tottenham Court Road tube. **Open** 10.30am-5.30pm Tue-Sat; noon-5.30pm Sun. **Admission** £3; free-£2 reductions. No credit cards. **Map** p139 D4 **❸**

On the ground floor of this transformed former dairy, the very best in British cartoon art is displayed in chronological order, starting with the early 18th century, through Britain's cartooning 'golden age' (1770-1830) and wartime cartoons, to modern satirists such as Gerald Scarfe, Ralph Steadman and the *Guardian*'s Steve Bell. Upstairs celebrates UK comic art, with Rupert the Bear, Dan Dare and

the Bash Street Kids all present and correct. There's a shop on site, but it isn't half as good as Gosh!, the comic store around the corner at 39 Great Russell Street.

Charles Dickens Museum

48 Doughty Street, WC1N 2LX (7405 2127/www.dickensmuseum. com). Chancery Lane or Russell Square tube. **Open** 10am-5pm Mon-Sat; 11am-5pm Sun. Tours by arrangement. **Admission** £5; £3-£4 reductions. No credit cards. **Map** p139 E3 **❹**

London is scattered with plaques marking the many addresses where the peripatetic Charles Dickens lived but never quite settled, but this is the only one of his London homes still standing. Dickens lived here for three years from 1837 while he wrote *Nicholas Nickleby* and *Oliver Twist*. Ring the doorbell to gain access to four floors of Dickens artefacts. The posters, personal letters, manuscripts and even Dickens' writing desk are exhibited in rooms decorated as they would have been at the time he occupied the house.

Foundling Museum

40 Brunswick Square, WC1N 1AZ (7841 3600/www.foundlingmuseum. org.uk). Russell Square tube. **Open** 10am-6pm Tue-Sat; noon-6pm Sun. **Admission** £5; free-£4 reductions. **Map** p139 D3 **❺**

Opened in 2004, the museum recalls the social history of the Foundling Hospital, set up in 1739 by shipwright and sailor Captain Thomas Coram, who was appalled by the number of abandoned children on London's streets. Securing royal patronage, he gained the artist William Hogarth and the composer GF Handel as governors; Hogarth decreed that the building should also be the first public art gallery, and artists including Gainsborough, Reynolds and Wilson donated their work. The museum uses pictures, manuscripts and objects to recount the social changes that occurred during the period. There are interactive exhibits, and mementos left by mothers for their babies.

Bloomsbury & Fitzrovia

❶ Sights & museums
❶ Eating & drinking
❶ Shopping
❶ Nightlife
❶ Arts & leisure

Numbered locations refer to the Bloomsbury and Fitzrovia sections on pp136-147

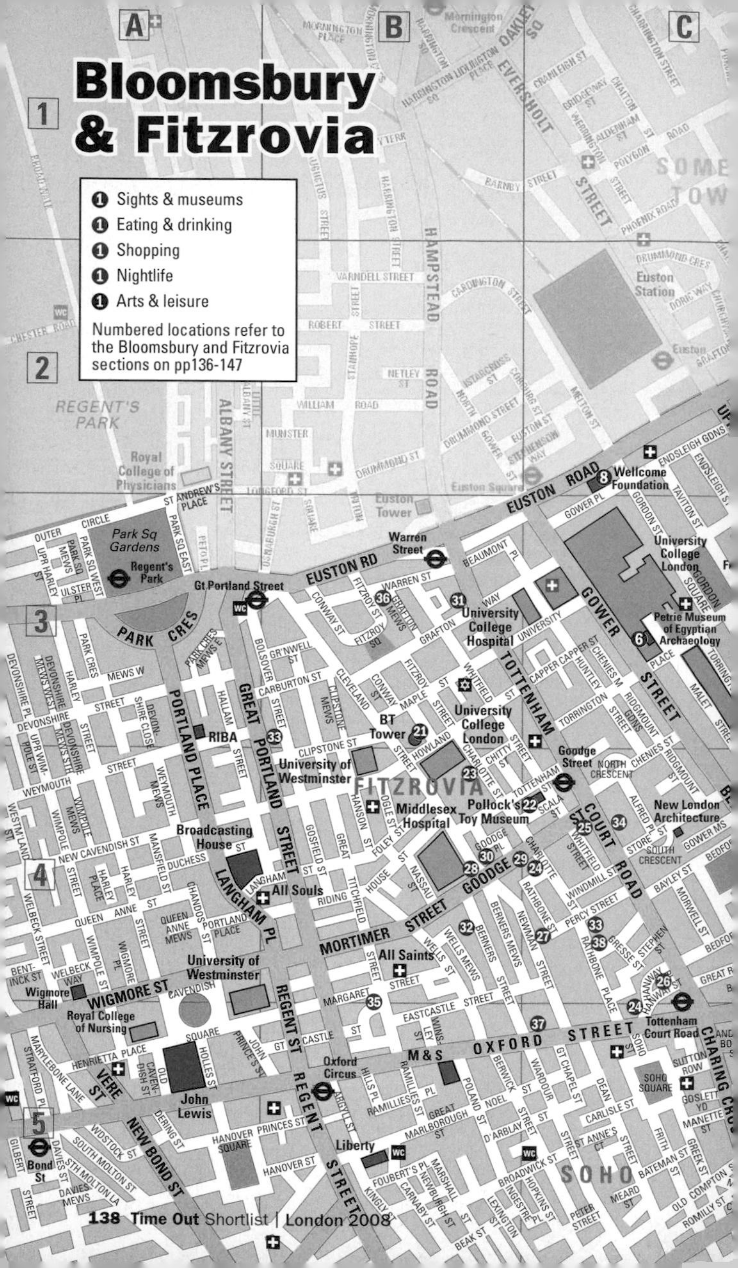

Petrie Museum of Egyptian Archaeology

University College London, Malet Place, WC1E 6BT (7679 2884/www.petrie. ucl.ac.uk). Euston Square, Goodge Street or Warren Street tube. **Open** 1-5pm Tue-Fri; 10am-1pm Sat. **Admission** free. **Map** p138 C3 ❻

The museum, set up in 1892 by eccentric traveller and diarist Amelia Edwards (*A Thousand Miles up the Nile*), is named after Flinders Petrie (pronounced 'pee-tree'), one of the most inexhaustible excavators of ancient Egyptian treasures. Where the British Museum's Egyptology collection is strong on the big stuff, the Petrie focuses on the minutiae of ancient life, such as pottery shards, grooming accessories, jewellery and primitive tools. Among the oddities are the world's oldest gynaecological papyrus and a 4,000-year-old skeleton of a man who was buried in an earthenware pot. It only adds to the fun that some corners of this small museum are so gloomy the staff provide torches.

St George's Bloomsbury

NEW *Bloomsbury Way (7405 3044/ www.stgeorgesbloomsbury.org.uk). Holborn or Tottenham Court Road tube.* **Open** 1-2pm Tue-Fri; 11.30am-5pm Sat; 2-5.30pm Sun. **Admission** free. **Map** p139 D4 ❼

Consecrated in 1730, St George is a grand and typically disturbing work by Nicholas Hawksmoor, with an offset, stepped spire inspired by the Mausoleum at Halicarnassus. It reopened in October 2006 following major renovations: highlights include the mahogany reredos, and 10ft-high sculptures of lions and unicorns clawing at the base of the steeple. As well as guided tours, there are regular concerts – and a weekday market should be getting underway.

Wellcome Collection

NEW *183 Euston Road, NW1 2BE (7611 2222/www.wellcomecollection. org). Euston Square tube/Euston tube/rail.* **Open** 10am-6pm Tue, Wed, Fri, Sat; 10am-10pm Thur; 11am-6pm Sun. *Library* 10am-6pm Mon, Wed, Fri; 10am-8pm Tue, Thur; 10am-4pm Sat. **Admission** free. **Map** p138 C2 ❽

See box p141.

Eating & drinking

Acorn House

NEW *69 Swinton Street, WC1X 9NT (7812 1842/www.acornhouse restaurant.com). King's Cross tube/rail.* **Open** 8am-10.30pm, noon-3pm, 6-10pm Mon-Fri; 10am-3pm, 6-11pm Sat. **££**. **British**. **Map** p139 E2 ❾

'Eco-restaurant' sounds terribly worthy, but Acorn House is far better than you might expect. With its banquettes, stylish interior and Riedel glasses, it looks like a grown-up restaurant, and ingredients are seasonal and well sourced (fish comes from sustainable stocks, meat is by Ginger Pig). Most dishes are successful, but the slow service is a reminder that this is a chef's training school as well as a restaurant.

Cigala

54 Lamb's Conduit Street, WC1N 3LW (7405 1717/www.cigala.co.uk). Holborn or Russell Square tube. **Open** noon-10.45pm Mon-Fri; 12.30-10.45pm Sat; noon-9.45pm Sun. **££**. **Spanish**. **Map** p139 E3 ❿

Chef/proprietor Jeff Hodges is an aficionado of classic Spanish cooking and it shows on the plate – although not in the clean-lined decor, which is bliss-fully free of Costa memorabilia. Fish and meat dishes are the stars, some served simply, others with a twist of innovation. The wine list goes well beyond Rioja, with fine examples from regions on the rise.

Konstam at the Prince Albert

NEW *2 Acton Street, WC1X 9NA (7833 5040/www.konstam.co.uk). King's Cross tube/rail.* **Open** 12.30-3pm, 7-10.30pm Mon-Sat. **££**. **British**. **Map** p139 E2 ⓫

The TV series *Urban Chef* made sure Oliver Rowe's new venture attracted a

Welcome, Wellcome

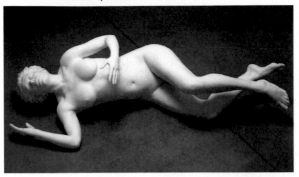

When we tell you that the £30 million **Wellcome Collection** (p140), due to open In June 2007, has been set up to encourage 'public engagement with health and well-being', you'd be forgiven for turning to the next page. But don't hurry away – the Wellcome should be really rather special.

In its quest to bring together medicine, modern art and people's ordinary lives, the Collection has a major headstart over other museums. Founder Henry Wellcome, when he wasn't amassing a huge fortune from his day job at the head of a pioneering pharmaceuticals company, spent his life collecting extraordinary objects from all over the world that related (sometimes rather tangentially) to medicine. Much of his booty is grisly – portions of tattooed human skin, delicately carved anatomical models of pregnant women, precious memento mori, voodoo dolls – but it is all fascinating.

To these original holdings the curators have been diligently adding serious works of modern art. One of the most arresting is John Isaacs' *I can't help the way I feel*, a six-foot-tall polystyrene, resin and steel statue of a man who appears to be in the process of burying himself in the fleshy folds of his own stomach. Horrid - but as a means of confronting the viewer with an image of obesity, hard to beat. More subtle, but no less interesting, is Marc Quinn's sculpture *Silvia Petretti – Sustiva, Tenofivir, 3TC (HIV)* (pictured). Graeco-Roman in style, the statue is of a woman with HIV... and the material used is mixed from the drugs she must take each day to stay alive. The contrast of smooth sculptural form and debilitating disease is striking.

The Wellcome will also host a rotating series of temporary exhibitions, beginning with 'The Heart'. This will use previously unseen religious images, drawings by Leonardo da Vinci, Andy Warhol prints, the Egyptian Book of the Dead and explorations of modern surgery to investigate our most important organ.

■ www.wellcomecollection.org

lot of attention before it opened in spring 2006. His gimmick is that nearly all the food on the daily-changing menu is produced within Greater London, taking the 'locally grown' mantra to a new level. In practice, the cooking can be a bit lacklustre, but desserts are a high point, and the drinks include excellent beers from the Greenwich-based Meantime Brewery. Rowe also runs the tiny Konstam café just around the corner.

Lamb

94 Lamb's Conduit Street, WC1N 3LZ (7405 0713/www.lambtavern.co.uk). Holborn or Russell Square tube. **Open** 11am-midnight Mon-Sat; noon-10.30pm Sun. **Pub**. **Map** p139 E3 ⑫

Founded in 1729, this beautifully restored etched glass and mahogany masterpiece is sheer class. Today, the snob screens have a decorative role above the horseshoe island bar, but, back in the days when music hall stars were regulars here, they were used to deflect unwanted attention. The Pit, a sunken back area, gives access to a summer patio.

Museum Tavern

49 Great Russell Street, WC1B 3BA (7242 8987). Holborn or Tottenham Court Road tube. **Open** 11am-11.30pm Mon-Thur; 11am-midnight Fri, Sat; noon-10.30pm Sun. **Pub**. **Map** p139 D4 ⑬

While cagouled Italian kids crocodile into the main entrance to the British Museum, canny drinkers can be found in the pub opposite. Former haunt of Orwell and Marx, the Museum Tavern has been a handsome beast ever since its sumptuous mid 19th-century refurb. Tourists come for tradition; locals for the splendid range of ales lined up along the room-length bar counter.

Shopping

The Brunswick, the compact 1970s housing development opposite Russell Square tube, reopened after a spruce-up in 2007. It's a neat agglomeration of mostly mid-brow chains, eating places and some oddities like **Skoob** (below).

French's Dairy

NEW *13 Rugby Street, WC1N 3QT (7404 7070/www.frenchsdairy.com). Holborn or Russell Square tube.* **Open** 11am-7pm Mon-Fri; 11am-5pm Sat. **Map** p139 E3 ⑭

A former dairy is an unlikely setting for a jewellery shop, but this isn't your ordinary bling. All budgets are covered, but major draws include chic costume pieces by jeweller-to-the-stars Philippe Ferrandis, while sumptuous clothing and accessories round out the stock.

James Smith & Sons

53 New Oxford Street, WC1A 1BL (7836 4731/www.james-smith.co.uk). Holborn or Tottenham Court Road tube. **Open** 9.30am-5.25pm Mon-Fri; 10am-5.25pm Sat. **Map** p139 D4 ⑮

A family umbrella business that has been on this site since 1830, James Smith still boasts charming Victorian fittings that were made by the brolly craftsmen themselves. As well as umbrellas, there's an excellent range of walking sticks and canes, and even shepherds' crooks.

London Review of Books

14 Bury Place, WC1A 2JL (7269 9030/www.lrb.co.uk/lrbshop). Holborn or Tottenham Court Road tube. **Open** 10am-6.30pm Mon-Sat; noon-6pm Sun. **Map** p139 D4 ⑯

This well-run shop, owned by the eponymous literary-political journal, is all polished wood, quiet conversations, passionate staff and a seriously informed selection of books. The range is extraordinary, from Alan Bennett's latest offerings and the most recent academic and political tomes, to up-to-date copies of the *New Yorker*, *Art Review* and *Smoke*, via excellent poetry, cookery and gardening titles. There are regular readings as well.

Skoob

NEW *Unit 66, The Brunswick (behind Waitrose), WC1N 1AE (7278 8760/ www.skoob.com). Russell Square tube.* **Open** 10am-8pm Mon-Sat; 11am-5pm Sun. **Map** p139 D3 ⑰

This back-to-basics second-hand book-store made a welcome return in spring 2007. Somewhat incongruous among the shiny chainstores, the new base-ment premises are all concrete and exposed piping, but to the point: some 50,000 titles, ranging from world his-tory to cultural studies, poetry to the occult, engineering to photography, arranged by the kind of loosely alphabetised themes beloved of book-browsers everywhere.

Nightlife

All-Star Lanes

Victoria House Place, WC1B 4DA (7025 2676/www.allstarlanes.co.uk). Holborn tube. **Open** 5-11.30pm Mon-Wed; 5pm-midnight Thur; noon-2am Fri, Sat; noon-11pm Sun. **Map** p139 D4 ⓭

The four bowling lanes are only part of the set-up here: alongside the alleys run diner-style booths at which to enjoy a trailer-chow menu and the spectacle of players bowling gutterballs. In the red-leather bar beyond, undulating circu-lar booths seat those warming down from a game, liquoring up in prepara-tion, or just enjoying a fine cocktail.

Fly

NEW *32-34 New Oxford Street, WC1A 1EP (7631 0862/www.barflyclub.com). Tottenham Court Road tube.* **Open** 5pm-midnight daily. **Map** p139 D4 ⓳

This sister venue to Camden's Barfly stages a similar mix of up-and-coming and never-will-be bands.

Arts & leisure

Place

17 Duke's Road, WC1H 9PY (7121 1000/www.theplace.org.uk). Euston tube/rail. **Map** p138 C2 ⓴

This internationally recognised dance venue provides top-notch professional training as well as classes in all genres for all levels. The 300-seat theatre pre-sents innovative contemporary dance from around the globe. Seating isn't numbered; it's a case of first come, first served. As a result, there's sometimes a scrum when the doors are thrown open ten minutes before the show starts. Since 2005, the Place has also sponsored an annual 'Place Prize', the British con-temporary dance equivalent of the liter-ary Booker or art world's Turner prizes.

Fitzrovia

Fitzrovia, west of Tottenham Court Road, has an enviable reputation as a gathering point for radicals, writers, boozers and and bohemians – but these days that reputation is little more than a historical artefact. Many of the current residents are wealthy media companies, which have drawn some of the capital's hippest restaurants and hotels, as well as inviting small shops, to the area, especially around strollable Charlotte Street or the increasing number of hip boutiques around Warren Street.

Sights & museums

BT Tower

60 Cleveland Street, W1. Goodge Street tube. **Map** p138 B3 ㉑

The BT Tower (previously known as the Post Office Tower) was designed to provide support for radio, TV and tele-phone aerials by means of microwave signals. It was opened in 1964 and its crowning glory was the revolving restaurant, the Top of the Tower, which closed to the public in 1971 after a bomb by the Angry Brigade. The building became Grade II-listed in 2003, but sadly the tower is still closed to the public.

Pollock's Toy Museum

1 Scala Street (entrance on Whitfield Street), W1T 2HL (7636 3452/www. pollockstoymuseum.com). Goodge Street tube. **Open** 10am-5pm Mon-Sat. **Admission** £3; free-£1.50 reductions. No credit cards. **Map** p138 C4 ㉒

Housed in a wonderfully creaky Georgian townhouse, Pollock's is named after Benjamin Pollock, the last of the Victorian toy theatre printers. By turns beguiling and creepy, the museum is a nostalgia-fest of old board games, tin trains, porcelain dolls and Robertson's gollies. It's fascinating for adults but possibly less so for children, for whom the displays are a bit static.

Eating & drinking

Boteca Carioca
93 Charlotte Street, W1T 4PY (7637 0050). Goodge Street tube. **Open** noon-3pm, 5.30-11pm Mon-Sat; 2-9.30pm Sun. **££. Brazilian.** Map p138 B4 ㉓
Service here is typically Brazilian, meaning friendly and laid-back. Food is cooked to order, so it may take 20 minutes for them to warm the stews slowly to keep the meats tender and allow the subtle flavours of Brazilian cooking – cashew, lemon, red peppers, coconut – to work their magic, but the wait is worth it. From prawn delicacies to fish stews to chicken concoctions, everything is superb, but try to save room for the equally toothsome desserts.

Bradley's Spanish Bar
42-44 Hanway Street, W1T 1UT (7636 0359). Tottenham Court Road tube. **Open** noon-11pm Mon-Sat; noon-10.30pm Sun. **Bar.** Map p138 C5 ㉔
This off-Oxford Street landmark is still a Spanish colony, even though a new generation (dreadlocked and/or pierced) mans pricey pumps of Spanish lager in the cramped, creaking, two-floor casket of velour. Punters spill on to the street in taxi-blocking bonhomie on summer nights. Top-quality jukeboxes.

Crazy Bear
26-28 Whitfield Street, W1T 2RG (7631 0088/www.crazybeargroup.co.uk). Goodge Street tube. **Open** noon-11pm Mon-Fri; 6-11pm Sat. **Bar.** Map p138 C4 ㉕
Über-stylish yet supremely comfortable. Ignore the upstairs restaurant and head down an ornate staircase to the opulent bar of cowhide swivel stools and red padded alcoves. The food and drinks are both exquisite, with lovely all-day dim sum for £4 and stunning cocktails, expertly and convivially mixed with high-end brands and innovative fruit purées.

Hakkasan
8 Hanway Place, W1T 1HD (7907 1888). Tottenham Court Road tube. **Open** noon-12.30am Mon-Wed; noon-1.30am Thur-Sat; noon-midnight Sun. **££££. Chinese.** Map p138 C4 ㉖
Hakkasan is still one of London's most glamorous restaurants, and the beauty of it can startle. The low lighting, dark oriental screens (seemingly stretching into infinity) and general buzz of this big basement are like nothing else. Dinner is expensive and you'll need to book well in advance, but for lunch on a weekday you can explore the innovative dim sum menu and spend a mere £15 per head. From the wonderful food to the cutting-edge cocktail list mixed by friendly barmen and in-house DJs who play music that's cool yet listenable, Hakkasan is pretty much faultless.

Newman Arms
23 Rathbone Street, W1T 1NG (7636 1127/www.newmanarms.co.uk). Goodge Street or Tottenham Court Road tube. **Open** noon-midnight Mon-Fri. **Pub.** Map p138 C4 ㉗
The narrow alley beside this former brothel was splendidly sinister in the 1960 film *Peeping Tom*, but don't expect maverick Fitzrovia bohemians these days. The poky downstairs bar is patronised by chuckling nine-to-fivers, and upstairs duvet-sized puffs of pastry cover any number of creative fillings in the Famous Pie Room.

Ooze
62 Goodge Street, W1T 4NE (7436 9444/www.ooze.biz). Goodge Street tube. **Open** noon-11pm Mon-Sat. **££. Risotto café.** Map p138 B4 ㉘
Ooze specialises in risotto, but takes it out of the familiar Italian ristorante setting into a modern 'risotto bar'. Other constituents – such as pan-fried sea bass, or pumpkin, hazelnut and sage – are added to the rice dish just before serving, and there are starters and top desserts for those who have a hearty appetite. With most risottos costing between £7 and £9, Ooze is good value, but the place can get noisy, so visit off-peak if you can.

Roka

37 Charlotte Street, W1T 1RR (7580 6464/www.rokarestaurant.com). Goodge Street or Tottenham Court Road tube. **Open** noon-11pm Mon-Fri; 12.30-11pm Sat; 12.30-10.30pm Sun. **£££**.
Japanese. Map p138 C4 ㉙

What started life as baby Zuma (p90) has grown into a confident, vital operation serving some of London's best modern Japanese food. From a central grill kitchen surrounded by brown wooden benching, head chef Nic Watts and his team serve the likes of succulent chicken wings or charred sea bream. Brilliant cocktails, focused on the eponymous vodka-like spirit, are mixed downstairs in the Shochu Lounge basement bar.

Salt Yard

54 Goodge Street, W1T 4NA (7637 0657/www.saltyard.co.uk). Goodge Street tube. **Open** noon-11pm Mon-Fri; 5-11pm Sat. **££**. **Spanish**. Map p138 B4 ㉚

This compact space is deftly furnished with a sleek, pared-down aesthetic of steely greys and chocolatey browns. The brief menu – divided into cold meats, bar snacks and tapas – and wine list demonstrate superb attention to detail, gathering the very best of Spain and Italy – corn-fed jamón ibérico and tangy chorizo meet delicate prosciutto and herb-flecked salami. Salt Yard is always busy, for all the right reasons.

Sardo

45 Grafton Way, W1T 5DQ (7387 2521/www.sardo-restaurant.com). Warren Street tube. **Open** noon-3pm, 6-11pm Mon-Fri; 6-11pm Sat. **£££**.
Sardinian. Map p138 B3 ㉛

Although it observes mainstream Italian aesthetics, there's an air of Sardinian separatism in this charming restaurant. Regional dishes such as spaghetti bottarga – a rich classic of fish roe and extra virgin olive oil – are enhanced by an almost Greek array of grilled fish and lamb. There's an intriguing selection of good Sardinian wine, temptingly priced.

All played out?

The announcement that the **Astoria** (p123) was under threat brought forth an astonishing gush of sentimental support. Astonishing when you consider the poor sound, sightlines and attitude of the staff, less so when you consider generations of music-lovers who have gathered to hear David Bowie, the Rolling Stones, Nirvana, the Sugarcubes, Radiohead… or perhaps Kylie, Madonna and Take That doing PAs at the long-running G.A.Y. club night.

Behind the passionate 'Save the Astoria' online petitions, the facts are simple. The place was bought by developers in 2006, starting rumours it would become a shopping complex, upmarket apartments, even a Crossrail station. Mean Fiddler holds the lease until 2008, however, so Megadeath and Tangerine Dream… your booking is safe.

London's mid-sized venues are dwindling, though: Hammersmith Palais is being demolished; the Hammersmith Apollo, Forum and Shepherd's Bush Empire look likely to be sold; adventurous Spitalfields venue the Spitz (www.spitz.co.uk) may well have become a gastropub before you get a chance to read this. Yet many of the city's smaller venues thrive: places like **Bardens Boudoir** (p181), the **Luminaire** (p173) and **Black Gardenia** (p124) are having the time of their lives, perhaps because they are quicker to respond to the rapid changes on this city's crazed music scene.

LONDON BY AREA

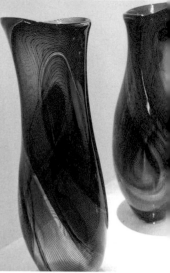

Contemporary Applied Arts

Suka

NEW *The Sanderson, 50 Berners Street, W1T 3NG (7300 1444). Oxford Circus tube.* **Open** 6.30am-11.30am, noon-2.30pm, 5.30pm-midnight Mon-Wed; 6.30am-11.30am, noon-2.30pm, 5.30pm-12.30am Thur-Sat; 6.30am-11.30am, noon-2.30pm, 5.30-10.30pm Sun. **££££**. **Malaysian**. **Map** p138 B4 **32**

The restaurant that used to be Spoon+ has been turned into a Malaysian-style, design-led restaurant charging big à la carte prices – but, being the Sanderson, you're likely to get 'wow' factor. The set lunch (£25 for two courses, £29 for three) brings things within reach.

Shopping

Tottenham Court Road has the city's main concentration of electronics and computer shops, but for tidy prices, advice and no hard sell, **John Lewis** (p101) is good.

Contemporary Applied Arts

2 Percy Street, W1T 1DD (7436 2344/ www.caa.org.uk). Tottenham Court Road or Goodge Street tube. **Open** 10.30am-5.30pm Mon-Sat. **Map** p138 C4 **33**

Museum and gallery curators buy and commission through CAA, so this should be your first stop if you're after contemporary applied art. There's a bespoke engagement/wedding ring service, the basement has craft items to suit all pockets, and the upper level is a gallery. Exceptional glassware.

Fopp

NEW *220-224 Tottenham Court Road, W1T 7PZ (7299 1640/www. fopp.co.uk). Goodge Street tube.* **Open** 10am-10pm Mon-Sat; noon-6pm Sun. **Map** p138 C4 **34**

The flagship store of this independent chain sells the latest CD releases for around £10 and loads of back catalogue for £5-£7. Books and DVDs retail at similarly low prices. The 250-capacity licensed bar/café downstairs, designed especially for in-store gigs (see box p183), has hosted the likes of Bert Jansch and Hot Chip.

Sniff

1 Great Titchfield Street, W1W 8AU (7299 3560/www.sniff.co.uk). Oxford Circus tube. **Open** 10am-7pm Mon-Wed; 10am-8pm Thur; 10am-6.30pm Fri, Sat; noon-6pm Sun. **Map** p138 B4 **35**

Conceived as an antidote to shops stocking identikit high-street shoes, Sniff sells established brands (Repetto, French Sole) but also pushes the eye-catching and adventurous, including its own brand of 1940s-inspired peep-and closed-toe wedges, fitted stilettos and platform boots.

Thorsten van Elten

22 Warren Street, W1T 5LU (7388 8008/www.thorstenvanelten.com). Warren Street tube. **Open** 10.30am-6.30pm Mon-Fri; 10.30am-6pm Sat. **Map** p138 B3 **36**

Among Warren Street's increasingly hip shopping options, Thorsten van Elten stands out with its passion, which has built a mighty reputation for products by young, London-based designers. We love Attua Aparicio Torino's Taz Ah mugs: take a slurp and reveal one of three animals' noses.

Nightlife

100 Club

100 Oxford Street, W1D 1LL (7636 0933/www.the100club.co.uk). Oxford Circus or Tottenham Court Road tube. **Open** 7.30pm-midnight Mon; 7.30-midnight Tue-Thur; 7.30pm-midnight Fri, Sat; 7.30-11pm Sun. **Map** p138 C5 **37**

This basement room has provided a home for jazzers, bluesmen, soulboys and punks (including the 1976 show that featured the Pistols, the Clash and the Damned). These days, expect jazz, swing-dance, indie and old rockers.

Wheatsheaf

25 Rathbone Place, W1T 1DG (7580 1585). **Open** 11.30am-11pm Mon-Fri; 12.30-6.30pm Sun. **Map** p138 C4 **38**

A perfectly decent boozer that happens to host what is probably the best improv comedy night in town: Grand Theft Impro happens every Thursday.

Magma p166

The City

The City

This was the original Londinium, and is full of history and heraldry, institutions and monuments – not least the deliciously spruced-up St Paul's Cathedral. The City of London, the self-governing 'square mile' that is England's financial heart, has pretty much exactly the same boundaries as the Romans gave it. It also has the offices to house, tall buildings to glorify and expensive restaurants to feed the incumbent financial establishment. Its pleasures lie in wandering the maze of streets whose ancient geography and names not even the Great Fire of London could eradicate, watching thrusting execs zoom about paying it no mind. The City is most itself at either end of the business day, when commuters plunge through the tube stations, but it's often more enjoyable to explore it at weekends and in the later evening, when the streets are eerily quiet. Many businesses don't bother to open at the weekend, although the handsome pedestrian bridge across the river between St Paul's and Tate Modern means things are getting busier.

City Information Centre

NEW *St Paul's Churchyard, EC4M 8BX (7332 1456). St Paul's tube.* **Open** phone to check. **Map** p150 C4 ❶
St Paul's tourist information centre is a brand new building on St Paul's Church Yard, just at the top of the steps leading from Tate Modern across the Millennium Bridge. Until it opens there are desks in the Museum of London (10am-5.50pm Mon-Sat; noon-5.50pm Sun) and St Paul's crypt shop (9am-5pm Mon-Sat; 10am-4.30pm Sun).

Sights & museums

Of the City's three landmark modern buildings, only the least visually arresting (and tallest) is open to the public: **Tower 42**, still almost universally known as the NatWest Tower, has a restaurant and the champagne bar Vertigo 42 (p156). But both 30 St Mary Axe ('the Gherkin', p153) and the Lloyd's of London building (p152) are well worth a look. And scour the Open House (p35) brochures for the occasional opportunity to peek inside.

Bank of England Museum

Entrance on Bartholomew Lane, EC2R 8AH (7601 5545/www.bankofengland. co.uk/museum). Bank tube/DLR. **Open** 10am-5pm Mon-Fri. **Admission** free. **Map** p151 E4 ❷

The bank, originally built by Sir John Soane in 1788, has been extensively remodelled over the years, and the restored Stock Office houses an amusing museum. As well as ancient coins and original artwork for banknotes, the museum offers a rare chance to lift a real gold bar (closely monitored by CCTV, more's the pity).

Bunhill Fields

Old Street tube/rail. **Admission** free. **Map** p151 E2 ❸

This was an important non-conformist burial ground until the 19th century, and it contains memorials to John Bunyan, Daniel Defoe and William Blake. Opposite, the home and chapel of John Wesley has been made into a quaint museum of Methodism (49 City Road, 7253 2262, www.wesleyschapel. org.uk); downstairs are some of the finest public toilets in London – built in 1899 and with original Victorian fittings by Sir Thomas Crapper.

Clockmakers' Museum

Guildhall Library, Aldermanbury, EC2V 7HH (7332 1868/ www.clockmakers.org). Mansion House or St Paul's tube/Bank tube/DLR/Moorgate tube/rail. **Open** 9.30am-4.45pm Mon-Sat. **Admission** free. **Map** p151 D4 ❹

Hundreds of ticking, chiming clocks and watches, all produced by members of the London Clockmakers' Company. You can see the marine chronometer of John Harrison (1693-1776), who solved the problem of longitude, and the watch Hillary carried to the top of Everest.

College of Arms

130 Queen Victoria Street, EC4V 4BT (7248 2762/www.college-of-arms.gov. uk). St Paul's tube/Blackfriars tube/rail. **Open** 10am-4pm Mon-Fri. **Admission** free. No credit cards. **Map** p150 C4 ❺

The first coats of arms were created to identify competing knights at medieval jousts, but heraldry soon became an integral part of family identity for the British gentry. Visitors interested in finding out about their family arms can consult the official register of arms and arrange tours to view the records.

Dr Johnson's House

17 Gough Square, off Fleet Street, EC4A 3DE (7353 3745/www. drjohnsonshouse.org). Chancery Lane tube/Blackfriars tube/rail. **Open** May-Sept 11am-5.30pm Mon-Sat. Oct-Apr 11am-5pm Mon-Sat. **Admission** £4.50; free-£3.50 reductions. No credit cards. **Map** p150 B4 ❻

Dr Samuel Johnson (1709-84) was the author of the enormously important *Dictionary of the English Language*, which established the method for all dictionaries that followed it – not that he enjoyed it much: 'to make dictionaries is dull work,' he wrote in his definition of the word 'dull'. You can tour his stately Georgian townhouse, or sit in the square outside with the bronze statue of his cat Hodge ('a very fine cat').

Guildhall Art Gallery

Guildhall Yard, off Gresham Street, EC2P 2EJ (7332 3700/www.guildhall-art-gallery.org.uk). Mansion House or St Paul's tube/Bank tube/DLR/Moorgate tube/rail. **Open** 10am-5pm Mon-Sat; noon-4pm Sun. **Admission**

The City

© Copyright Time Out Group 2007

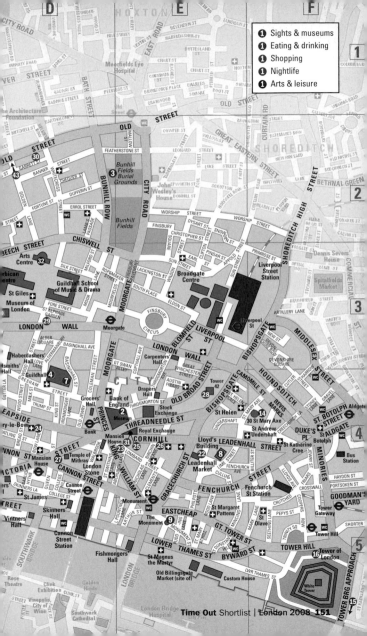

£2.50; free-£1 reductions. No credit cards. **Map** p151 D4 **7**

Most of what's here is stuffy portraiture of royals and politicians, with the centrepiece John Copley's *Siege of Gibraltar* – the largest painting in Britain – which spans two floors of the gallery. There is a delightful collection of Pre-Raphaelite paintings in the basement, and works by Constable and Reynolds. In a sub-basement are the ruins of London's Roman amphitheatre, from AD 70.

Lloyd's of London

1 Lime Street, EC3M 7HA (www. lloyds.com). Monument tube. **Map** p151 E4 **8**

Lord Rogers' high-tech Lloyd's of London building has all its mechanical services (ducts, stairwells, lift shafts and even loos) on the outside, making it look like a disassembled washing machine. The original Lloyd's Register of Shipping, decorated with bas-reliefs of sea monsters and nautical scenes, is around the corner on Fenchurch Street.

Monument

Monument Street, EC3R 8AH (7626 2717/www.towerbridge.org.uk). Monument tube. **Open** 9.30am-5pm daily. **Admission** £2; free-£1 reductions. No credit cards. **Map** p151 E5 **9**

The Monument is the world's largest free-standing Doric column. It was designed by Sir Christopher Wren and Robert Hooke as a memorial to the Great Fire of London, its 202 feet in height matching the distance to Farriner's bakery in Pudding Lane, where the fire began. Inside, a spiral staircase winds up 311 steps to a narrow gallery with fantastic views. A much-improved public space at the base of the Monument was unveiled in January 2007, the first phase of an 18-month, £5 million scheme to set up a permanent exhibition space there.

Museum of London

150 London Wall, EC2Y 5HN (0870 444 3851/www.museumoflondon.org. uk). St Paul's or Barbican tube. **Open** 10am-5.50pm Mon-Sat; noon-5.50pm Sun. **Admission** free; suggested donation £2. **Map** p151 D3 **10**

Reached through a brick bastion in the middle of a roundabout on London Wall, this expansive museum traces the history of the capital from its prehistoric settlements to the outbreak of World War I; the favourite displays have always been those on the Great Fire and Black Death. An impressive two-year expansion project began in early 2007 with the closure of the downstairs galleries. As well as creating 25% more space for previously unseen exhibits, the £20 million 'Capital City' project will add an inviting new glass entrance to the museum. In the interim, temporary foyer exhibits will complement an improved, interactive Great Fire section on the ground floor, which takes its place alongside the familiar displays.

Event highlights 'London's Burning' (until 2008).

St Bartholomew-the-Great

West Smithfield, EC1A 9DS (7606 5171/www.greatstbarts.com). Barbican tube/Farringdon tube/rail. **Open** 8.30am-5pm Tue-Fri (until 4pm Nov-Feb); 10.30am-1.30pm Sat; 8.30am-1pm, 2.30-8pm Sun. **Admission** free. **Map** p150 C3 **11**

Probably the City's finest medieval church. Parts of the building belong to the 12th-century priory hospital of St Bartholomew, founded by Prior Rahere, a former courtier of Henry I. The church was chopped about during Henry VIII's reign and the interior is now firmly Elizabethan. Benjamin Franklin trained here as a printer in 1724.

St Paul's Cathedral

Ludgate Hill, EC4M 8AD (7236 4128/ www.stpauls.co.uk). St Paul's tube. **Open** 8.30am-4pm Mon-Sat. *Galleries, crypt & ambulatory* 9.30am-4pm Mon-Sat. *Tours* 11am, 11.30am, 1.30pm, 2pm Mon-Sat. **Admission** *Cathedral, crypt & gallery* £9.50; free-£8 reductions. *Tours* £3.50; £1-£3 reductions. No credit cards. **Map** p150 C4 **12**

London's most famous cathedral has grown more radiant for its 300th anniversary. A decade of restoration has stripped off the Victorian grime and the extravagant main façade looks as brilliant today as it must have when first unveiled in 1708. Sir Christopher Wren had to fight to get his plans for this epic cathedral past the authorities – many dignitaries thought it too large and expensive – and he changed his mind halfway through to create the massive dome for which it is now famous. In fact, there are three domes – the inner and outer domes are separated by a hidden brick dome that supports the entire structure (believed to weigh 64,000 tons).

Most visitors walk around in wonder at the vast open spaces and memorials to such heroes of empire as Nelson, Wellington and Lawrence of Arabia, but you can also look down from the Whispering Gallery, reached by 259 steps from the main hall (the acoustics allow a whisper to be bounced clearly to the other side of the dome). Steps continue to the outdoor Golden Gallery (530 steps), which offers giddying views over the City. Keep an eye out for 18th-century graffiti as you climb.

Before leaving St Paul's, head down to the maze-like crypt, which contains the small, plain tombstone of Wren, inscribed 'Reader, if you seek a monument, look around you'. Tours of the Triforium – visiting the library and Wren's 'Great Model' – must be pre-booked on 7246 8357 (£14).

Temple Church & the Inns of Court

King's Bench Walk, EC4Y 7BB (7353 8559/www.templechurch.com). Temple tube. **Open** 11am-12.30pm, 1-4pm Mon, Tue; 2-4pm Wed; 11am-12.30pm, 2-4pm Thur, Fri; 11am-12.30pm Sat, Sun. **Admission** free. **Map** p150 B4 ⑬
Inspired in its style by Jerusalem's Church of the Holy Sepulchre and consecrated in 1185, the Temple Church was the private chapel of the mystical Knights Templar – and hence gained sudden, unsought notoriety as The Da Vinci Code church. It's the only round church in London and contains the worn gravestones of several Crusader knights, but you might have more fun exploring the Inns of Court than poring over the church. Middle Temple (7427 4800, www.middletemple.org.uk) and Inner Temple (7797 8183, www.innertemple.org.uk) aren't open to the public, but you can still potter through the courtyards; Inner Temple has fine buildings and lovely lawns for a peaceful picnic. North of the Royal Courts, Lincoln's Inn (7405 1393, www.lincolnsinn.org.uk) is a catalogue of architectural styles (its Old Hall is well over 500 years old) surrounding London's largest public square, while the gardens of the serene Gray's Inn (7458 7800, www.graysinn.org.uk) are open to the public on weekday mornings.

30 St Mary Axe

(www.30stmaryaxe.com). Liverpool Street tube/rail. **Map** p151 F4 ⑭
Having only opened in 2004, it is extraordinary how swiftly Lord Foster's skyscraper has become a cherished icon of modern London. The appropriateness of its 'Erotic Gherkin' nickname is immediately apparent; the sophistication of the technology within much less so – it cools and heats itself with maximum efficiency, as well as reducing fuel wastage by making the most of any available natural light.

Tower Bridge

Tower Bridge, SE1 2UP (7403 3761/www.towerbridge.org.uk). Tower Hill tube/Tower Gateway DLR. **Open** Apr-Sept 10am-6.30pm daily. Oct-Mar 9.30am-6pm daily. **Admission** £6; free-£4.50 reductions. **Map** p151 F5 ⑮
In its day the bridge was a triumph of Victorian technology, and even though it's only opened a few times a week these days, it still performs its drawbridge trick magnificently. Both of the towers and the west walkway that connects them have been converted into the Tower Bridge Exhibition, the views from the top of which are nothing short of stupendous.

Tower of London

Tower Hill, EC3N 4AB (0870 756 6060/www.hrp.org.uk). Tower Hill tube/ Tower Gateway DLR/Fenchurch Street rail. **Open** *Mar-Oct* 10am-6pm Mon, Sun; 9am-6pm Tue-Sat. *Nov-Feb* 10am-5pm Mon, Sun; 9am-5pm Tue-Sat. **Admission** £15; free-£12 reductions. **Map** p151 F5 ⑯

Over the centuries, the Tower of London has served a number of functions: it's been a fortress, a royal palace, a prison and an execution site for traitors to the state – not to mention a couple of Henry VIII's wives. Despite being insanely crowded and blighted by poor disabled access (an unfortunate consequence of 900 years of fortification), this is one of the best-value attractions in London. There's so much to see that many visitors make a day of it. Tickets are sold in the modern kiosk just to the west of the palace and visitors enter through the Middle Tower, but there's also a free audio-visual display in the modernist Welcome Centre outside the walls. There are two ways to see the Tower: you can go it alone – with or without audio tour – and stand some chance of having the displays to yourself, or join a free hour-long tour led by a Yeoman Warders (Beefeaters), who also care for the Tower's most famous residents, the ravens. Children love the tours, especially gruesome stories of treason, torture and execution delivered by these cheery, red-coated former soldiers.

The highlight of any visit will probably be the Crown Jewels, which you glide past on airport-style travelators; the other big attraction is the armoury in the White Tower, with its array of swords and cannons, suits of armour and executioner's axe. Executions were actually carried out on the green in front of the Tower – this gruesome site is now marked by a glass pillow, sculpted by the artist Brian Catling in 2006. New developments in 2007 included an impressive re-creation of Edward I's chambers in the Medieval Palace, complete with sound effects and a CGI film of medieval palace life.

Eating & drinking

Bar & Grill

2-3 West Smithfield, Clerkenwell, EC1A 9JX (7246 0900/www.barandgrill. co.uk). Farringdon tube/rail. **Open** noon-11pm daily. **£££. North American**. **Map** p150 C3 ⑰

The Bar & Grill opened in 2005 with a rush of publicity for its 'Kobe' beef and big steaks. It offers all the usual cuts for reasonable prices, plus the fabled wagyu steak (£50 for 8oz – cheat and have the £16.95 wagyu steak burger). On a Friday night, the cocktail bar fills with men loosening ties and women who've brought heels to change into.

Black Friar

174 Queen Victoria Street, EC4V 4EG (7236 5474). Blackfriars tube/rail. **Open** 11am-11pm Mon-Wed, Sat; 11am-11.30pm Thur, Fri; noon-10.30 pm Sun. **Pub**. **Map** p150 C4 ⑱

Built in 1875, the Black Friar was remodelled by Arts and Crafts Movement devotees in 1905. The result is a pale green mosaic exterior, a billowing white marble-topped bar and an odd anteroom with glorious lush carpet and gold and jade mosaic ceiling. Possibly London's most beautiful pub – with a good selection of real ales.

De Gustibus

53-55 Carter Lane, EC4V 5AE (7236 0056/www.degustibus.co.uk). St Paul's tube/Blackfriars tube/rail. **Open** 7am-5pm Mon-Fri. **£. Bakery café**. **Map** p150 C4 ⑲

This award-winning baker supplies upmarket restaurants with a mouthwatering range of artisan breads, also used to make deep-filled sandwiches or accompany own-made soups. Full breakfasts are served too.

Flâneur

41 Farringdon Road, EC1M 3JB (7404 4422/www.flaneur.com). Farringdon tube/rail. **Open** 8.30am-10pm Mon-Sat; 10am-6pm Sun. **££. Modern European/deli**. **Map** p150 B3 ⑳

Don't be deterred by the unassuming storefront; inside there's a capacious

Pho p163

food hall, its towering shelves lined tidily with gourmet goodies and artisanal delights, and a terrific restaurant. The kitchen staff are kept on their toes by a pair of menus that often change: one lists appetising breakfasts; the other encompasses lunches and dinners with a Mediterranean influence.

Fryer's Delight
19 Theobald's Road, WC1X 8SL (7405 4114). Chancery Lane or Holborn tube. **Open** noon-10pm Mon-Sat. No credit cards. **£. Fish & chips.** Map p150 A3 ㉑
A cabbies' favourite, this no-frills Formica-clad chippie comes with low-wattage lighting and unforgiving bench seating. The menu is short but sweet: fish, chips and accompaniments.

Lamb Tavern
10-12 Leadenhall Market, EC3V 1LR (7626 2454). Monument tube/Bank tube/DLR. **Open** 11am-midnight Mon-Fri. **Pub.** Map p151 E4 ㉒
In the 18th-century glory days of this photogenic pub, it kept the market's stallholders lubricated; these days most local traders deal not in fruit and veg but in stocks and shares. The matey main space is little more than a

room with a bar in it, but there are tables on the gallery above, and a restaurant at the top.

1 Lombard Street
1 Lombard Street, EC3V 9AA (7929 6611/www.1lombardstreet.com). Bank tube/DLR. **Open** 11am-11pm Mon-Fri. **££** Brasserie. **£££** Restaurant. **French.** Map p151 E4 ㉓
By no means the only former banking hall to have been remodelled into a restaurant, 1 Lombard Street is set apart by its Michelin star. The rear restaurant is calm and secluded; the larger front brasserie more approachable and anchored by a circular bar beneath a domed skylight. Food is terrific in both.

Place Below
St Mary-le-Bow, Cheapside, EC2V 6AU (7329 0789/www.theplacebelow.co.uk). St Paul's tube/Bank tube/DLR. **Open** 7.30-11am, 11.30am-3pm Mon-Fri. **£.** **Vegetarian.** Map p151 D4 ㉔
Located in the crypt of St Mary-le-Bow church, this smart canteen, with its domed ceiling, columns and cosy alcoves, is a hit with the area's stockbrokers and fund managers. The quality of the food varies but it's always

LONDON BY AREA

imaginatively prepared and often scores highly. In fine weather, sit outside in the churchyard.

Royal Exchange Grand Café & Bar

The Royal Exchange, EC3V 3LR (7618 2480/www.royalexchangegrandcafeand bar.com). Bank tube/DLR. **Open** 8-11am, 11.30am-10pm Mon-Fri. **££.**
Mediterranean. Map p151 E4 ㉕
Hidden from the street, this smart venture mutates from calm breakfast haunt to lively cocktail bar. A mezzanine looks down on the action in the grand concourse with its oval bar. The food can be workaday, but the premises are among the grandest in London. The understated, excellent French restaurant Sauterelle (7618 2483) is also here.

Simpson's Tavern

382 Cornhill, EC3V 9DR (7626 9985). Bank tube/DLR. **Open** 11.30am-5pm Mon-Fri. *Food served* noon-3pm Mon-Fri. **££. British**. Map p151 E4 ㉖
Established in 1757, this venerable City tavern is tucked away in a tiny courtyard. The upstairs dining room, with its waft of Dickensian victuals from the smoky grill, has communal tables packed with former public schoolboys. A City essential.

Sweetings

39 Queen Victoria Street, EC4N 4SA (7248 3062). Mansion House tube. **Open** 11.30am-3pm Mon-Fri. **£££. Fish**. Map p151 D4 ㉗
In business since 1830 and settled on this site for a century, Sweetings is another City institution. Perch on a stool at the high counter in the charmingly shabby and cramped interior to scoff potted shrimps, washed down with a silver tankard of ale, or slurp down the exquisite all-native oysters.

Vertigo 42

Tower 42, 25 Old Broad Street, EC2N 1HQ (7877 7842/www.vertigo42.co.uk). Bank tube/DLR/Liverpool Street tube/rail. **Open** noon-3pm, 5-11pm Mon-Fri. **Champagne bar**. Map p151 E4 ㉘

Check in at reception, pass through the metal detectors, and take an express lift up 42 floors to this champagne bar. The decor is a bit like an airport executive lounge, but the 360° panorama through floor-to-ceiling windows is everything you could wish for. The views from Rhodes Twenty Four (7877 7703, www.rhodes24.co.uk) are roughly half as exciting – seeing as it's on the 24th floor.

Wood Street

Wood Street (corner of Fore Street), EC2Y 5EJ (7256 6990/www.woodstreet bar.com). Moorgate or Barbican tube/rail. **Open** 11am-11pm Mon-Fri. **£££. Wine bar**. Map p151 D3 ㉙
Lacklustre decor, variable service. So why bother with Wood Street? Because of the windowed view of the Barbican's lake and terrace. The pan-European food shows discernible signs of passion, at least, and there's a decent range of drinks.

Shopping

Bread & Honey

205 Whitecross Street, EC1Y 8QP (7253 4455/www.breadnhoney.com). Barbican tube/Old Street tube/rail. **Open** 10am-6.30pm Mon-Wed, Fri; 10am-7pm Thur; 11am-5pm Sat. **Map** p151 D2 ㉚
Owned by streetwear expert Laurent Roure and club promoter Laurent Chaumer, this boutique sells upscale sports and casualwear. Check out, particular, the Baracuta G9 Harrington jacket, as worn by Steve McQueen, and military-inspired bags from QWST.

Wint & Kidd

Courtyard, Royal Exchange, EC3V 3LQ (7908 9990/www.wintandkidd.com). Bank tube. **Open** 10.30am-5.30pm Mon-Fri. **Map** p151 E4 ㉛
Wint & Kidd deals exclusively in diamonds. There's a vast selection and help is at hand if you need instructions on how to wear your gem. The emphasis here is on discreet bespoke service, although there are ready-to-wear pieces available too.

Arts & leisure

Throughout the year young musicians give low-key lunchtime recitals in the City's churches. Watch out for the Wednesday night organ concerts at **Temple Church** (p153), for example, or get a programme from **St Bride's** (7427 0133, www.stbrides.com), **St Margaret Lothbury** (7606 8330, www.stml.org.uk) or **St Mary-le-Bow** (7248 5139, www.stmary lebow.co.uk).

Barbican Centre

Silk Street, EC2Y 8DS (7638 4141/ box office 7638 8891/www.barbican. org.uk). Barbican tube/Moorgate tube/ rail. **Map** p151 D3 ⬛32

The Barbican recently spent millions of pounds on a refurbishment aimed at making its labyrinthine array of public spaces more welcoming and easier to navigate. It hasn't really helped; indeed, returning visitors will take one look and wonder where the money went. The reworking of the acoustics in the arts centre's main concert hall has proved rather more successful, making the Barbican's already excellent music programming still more attractive. At the core of the music roster, performing 90 concerts a year, is the London Symphony Orchestra (LSO), but the BBC Symphony Orchestra is a frequent visitor and there are frequent guest soloists and ensembles from around the world. The modern music programme takes in jazz, rock, world and country, and it's all supplemented by free performances in the foyer. There are also three well-programmed cinemas and an impressively curated art gallery.

Event highlights Philip Glass & Patti Smith (19 Oct 2007); BITE season; Michael Clark's Stravinsky Project Part 3 (31 Oct - 10 Nov 2007).

Holborn & Clerkenwell

Sandwiched between the City and the West End, Holborn and Clerkenwell were, for most of their history, places where the mean folk of London pursued their little-respected trades. **Clerkenwell**,

Courtauld Institute of Art Gallery p159

Cézanne revealed

For it's 75th birthday, the charmingly intimate **Courtauld Institute** (p159) is for the first time to display all its holdings of Paul Cézanne, the finest such collection in Britain.

Born in Aix-en-Provence in 1839, Cézanne's paintings were little appreciated in his lifetime, with the Paris Salon rejecting his work for most of the 1860s. It wasn't until the 1890s that he began to gain public recognition, by which time the painter had left Paris for the seclusion of Provence. These days, his mastery of composition and colour, and his attempt to see the geometric structure that underpinned reality, are seen as a vital link between the 19th-century Impressionists and the Cubists of the 20th century; Picasso and Matisse were admirers, and he has been called 'the father of modern art'.

It's a stroke of luck that in the 1920s industrialist Samuel Courtauld went against prevailing artistic tastes in Britain to buy his Cézannes, which include key paintings *Montagne Sainte-Victoire* (1887) and *Card Players* (1892-5). This exhibition will show all ten of the paintings, as well as drawings and watercolours. Further insight will be supplied by displays of previously unexhibited letters in which Cézanne explains his artistic principles and new research into his methods, including X-ray techniques.
■ 'The Courtauld Cézannes' (26 June-21 Sept 2008).

north-west of the City across from Smithfields meat market, has a particularly bloody history, taking in plague and burnings-at-the-stake – today you'll burn nothing more dangerous than the dancefloors of a clutch of clubs. The area is now a relatively residential inner-city neighbourhood with great pubs, bars and restaurants on characterful streets. South of Clerkenwell, **Holborn** (pronounced 'Hoe-bun') is a legal district, home to the Courts of Justice and the quadrangles of the medieval Inns of Court (p153), not to mention shops full of wigs, gowns and weighty, terrifyingly dry-looking tomes.

Sights & museums

Hunterian Museum

Royal College of Surgeons, 35-43 Lincoln's Inn Fields, Holborn, WC2A 3PE (7869 6560/www.rcseng.ac.uk/ museums). Holborn tube. **Open** 10am-5pm Tue-Sat. **Admission** free. **Map** p150 A4 ❸

John Hunter (1728-93) was a pioneering surgeon and anatomist who amassed a huge collection of medical specimens and related artworks. After he died, the collection was enhanced and expanded by others; today, it can be viewed in a bright modern space. Check out the brain of 19th-century mathematician Charles Babbage and dentures worn by Winston Churchill.

Museum & Library of the Order of St John

St John's Gate, St John's Lane, Clerkenwell, EC1M 4DA (7324 4000/ www.sja.org.uk/museum). Farringdon tube/rail. **Open** 10am-5pm Mon-Fri; 10am-4pm Sat. *Tours* 11am, 2.30pm Tue, Fri, Sat. **Admission** free. Suggested donation £5; £4 reductions. **Map** p150 C2 ❸

Today, the Order of St John is best known in London for its provision of ambulance services, but in fact it can trace its history all the way back to early Christian medical practice during the Crusades. This fascinating collection of objects and artworks charts the evolution of the medieval Order of Hospitaller Knights through Jerusalem, Malta and other far-flung outposts of the Ottoman Empire.

Sir John Soane's Museum

13 Lincoln's Inn Fields, Holborn, WC2A 3BP (7405 2107/www. soane.org). Holborn tube. **Open** 10am-5pm Tue-Sat; 10am-5pm, 6-9pm 1st Tue of mth. *Tours* 2.30pm Sat. **Admission** free; donations appreciated. *Tours* £3; free reductions. **Map** p150 A3 ⓭

Architect Sir John Soane (1753-1837) obsessively collected art, furniture and architectural ornamentation. In the early 19th century, he turned his house into a museum to which 'amateurs and students' should have access. Rooms arc modestly sized but modified by Soane with ingenious devices to enhance natural daylight and to expand available space, including walls that open out like cabinets to display paintings (including Canalettos, Turners and two series by Hogarth). The real wow is the Monument Court, a multi-storey affair stuffed with sculpted stone from ancient buildings and a sarcophagus of alabaster carved for the pharaoh Seti I (1291-78 BC).

Somerset House

Strand, WC2R 1LA (7845 4600/www. somerset-house.org.uk). Temple tube (closed Sun)/Charing Cross tube/rail. **Open** 10am-6pm daily. **Admission** *Courtyard & terrace* free. *Exhibitions* £5; £4 reductions. No credit cards. **Map** p150 A4/5 ⓲

The original Somerset House was a Tudor palace commissioned by the Duke of Somerset in 1547, but it was demolished 1775 to make way for an entirely new building. The architect Sir William Chambers spent the last 20 years of his life working on the neoclassical mansion that now peers out over the Thames. It accommodated learned societies such as the Royal Academy and various governmental offices, including the Inland Revenue. The taxmen are still here, but the rest

Ambassador p160

of the building is open to the public, and houses three formidable museums, a brilliant fountain court, a little café and a very high-class restaurant. And an ice rink is erected in the courtyard for a couple of months each winter.

Courtauld Institute of Art Gallery

7848 2526/www.courtauld.ac.uk/gallery. The Courtauld, one of the world's leading centres for research in the history of art, also has one of Britain's most important collections of paintings. The gallery is diverse, yet on a more manageable scale than, say, the National. Old Masters, Impressionists and Post-Impressionists are here, with famous works including Manet's *A Bar at the Folies Bergère* and Van Gogh's *Self-Portrait with Bandaged Ear*. The 20th-century collection has been expanded with pieces by Kandinsky, Matisse and Barbara Hepworth.

Event highlights 'Walter Sickert: The Camden Town Nudes' (25 Oct 2007-20 Jan 2008); 75th anniversary show 'The Courtauld Cézannes' (26 June-21 Sept 2008; see box p158).

Café Kick

Gilbert Collection

7420 9400/www.gilbert-collection.org.uk.
In 1949, British-born Sir Arthur Gilbert
uprooted to California, where he made
his millions in real estate. He developed
a predilection for silver, gold and all
sorts of gemmed, gilded and shiny
objects. In 1996, the country of his birth
became the beneficiary of this obsession when Gilbert donated his entire
collection, saying 'I felt it should return
to the country of my birth'. And he con-
tinued buying new pieces after the
museum had been opened. The collection's two floors are dazzlingly
bedecked with candelabras, mosaics,
vases, urns, plates, mosaics and even-
snuff boxes.

Hermitage Rooms

7845 4630/www.hermitagerooms.co.uk.
The Hermitage Rooms host a rotating
programme of exhibitions of items
belonging to the Winter Palace in St
Petersburg. The rooms in this corner
of Somerset House even recreate in
miniature the sumptuous decor of their
Russian twin. New shows arrive twice
a year and can include everything from
paintings and drawings to decorative
art and fine jewellery.

Eating & drinking

Ambassador

*55 Exmouth Market, Clerkenwell,
EC1R 4QL (7837 0009/www.the
ambassadorcafe.co.uk). Angel tube/
Farringdon tube/rail/19, 38 bus.*
Open 8.30am-10.15pm Mon-Fri;
11am-4pm Sat, Sun. **££. Modern
European**. Map p150 B1 ❸
This easygoing incarnation of an ide-
alised bistro was a worthy runner-up
for *Time Out*'s Best New Restaurant of
2006. You can just have a drink, or add
a bar plate or two, or order a full meal
from a short but tempting menu that is
matched by an interesting wine list
(with plenty by the glass). Breakfast is
also served, plus brunch at weekends.

Bountiful Cow

*51 Eagle Street, Holborn, WC1R
4AP (7404 0200). Holborn tube.*
Open/food served 11am-11pm
Mon-Sat. **Diner**. Map p150 A3 ❸
This sassy two-floor diner has a witty
and well-sourced bovine theme – retro
Vache Qui Rit and Bovril ads, film
posters for *Urban Cowboy* and *Cattle
Queen*. The steaks, both ribeye (£13)
and sirloin (£14), are 9oz and succulent

to a T, and are sourced from selected beef hung for two weeks at least, but daily specials mean it's not all beef, beef, beef. Wines are well chosen and there's real ale for the discerning beer drinker too.

Café Kick

43 Exmouth Market, Clerkenwell, EC1R 4QL (7837 8077/www.cafe kick.co.uk). Angel tube/Farringdon tube/rail/19, 38 bus. **Open** noon-11pm Mon-Thur; noon-midnight Fri, Sat; 4-10.30pm Sun (spring/summer only). **£**. **Café/bar**. Map p150 B1 ③⑨
Enjoyably boisterous and noisy, Café Kick has three babyfoot tables at the front of a narrow bar that stocks a good range of international bottled beers. An especially great destination in summer, when the bay doors open to the street.

Club Gascon

57 West Smithfield, Clerkenwell, EC1A 9DS (7796 0600). Barbican tube/Farringdon tube/rail. **Open** noon-2pm, 7-10pm Mon-Thur; noon-2pm, 7-10.30pm Fri; 7-10.30pm Sat. **££££**. **French**. Map p150 C3 ④⓪
Club Gascon has quietly become one of London's great restaurants. Sure, it has spun off a neighbouring wine bar (Cellar Gascon) and a deli-restaurant (Le Comptoir Gascon, 61-63 Charterhouse Street), but it remains low-key. The room is atmospheric, and the food artistically conceived and beautifully presented. Foie gras is the house speciality.

Dovetail

9 Jerusalem Passage, Clerkenwell, EC1V 4JP (7490 7321/www. belgianbars.com). Farringdon tube/rail. **Open** noon-11pm Mon-Sat; noon-5pm Sun. **Pub**. Map p150 C2 ④①
The only beer served at Dovetail is Belgian – in 101 varieties. Taps supply Leffe Blonde and Brune, Jupiler and Maes Pils, and the drinks menu makes a good guidebook for the intrepid beer explorer. The Trappist brews fit in spirit with the stone-flagged floors and pew-style seating. Hearty food is also served.

Eagle

159 Farringdon Road, Clerkenwell, EC1R 3AL (7837 1353). Farringdon tube/rail. **Open** noon-11pm Mon-Sat; noon-5pm Sun. **££**. **Gastropub**. Map p150 B2 ④②
In the early 1980s Michael Belben and David Eyre came up with a radical notion – why not serve restaurant-quality food in a pub? So this is where the whole gastropub boom began – and it's no historical artefact. The place buzzes, with the chefs in the tiny kitchen area behind the bar delivering a daily changing, blackboard menu of Med dishes. There's good beer, decent wines by glass and bottle, and a laid-back feel.

Fish Central

149-155 Central Street, Clerkenwell, EC1V 8AP (7253 4970/www.fish central.co.uk). Angel tube/Old Street tube/rail/55 bus. **Open** 11am-2.30pm, 5-10.30pm Mon-Thur; 11am-2.30pm, 5-11pm Fri, Sat. **£**. **Fish & chips**. Map p151 D2 ④③
Miles from anywhere, Fish Central is nonetheless packed by Londoners who travel from all over for what they reckon is the best chippie in town.

Hat & Feathers

NEW *2 Clerkenwell Road, Clerkenwell, EC1M 5PQ (7490 2244). Barbican tube/Farringdon tube/rail.* **Open** noon-2.30pm, 6-10.30pm Mon-Fri; 6-10.30pm Sat. **££**. **Gastropub**. Map p150 C2 ④④
Once derelict, this Victorian boozer has been handsomely restored – lovely acid-etched windows, wood panelling, gold leaf on the cornicing and even atmospheric gas lighting – but with distinctly contemporary accents – black leather chairs and faux ostrich-skin banquettes. Fine modern European food is served upstairs; the pub grub (Gressingham duck risotto, say) is certainly no slouch.

Jerusalem Tavern

55 Britton Street, Clerkenwell, EC1M 5UQ (7490 4281/www.stpetersbrewery. co.uk). Farringdon tube/rail. **Open** 11am-11pm Mon-Fri. **Pub**. Map p150 C2 ④⑤

Wines buffed

The new breed of wine bar that's taking over Clerkenwell.

Vinoteca

Vivat Bacchus

Finally it's happened: London's wine bars are losing their associations of would-be suburban sophistication and yuppie smugness and becoming places where – surely it can't be true? – you might be able to enjoy tasting top-quality wine.

It's no coincidence that *Time Out*'s Eating & Drinking awards in 2006 dished out their first gong for Best Wine Bar: there suddenly seemed to be a wealth of contenders in what had previously been far too narrow a field. Foremost among them is our prize-winner **Vinoteca** (p166), a variation on the increasingly popular Italian enoteca concept – you can buy wines in the bar to drink on the spot, or from a shop in the same building. **Vivat Bacchus** (p166) is another classy operation, with tasting and teaching rooms on the premises. Both also serve good food.

That these venues should both have appeared in Clerkenwell is perhaps down to a worthy predecessor – the excellent, stylish **Cellar Gascon** (p161), which has been doing sterling work with a list that focuses on the wines of south-west France – assisted by foodies' favourite **St John** (p164), offering favourable rates on takeaway bottles from its restaurant winelist.

This would be no more than a minor revolution if all the action were confined to Clerkenwell, but happily this isn't so. Borough Market's **Wine Wharf** (p68) was another contender for the prize, and **Bedford & Strand** (1A Bedford Street, WC2E 9HH, 7836 3033, www.bedford-strand.com) just off the Strand, **Vinifera** (20-26 Bedford Road, SW4 7HJ, 7498 9648) in Clapham and Fortnum's **1707** (see box p80) are all welcome new ventures.

This exemplary former coffeehouse serves fine booze from St Peter's Brewery in a fabulously wonky setting. Lurking behind a shopfront dating from 1810, interior is tight and cosy, with green-painted wood, chipped walls and candles complementing the original tilework.

Match

45-47 Clerkenwell Road, Clerkenwell, EC1M 5RS (7250 4002/www.match bar.com). Farringdon tube/rail. **Open** 11am-midnight Mon-Fri; 5pm-midnight Sat. **Cocktail bar**. Map p150 C2 **46**
Now one of the Clerkenwell's old guard, Match's continuing success is down to Dale DeGroff's definitive and frequently changing cocktail list – value for money at up to £12. A table-lined balcony overlooks the sunken standing and dancing space, which in turn faces an excellently stocked and styled bar.

Medcalf

40 Exmouth Market, Clerkenwell, EC1R 4QE (7833 3533/www.medcalf bar.co.uk). Angel tube/Farringdon tube/rail. **Open** noon-11pm Mon-Thur, Sat; noon-12.30am Fri; noon-5pm Sun. **££. British**. Map p150 B1 **47**
Medcalf occupies long thin premises that used to be a butcher's, with a bar extension next door. The focused kitchen turns out a short, top-quality, regularly changing menu. Save room for dessert, and be sure to book.

Moro

34-36 Exmouth Market, Clerkenwell, EC1R 4QE (7833 8336/www.moro. co.uk). Farringdon tube/rail/19, 38 bus. **Open** 12.30-10.30pm Mon-Sat. **£££**. **Spanish**. Map p150 B2 **48**
Moro's Spanish/North African cooking has become part of London's foodie lexicon over the last decade. You'll wait up to three weeks for a booking, but you can settle instead for tapas at the zinc bar. Moro also now opens for Saturday lunch, offering tasting menus with matched sherries. Pure quality.

Pho

86 St John Street, Clerkenwell, EC1M 4EH (7253 7624). Barbican tube/ Farringdon tube/rail. **Open** noon-3pm, 6-10pm Mon-Fri. **£**. **Vietnamese**. Map p150 C2 **49**

Seven Stars p164

The English owners of this appealing little café have taken a few Vietnamese street snacks, and turned them into a 'concept'. Pho, the beef broth and noodle soup, is the mainstay, coming in a dozen excellent variations. Drinks include wines, Vietnamese-style iced coffee and the expensive 'weasel coffee' – the beans have supposedly been through the alimentary tract of an Asian rodent, a myth perpetuated by the canny Vietnamese makers.

Portal

88 St John Street, Clerkenwell, EC1M 4EH (7253 6950/www. portalrestaurant.com). Barbican tube/Farringdon tube/rail. **Open** noon-3pm, 6-10.15pm Mon-Fri; 6-10.15pm Sat. **£££. Modern European.** Map p150 C2 ⓾

The name is a homage to Douro-based winemakers Quinta da Portal and, although there's no official collaboration, a selection of the company's bottles shows up on the unusual and Iberian-leaning wine list. The food is every bit as imaginative as the wine selection. Exposed brickwork and trendy curved chairs look sleek and relaxed, and there's a wonderful glass-roofed dining room at the back.

St John

26 St John Street, Clerkenwell, EC1M 4AY (7251 0848/4998/www.stjohn restaurant.com). Farringdon tube/rail. **Open** 11am-11pm Mon-Fri; 6-11pm Sat. **£££. British.** Map p150 C3 ⓾

The look of the internationally renowned home of 'nose-to-tail' dining is quite basic, with whitewashed walls and rickety chairs, but that's in keeping with the ethos of the menu: simply described British dishes, incorporating all manner of offal, beautifully cooked. A more snacky version of the menu is served in the affable ground-floor bar.

Seven Stars

53 Carey Street, Holborn, WC2A 2JB (7242 8521). Chancery Lane or Temple tube. **Open** 11am-11pm Mon-Fri; noon-11pm Sat; noon-10.30pm Sun. **££. Gastropub.** Map p150 A4 ⓾

A fabulous little Holborn pub that squeezes the best real ales, wines and food into a tiny, impressively narrow interior. It's low-ceilinged and cramped, but nobody minds because the food's so good. There's a blackboard of gastronomic fare prepared by proprietress, raconteur and TV chef Roxy Beaujolais.

Smiths of Smithfield

67-77 Charterhouse Street, Clerkenwell, EC1M 6HJ (7251 7950/www.smithsof smithfield.co.uk). Farringdon tube/rail. **Open** 7am-11pm Mon-Wed; 7am-12.30am Thur, Fri; 10am-12.30am Sat; 9.30am-10.30pm Sun. **£** Bar. **££** Brasserie. **£££** Restaurant. **Modern European.** Map p150 C3 ⓾

Vibrant and roomy, SOS sprawls over four floors of a listed building right opposite Smithfield Market. The ground floor is where the buzzy after-work crowd drink and eat, but there's also a small café cocktail bar on the first floor, the second-floor Dining Room and the calmer, classier, Brit-slanted Top Floor, with its dramatic views. Expert cooking allows first-rate ingredients – the meat, especially – to shine. DJs play from 8pm Wednesday to Saturday; the decor throughout is industrial warehouse chic.

Terrace

NEW *Lincoln's Inn Fields, Holborn, WC2A 3LJ (7430 1234/www.the terrace.info). Holborn tube.* **Open** 8-11am, noon-3pm, 5.30-8.30pm Mon-Fri; 11am-8.30pm Sat. **££. Modern European.** Map p150 A3 ⓾

Beautifully situated in Lincoln's Inn Fields, Terrace looks a like a large, sleek, light-filled garden shed – and there's a touch of greenhouse about it on sunny days, when it's best to head to the outdoor tables. The menu is wide-ranging and tantalising, offering huge portions that are usually as mouth-watering as they look.

Three Kings of Clerkenwell

7 Clerkenwell Close, Clerkenwell, EC1R 0DY (7253 0483). Farringdon tube/

Terrace

rail. **Open** noon-11pm Mon-Fri; 7-11 pm Sat. No credit cards. **Pub**. **Map** p150 B2 ⑤⑤
Welcome to slacker HQ, where shambling, creative souls congregate for happy pints under the watchful eye of a papier-mâché rhino head thrusting out over the open fire. Decorations run to glitter balls, fairy lights and candles, with a glass cabinet of snowdomes and a mighty Prestige jukebox in the slightly grungy upstairs rooms.

Vinoteca

7 St John Street, Clerkenwell, EC1M 4AA (7253 8786/www.vinoteca.co.uk). Farringdon tube/rail. **Open** 11am-11pm Mon-Sat. **Wine bar**. **Map** p150 C3 ⑤⑥
Vinoteca has 'wine lover' written all over it: lovely staff, a nice atmosphere and one of the best wine lists we've seen in a London bar – flat-rate rather than percentage mark-ups make the expensive bottles more accessible. The Europhile bar food's good too.

Vivat Bacchus

47 Farringdon Street, Clerkenwell, EC4A 4LL (7353 2648/www.vivat bacchus.co.uk). Chancery Lane tube/ Farringdon tube/rail. **Open** noon-10.30pm Mon-Fri. *Restaurant* noon-2.30pm, 6.30-9.30pm Mon-Fri. **£** Bar. **£££** Restaurant. **Wine bar**. **Map** p150 B3 ⑤⑦
One of the most ambitious wine operations in the capital. The firm originated in Johannesburg, so there's a fine selection of South African wines. The by-the-glass selection is relatively small, but if you show a keen interest, the manager might guide you round the cellars and let you choose your bottle. Impressive cheeseboard.

Ye Old Mitre

1 Ely Court, Ely Place, Clerkenwell, EC1N 6SJ (7405 4751). Chancery Lane tube/Farringdon tube/rail. **Open** 11am-11pm Mon-Fri. **Pub**. **Map** p150 B3 ⑤⑧
A gruffly cheerful and efficient Scottish barman pulls quality pints amid the wood panels and exposed beams of this deliciously hidden pub (it's down a tiny alley, marked only by a little pub sign between jewellers' shops). There's even a snug sized for half a dozen close friends. The upstairs room has least character and is thus usually less busy.

Shopping

Brill

27 Exmouth Market, Clerkenwell, EC1R 4QL (7833 9757). Angel tube/ Farringdon tube/rail. **Open** 10.30am-6.30pm Mon-Fri; 10.30am-5.30pm Sat. **Map** p150 B1 ⑤⑨
A CD shop-cum-café, Brill uses its small size selectively: if it's stocked here, it's going to be good. If there were any prizes going for friendly and well-informed staff, then this place would be guaranteed a podium finish.

Brindisa

32 Exmouth Market, Clerkenwell, EC1R 4QE (7713 1666/www. brindisa.com). Angel tube/Farringdon tube/rail. **Open** 10am-6pm Mon; 9.30am-6pm Tue-Sat. **Map** p150 B2 ⑥⓪
Brindisa imports food from some of Spain's best producers. Wooden shelves are stacked with chocolates, wine, sherry, paella pans and cookery books. There's also an unrivalled selection of Iberico and Serrano hams, as well as a range of utensils, including paella dishes.

ec one

41 Exmouth Market, Clerkenwell, EC1R 4QL (7713 6185/www.econe.co. uk). Farringdon tube/rail. **Open** 10am-6pm Mon-Wed, Fri; 11am-7pm Thur; 10.30am-6pm Sat. **Map** p150 B1 ⑥①
Jos and Alison Skeates showcase jewellery from more than 50 designers. Jos Skeates's own designs are serious statement pieces, while Emma Craig makes impossibly delicate rings and bangles.

Magma

117-119 Clerkenwell Road, Clerkenwell, EC1R 5BY (7242 9503/wwwmagmabooks.com).

Chancery Lane tube/Farringdon tube/ rail. **Open** 10am-7pm Mon-Sat. **Map** p150 B2 ❻❷

Blurring the boundary between bookshop and gallery, this beautifully designed, multi-functional space is a first port of call for books on design, architecture, photography, film, animation, fine art and graffiti, with fun stuff alongside the obscurities.

Nightlife

Fabric

77A Charterhouse Street, Clerkenwell, EC1M 3HN (7336 8898/www.fabric london.com). Farringdon tube/rail. **Open** 9.30pm-5am Fri; 10pm-7am Sat. **Admission** £12-£15. **Map** p150 C3 ❻❸

Fabric is the club that most party people come to see in London. Fridays belong to the bass, while Saturdays are techy, minimal, deep house. DTPM, the original Sunday afternoon club, is still here too, playing house and R&B to a mixed gay/straight crowd.

Turnmills

63B Clerkenwell Road, Clerkenwell, EC1M 5PT (7250 3409/www.turnmills. com). Farringdon tube/rail. **Open** 9pm-2am Thur; 10.30pm-7.30am Fri; 10pm-6am Sat; 9pm-3am Sun. **Admission** £8-£15. **Map** p150 B2 ❻❹

Turnmills is a true hedonists' playground. The Gallery draws the hard dance and trance kids every Friday, while Saturdays bill more credible fare, including the bi-monthly, festival-inspired Together and superstar DJs like Roger Sanchez.

Volupté

NEW *9 Norwich Street, Holborn, EC4A 1EJ (7831 1622/www.volupte-lounge.com). Chancery Lane tube.* **Open** noon-late Tue-Sat. **Admission** £8-£12. **Map** p150 B3 ❻❺

Expect to suffer extreme wallpaper envy as you enter this ground-floor bar then descend to the club proper. Tables are set under absinthe-inspired vines, surrounded by lush curtains, from where punters enjoy some of the best cabaret talent in town. See box p134.

Supersize me!

Enough of the backroom mash-up – let's go large.

It was bound to happen. After the death of the superclub, if there were more than 100 on a London dancefloor, the kids who preferred raving in the back rooms of pubs would sneer. Still, no amount of illegal partying can match the electricity of a monster club night. A couple of thousand folk screaming as the killer break fires on and on? Yes, please!

We've loved seeing the inspired Together at **Turnmills** (p167). London's friendliest venue throws open each of its six rooms for a festival-within-a-club. And just like at festivals, you're guaranteed to lose your friends and make new ones in the loos.

Chalk at the **Scala** (p173) is a recent addition to the scene and attracts a younger crowd – if you're either side of 18-21, you might not want to bother. The area round **Canvas**, the **Key** and the **Cross** (pp172-3) comes together each August Bank Holiday for the Cross Central festival; visit www.crosscentral. co.uk in June to check the all-day, all-night line-ups.

But there's one club in town that still sees well over a thousand jumping party people every weekend of the year, and that's **Fabric** (p167). Just how this legendary clubbing space does it, we're not sure, but queues are still around the block, and London's clubbing wouldn't be the same without it.

Neighbourhood London

Londoners tend to live, rest and above all play where the rents are cheapest, which is generally anywhere but the city centre. This means restaurants and bars are often more vital – and exciting scenes more apt to develop – on the periphery than around the parts of town most familiar to tourists. So the city's nightlife hotspots are around King's Cross/Camden to the north and Shoreditch/Hoxton in the east, and excellent clusters of eating and drinking options crop up in residential areas like Clapham to the south. In maritime Greenwich, Kew's Royal Botanic Gardens and Hampton Court, neighbourhood London also has tourist attractions that could easily fill a sightseeing day each on their own.

North London

Islington's main drag Upper Street isn't much to look at but a reliable stream of visitors patronise its cafés, gift, clothes and antiques shops. Things are really perking up around **Camden**, though, perhaps in part fuelled by the new Eurostar Terminal opening to the south in St Pancras station. In addition to the market, one of London's biggest tourist draws, there is a growing number of ambitious venues – with fine food and cocktails joining the roster of scuzzy indie pubs and banging clubs.

Hampstead and **Highgate** remain as ever they were: prettily leafy, well-off villages either side of the magnificent heath.

Lock Tavern p171

Sights & museums

Hampstead Heath

Hampstead Heath or Gospel Oak rail.
Inspiration for CS Lewis's Narnia, the heath's charming contours and woodlands make it feel far larger and more rural than it is. The views of London from the top of Parliament Hill are wonderful and on hot days the murky bathing ponds (men's, women's and mixed, open daily all year) are a godsend. The heath is popular for flying kites and sailing model boats too. The information points can advise you of concerts held at the two bandstands on Sundays in summer. At the north end of the park is Kenwood House (below).

Highgate Cemetery

Swains Lane, Highgate, N6 6PJ (8340 1834/www.highgate-cemetery.org). Highgate tube. **Open** *East Cemetery* Apr-Oct 10am-4.30pm Mon-Fri; 11am-4.30pm Sat, Sun. Nov-Mar 10am-3.30pm Mon-Fri; 11am-3.30pm Sat, Sun. *West Cemetery* tours only. *Tours* Dec-Feb 11am, noon, 1pm, 2pm, 3pm, 4pm Sat, Sun; Mar-Nov 2pm Mon-Fri. **Admission** £2. *Tours* £5. No credit cards.

With its dramatic tombs topped by towering angels, shrouded urns and broken columns, Highgate exudes a romantic atmosphere of ivy-covered neglect. The original 1839 West Cemetery (by tour only; book at weekends) is breathtaking, but it's the East Cemetery that has memorials to Karl Marx and George Eliot. The cemetery closes during burials, so call ahead.

Kenwood House

Hampstead Lane, Hampstead, NW3 7JR (8348 1286/www.english-heritage. org.uk). Hampstead tube/Golders Green tube then 210 bus. **Open** *Apr-Sept* 11am-5pm daily. *Nov-Mar* 11am-4pm daily. **Admission** free. *Tours* £5; £4-£3 reductions.
Built in 1616, Kenwood House was bought in 1925 by brewing magnate Edward Guinnes, who filled it with his amazing art collection – a Vermeer and a Rembrandt are among the treasures. Outside, the landscaped grounds remain mostly unchanged from their creation in 1793, with a terrace giving lovely views over the lakes. The café does a terrific breakfast.

Akari

Lord's Tour & MCC Museum

*St John's Wood Road, St John's Wood,
NW8 8QN (7616 8595/MCC 7289
1611/www.lords.org). St John's Wood
tube.* **Tours** *Oct-Mar* noon, 2pm daily.
Apr-Sept 10am, noon, 2pm daily.
Admission £10; £6-£7 reductions.

The wearers of the famous egg-and-
bacon striped tie have come to love the
NatWest Media Centre, the funky
raised pod that dominates the home of
cricket. The centre is part of the guided tour (book ahead), as are WG Grace
ephemera and the Ashes urn.

Eating & drinking

Akari

NEW *196 Essex Road, Islington, N1
8LZ (7226 9943). Essex Road rail.*
Open noon-11pm Tue-Sun. **££**.
Japanese.

This pub-turned-bistro-turned-izakaya
still looks like its first incarnation, with
Japanese modifications such as attrac-
tively faded Asahi and Kirin beer
posters. The menu is short on raw fish
but long on comfort food such as noo-
dles, tempura and stewed pork belly.

At Proud

NEW *The Gin House, Stables Market,
Chalk Farm Road, NW1 8AH (7482
3867/www.proud.co.uk). Chalk Farm or
Camden Town tube.* **Open** 11am-1am
Mon-Wed, Sun; 11am-3am Thur-Sat.
Bar.

Brilliantly urban and a little like a mar-
quee, At Proud is a rock 'n' roll bar that
puts on gigs and art exhibitions.
There's a fine terrace too.

Charles Lamb

NEW *16 Elia Street, Islington, N1 8DE
(7837 5040). Angel tube.* **Open** noon-
11pm Tue-Sat; noon-10.30pm Sun. **££**.
Gastropub.

Occupying a small, pretty space, the
Charles Lamb is divided in two for
drinkers (newspapers, real ales) and
eaters (a light-wood dining room, with
Sunday roasts and other solid fare).
Decorative touches are perky, and staff
super-friendly. Worth seeking out.

Gilgamesh

NEW *Stables Market, Chalk Farm
Road, Camden, NW1 8AH (7482
5757/www.gilgameshbar.com). Chalk
Farm tube.* **Open** *Bar* noon-2.30am

Mon-Sat; noon-1.30am Sun. *Restaurant* 6pm-midnight Mon-Thur; noon-3pm, 6pm-midnight Fri; noon-midnight Sat, Sun. *Tea house* noon-3pm Mon-Thur. **£££** Restaurant. **£** Tea house. **Asian bar/restaurant**.

Ian Pengelley's bar/restaurant is apparently the biggest in London. The decor features intricately carved wood, super-sized statuary, inlaid tables and friezes, and a 40ft glass ceiling that opens up. Food in both restaurant and bar is impressive, as are the cocktails, but service can be confused.

Holly Bush

22 Holly Mount, Hampstead, NW3 6SG (7435 2892/www.hollybushpub.com). Hampstead tube. **Open** noon-11pm Mon-Sat; noon-10.30pm Sun. **Pub**.
Tucked away up a hill from the main drag, the Holly Bush isn't easy to find, but it's worth it. Dating from the 1800s, it has capacious, dim-lit front rooms and lighter but no less charming rooms out back. Additional bonuses? No music, no fruit machine, splendid pies.

Lock Tavern

35 Chalk Farm Road, Camden, NW1 8AJ (7482 7163/www.lock-tavern.co. uk). Camden Town or Chalk Farm tube. **Open** noon-midnight Mon-Thur; noon-1am Fri, Sat; noon-11pm Sun. **Bar**.
Don't be intimidated by the fiercely fashionable punters and icily gorgeous staff: this is a brilliant boozer. There's a garden and DJ sessions that guarantee a full house from Thursday to Sunday; upstairs is a more intimate space, with a quiet roof terrace.

Odette's

NEW *130 Regent's Park Road, Primrose Hill, NW1 8XL (7586 8569). Chalk Farm tube.* **Open** 12.30-2.30pm, 6.30-10.30pm Tue-Sat; 12.30-2.30pm Sun. **££££. Modern European**.
A new owner has tastefully redecorated this long-established restaurant and installed top-class chef Bryn Williams. The menu is brief, with around half-a-dozen seasonal choices at each course, but everything we tried was spot-on. Pricey, but worth every penny.

Ottolenghi

287 Upper Street, Islington, N1 2TZ (7288 1454/www.ottolenghi.co.uk). Angel tube/Highbury & Islington tube/rail. **Open** 8am-11pm Mon-Sat; 9am-7pm Sun. **££. Mediterranean**.
Simple but not plain, Ottolenghi looks stunning. The entrance area, a bakery shop and deli, leads into a bright white room with long tables and clever art. At night, it shifts from café to restaurant, with a daily changing menu of small dishes that imaginatively combine modern Mediterranean flavours.

Shopping

Camden Market

Camden Canal Market *off Chalk Farm Road, south of the junction with Castlehaven Road, NW1 9XJ (7485 8355/www.camdenlock.net).* **Open** 10am-6pm daily.
Camden Lock *Camden Lock Place, off Chalk Farm Road, NW1 8AF (7485 3459/www.camdenlockmarket. com).* **Open** 10am-6pm Mon-Wed, Fri-Sun; 10am-7pm Thur.
Camden Market *Camden High Street, junction with Buck Street, NW1 (7278 4444).* **Open** 9.30am-5.30pm daily.
Electric Ballroom *184 Camden High Street, NW1 8QP (7485 9006/www. electric-ballroom.co.uk).* **Open** 10.30am-3.30pm Fri; 10am-6pm Sat, Sun.
Stables *off Chalk Farm Road, opposite junction with Hartland Road, NW1 8AH (7485 5511/www.camden lock.net).* **Open** 10am-6pm daily.
All *Camden Town or Chalk Farm tube.*
Camden Market, just next to the tube station, flogs cheap sunglasses and cut-price versions of current fashions, while the unimpressive Electric Ballroom sells second-hand clothes, young designers' wares and cheap CDs. Camden Lock market is much better, with an attractive courtyard beside Regent's Canal. There are cafés, good bars and shops selling things you might actually want to buy. Crafty stalls sell funky lighting and ethnic homeware, art and antiques. North of the courtyard are the Stables, with more permanent stalls and food huts.

LONDON BY AREA

Some of Camden's best shopping is here, with a whole row of vintage clothing and clubwear shops housed underneath the railway arches. Even better are the antiques and contemporary designer furniture sold in the most northerly portion, by the Horse Hospital.

Equa

28 Camden Passage, Islington, N1 8ED (7359 0955/www.equaclothing.com). Angel tube. **Open** noon-6pm Mon; 11am-6pm Tue; 11am-6.30pm Wed-Fri; 10am-6pm Sat; noon-5pm Sun.

London's first stand-alone shop to dedicate itself entirely to fairly traded and organic fashion is a cute clothes boutique. The collection is tiny and prices are quite high, but the selection process has clearly been rigorous.

Sefton

196 Upper Street, Islington, N1 1RQ (7226 7076). Highbury & Islington tube/rail. **Open** 10am-6.30pm Mon-Wed; 10am-7pm Thur, Fri; 10am-6.30pm Sat; noon-6pm Sun.

If you like your clothes high-end but don't have the energy for big-hitters like Harvey Nichols, Sefton could be the answer. Costume National and Miu Miu are prominent, and a good selection of Junk de Luxe and Yohji Yamamoto pleases those of quieter taste and slimmer wallet.

Nightlife

Multi-arts venue the **Roundhouse** (p173) stages impressive gigs.

Barfly

49 Chalk Farm Road, Chalk Farm, NW1 8AN (7691 4244/www.barflyclub.com). Chalk Farm tube. **Open** 7.30pm-1am Mon-Thur; 7.30pm-3am Fri, Sat; 7-10.30pm Sun. *Gigs* 7.30pm daily.
Admission £6-£8. No credit cards.

Barfly is a big part of the reason why indie guitar-meets-electro parties are doing well. The battered upstairs/downstairs space is packed with local 'faces' and kids sporting cool haircuts and skinny jeans, who come for the next-big-thing bands. Kill Em All Let

God Sort It Out and Adventures In The Beetroot Field are outstanding indie/dance mash-ups.

Big Chill House

257-259 Pentonville Road, King's Cross, N1 9NL (7427 2540/www.bigchill.net). King's Cross tube. **Open** noon-midnight Mon-Wed, Sun; noon-1am Thur; noon-4am Fri, Sat. **Admission** £5 after 9pm Fri, Sat.

With its stylishly playful interior (two main rooms, plus themed nooks and crannies), Big Chill House has been an instant hit, packed at weekends with long, long queues. Music is top priority, the festival-running owners having booked an eclectic calendar covering countless genres. Food is served and, at quieter times, the main room offers a decent lounge for coffee and chat.

Canvas

King's Cross Goods Yard, off York Way, King's Cross, N1 0UZ (7833 8301/www.canvaslondon.net). King's Cross tube/rail. **Open** 8pm-midnight Thur; 8pm-2am Fri; 10pm-6am Sat. **Admission** £10-£20.

Old ravers know this former warehouse as Bagley's, but now it's a beautifully revamped three-room club that's even got a pretty terrace for summer sunnin'. Roller Disco every Thursday and Friday is great fun, irregular one-offs fill out the rest of the year.

Cross

The Arches, 27-31 King's Cross Goods Yard, off York Way, King's Cross, N1 0UZ (7837 0828/www.the-cross.co.uk). King's Cross tube/rail. **Open** 10pm-6am Fri, Sat.

This stylish bricks 'n' arches space was the first of the trio of clubs now lodged in the Goods Yard, and it's still a firm favourite with a beautiful international crowd. The focus is on house: Fridays are for polysexual Fiction, while Saturday parties include Renaissance and X-Press 2's Muzikism.

EGG

200 York Way, King's Cross, N7 9AP (7609 8364/www.egglondon.net). King's Cross tube/rail. **Open** 10pm-10am Fri; 10pm Sat-2pm Sun.

With its Med-styled three floors, garden and enormous terrace (complete with a pool), EGG is big enough to lose yourself in, but somehow retains an intimate atmosphere. The upstairs bar in red ostrich leather is elegant, while the main dancefloor downstairs has a warehouse rave feel. Club nights range from dark electro synth raves to house.

Key

King's Cross Freight Depot, King's Cross, N1 OUZ (7837 1027/www.the keylondon.com). King's Cross tube/rail. **Open** 11pm-5am Fri; 10pm-6am Sat. The flashing disco dancefloor of this intimate space is typically filled with cracking house, electro and minimal parties, such as DDD, Chicken Nickers and the after-hours Formulate.

KOKO

1A Camden High Street, Camden, NW1 7JE (0870 432 5527/www.koko. uk.com). Camden Town or Mornington Crescent tube. **Open** 10pm-3am Fri. The erstwhile Camden Palace has scrubbed up nicely after its refit a few years back, and has built up a roster of events to match. There are a fair few club nights alongside an indie-heavy (but still interesting) gig programme: check out Sean Rowley's cheesetastic (and very popular) Guilty Pleasures.

Luminaire

307-311 Kilburn High Road, Kilburn, NW6 7JR (7372 8668/www.theluminaire. co.uk). Kilburn tube/Brondesbury rail. **Open** 7pm-midnight Mon-Wed, Sun; 7pm-1am Thur; 7pm-2am Fri, Sat. This newcomer won *Time Out* magazine's Live Venue of the Year award for 2006, and with good reason. The booking policy is fantastically broad, the sound system is well up to scratch, the decor is stylish, the drinks are fairly priced, and the staff are actually approachable, even friendly. If only all venues were built this way.

Scala

275 Pentonville Road, King's Cross, N1 9NL (7833 2022/www.scala-london. co.uk). King's Cross tube/rail.

This capacious building stages a laudably broad range of shows: 2006 saw appearances by everyone from Scritti Politti to the Melvins. Unlike many venues of similar size (around 1,145 bodies), the sound quality is decent and the staff personable. Regular club nights include Friday's Popstarz, the original gay indie party.

Arts & leisure

Arsenal Football Club

NEW *Emirates Stadium, Ashburton Grove, N7 7AF (7704 4040/www. arsenal.com). Arsenal tube.* Arsenal moved to a sparkling new 60,000-capacity ground at Ashburton Grove in 2006 – more than two million fans were thus able watch their team over the season. There's a spruced-up museum describing the club's history and paying homage to its biggest stars. An unimpressive season has taken the gloss off Arsenal's excellent record under manager Arsène Wenger, but the young squad shows prodigious talent – if not yet consistency.

Roundhouse

Chalk Farm Road, Camden Town, NW1 8EH (0870 389 1846/www. roundhouse.org.uk). Chalk Farm tube. In 1966, the Greater London Council turned a former railway engine shed into an arts venue; the Doors, Hendrix and Pink Floyd all played here, but the venue fell on hard times. Completed in 2006, a £30 million refit has perked up the lower passageways and restyled the auditorium, added a café and bars, and given the place an exterior facelift. Downstairs, there's a new black-box theatre. Performances have so far included top-drawer gigs and breathtaking dance and theatre collaborations.

Sadler's Wells

Rosebery Avenue, Finsbury, EC1R 4TN (0870 737 7737/www.sadlerswells.com). Angel tube. One of the world's premier dance venues, with the most exciting line-up in town. Top companies and dancers, from the Nederlands Dans Theater to Carlos Acosta, are showcased throughout the year, and a major new initiative has brought important British dancemakers into the fold.

Wembley Stadium

NEW *Stadium Way, Wembley, Middx HA9 0WS (8795 9000/www.wembley stadium.com). Wembley Park tube/ Wembley Stadium rail.*

The old stadium, with its famous twin towers, staged its last major football match in October 2000, after which the extensive rebuilding process was plagued by disputes and delay after delay. The 90,000-seat venue, designed by Lord Foster, was eventually finished in 2007, in time to host the FA Cup Final on 19 May 2007. The huge steel arch spanning the stadium is already an established landmark.

East London

On the doorstep of the City, **Spitalfields** has become a major tourist attraction over the last decade. Centred on the Victorian covered market are chic boutiques, gourmet food shops, restaurants and bars. Alongside it to the east is **Brick Lane**, famous as the British home of curries (no longer notably cheap and rarely particularly cheerful). It's an enjoyable mix of new fashion and music with long-standing immigrant communities. **Bethnal Green**, slightly further out, has a more residential feel.

North of Spitalfields in **Shoreditch** and **Hoxton**, the bars and clubs take off. Don't expect the area to look like much: it was the cheap rent on deserted industrial buildings that brought in the artists and clubbers in the 1990s, and the bleak aesthetics haven't changed.

East London's other major focus is **Docklands**. Centred on Canary Wharf's iconic tower, One Canada Water, there now some good places to eat – and even a proper museum.

Sights & museums

For a tour round East London's art galleries, see p52.

Dennis Severs' House

18 Folgate Street, Spitalfields, E1 6BX (7247 4013/www.dennissevershouse. co.uk). Liverpool Street tube/rail. **Open** 2-5pm 1st & 3rd Sun of month; noon-2pm Mon following 1st & 3rd Sun of month; Mon evenings (times vary). **Admission** £8 Sun; £5 noon-2pm Mon; £12 Mon evenings.

This Huguenot house recreates, down to the smallest detail, snapshots of life in Spitalfields between 1724 and 1914. A tour through this compelling 'still-life drama', as creator Dennis Severs dubbed it, takes you through room after room, with hearth and candles burning, smells lingering and objects scattered haphazardly. It's as if the inhabitants left just moments before.

Geffrye Museum

Kingsland Road, Shoreditch, E2 8EA (7739 9893/recorded information 7739 8543/www.geffrye-museum.org.uk). Liverpool Street tube/rail then 149, 242 bus/Old Street tube/rail then 243 bus. **Open** 10am-5pm Tue-Sat; noon-5pm Sun. **Admission** free. *Almshouse tours* £2; free under-16s.

Housed in a set of converted alms-houses, the Geffrye is a marvellous physical history of the English interior. It recreates typical English living rooms from the 17th century to the present, and has a series of lovely gardens designed along similar chronological lines. There's an airy restaurant, and special temporary exhibitions.

Kinetica

NEW *SP2 Pavilion, Old Spitalfields Market, E1 6AA (7392 9674/www. kinetica-museum.org). Liverpool Street tube/rail.* **Open** 11am-6pm Wed-Sun. **Admission** varies.

A glass-walled gallery that focuses on new media and kinetic art. Expect to see early 20th-century automata or hear phrases like 'skeletal electrolumi-nescent chaise-longue' in connection with artworks using moving light.

Shiny happy Camden?

The words 'Camden' and 'boulevard' haven't often appeared in the same sentence – teenage goth, scuzzy indie pub, yes, but boulevard? Yet Camden council has spent £24 million on a much-lauded Boulevard Project (pictured), a five-year scheme to improve the area through tree-planting, improved street lighting, more cycle lanes and pavements resurfaced as fashionable, washable 'boulevards'. 'They spent £150,000 on improving the street aspect between Chalk Farm and Camden Lock bridge,' says Alex Proud, owner of At Proud (p170) and chair of regeneration organisation Camden Town Unlimited (CTU). 'It's making the place look nicer and feel safer. If you were down here at 1am a few years ago, you were terrified. Now it's vibrant. But not like Soho, full of idiots vomiting.'

It seems developers have woken up to Camden's commercial potential. The hedonistic mix of stores, bars and head shops has made it one of the busiest places in the capital, especially at the weekend. And smart new venues like Gilgamesh (p170) have begun to spring up, along with high-street giants like Virgin and Gap.

Proposals to redevelop the Stables area of the Camden Market (p171) as a four-storey shopping centre, granted planning permission in 2007, have met resistance. Chris Jakubiac of the Save Stables campaign fears Camden will become a clone town: 'Camden works because of the way it is. People go there and dress as they want, act like they want. It's got that vibe because it's not a big commercial centre.' Proud counters that the area won't become 'a horrifying, north London version of Covent Garden.'

Whatever the truth, work on Stables was due to begin in summer 2007. According to the plans, the beautiful Victorian 'coal' arches will be preserved and the traders safeguarded, with space for stalls opened up beneath the Gilgamesh building. Intriguingly, the council is looking at opening up underground horse tunnels beneath Lock Market. Proud goes so far as to suggest market forces are on the side of independent traders. 'If you're a developer and you have 500,000 people coming through your land, you're not going to destroy that. I know most of the developers in Camden Town and they love the markets.'

Museum in Docklands

No.1 Warehouse, West India Quay, Hertsmere Road, Docklands, E14 4AL (recorded information 0870 444 3856/ www.museumindocklands.org.uk). West India Quay DLR/Canary Wharf tube. **Open** 10am-6pm daily. **Admission** £5; free-£3 reductions.

In a former warehouse, this large museum follows the history of London's docklands over two millennia. Many exhibits are narrated by people who saw the changes; the Docklands at War section is particularly moving. There are also full-scale mock-ups of a quayside and a dingy riverfront alley. A new permanent gallery explores the slave trade, paying particular attention to West India Dock.

V&A Museum of Childhood

NEW *Cambridge Heath Road, Bethnal Green, E2 9PA (8983 5200/recorded information 8980 2415/www.museum ofchildhood.org.uk). Bethnal Green tube/rail/Cambridge Heath rail.* **Open** 10am-5.45pm daily. **Admission** free.

Part of the Victoria & Albert Museum (p86), the Museum of Childhood came to the end of a five-year refurbishment programme in early 2007, creating a new entrance, art gallery and exhibition of moving toys. A massive collection of toys, dolls' houses, games and costumes have been amassed since the museum opened in 1872, and there are lots of hands-on activities for kids, including dressing-up boxes.

Whitechapel Art Gallery

80-82 Whitechapel High Street, Whitechapel, E1 7QX (7522 7888/ www.whitechapel.org). Aldgate East tube. **Open** *Main gallery* closed until 2008. *Laboratory* 11am-6pm Wed-Sun. **Admission** free.

Whitechapel's architecturally impressive art gallery has presented forward-thinking exhibitions for over a century. The venue is enjoying an impressive renovation as it expands into the historic former library next door, but it won't reopen until at least summer 2008. In the meantime, duck down Angel Alley beside the gallery: there the Laboratory shows lens-based work, and hosts a variety of night-time music and poetry events.

Eating & drinking

Kingsland Road is the centre of London's Vietnamese restaurants – try **Sông Quê** (no.134, 7613 3222) or **Thang Loi** (no.122, 7729 3074).

Bistrotheque

23-27 Wadeson Street, Bethnal Green, E2 9DR (8983 7900/www.bistrotheque. com). Bethnal Green tube/rail/Cambridge Heath rail/55 bus. **Open** *Bar* 5.30pm-midnight Mon-Sat; 1pm-midnight Sun. *Restaurant* 6.30-10.30pm Mon-Fri; 11am-4pm, 6.30-10.30pm Sat, Sun. **£££. French**.

Bistrotheque has an unaffected warehouse charm. Downstairs is an agreeable bar, with an eccentric baronial ambience, and a cabaret room that's a prime mover in the east London scene. Upstairs is the restaurant: simply styled with marble-topped tables, soft hanging lights and statement flowers. The food is simple and direct, with every taste speaking for itself. Spot-on staff and good-value house wines.

Brick Lane Beigel Bake

159 Brick Lane, E1 6SB (7729 0616). Liverpool Street tube/rail/8 bus. **Open** 24hrs daily. **£. No credit cards. Bakery**.

A charismatic East End institution rolling out perfect bagels, both plain and filled (egg, cream cheese, herring, mountains of salt beef), superb bread and magnificently moreish cakes.

Catch

22 Kingsland Road, Hoxton, E2 8DA (7729 6097/www.thecatchbar.com). Old Street tube/rail/55 bus. **Open** 6pm-midnight Tue, Wed; 6pm-2am Thur-Sat; 6pm-1am Sun.

Its cool location and the fact that it doesn't charge admission explain why Catch often has a queue outside after kicking-out time elsewhere. Amiable bouncers usher in a mixed crowd, who jockey for the seating spots or mob the

V&A Museum of Childhood

bar. Later, booty shakers dance to excellent DJs playing everything from disco to punk and R&B.

dreambagsjaguarshoes

34-36 Kingsland Road, Hoxton, E2 8DA (7729 5830/www.dreambags jaguarshoes.com). Old Street tube/rail. **Open** 5pm-midnight Mon; noon-1am Tue-Fri; 5pm-1am Sat; noon-12.30am Sun. **Bar**.

This bar was once two retail outlets (hence the name), but there's little left of them except the old signs. Now concrete walls are softened by mellow lighting and a changing array of graffiti, manga figures or giant tattoos. DJs play everything from soft metal to rockabilly, and the place is reliably packed at the weekends.

E Pellicci

332 Bethnal Green Road, Bethnal Green, E2 0AG (7739 4873). Bethnal Green tube/8 bus. **Open** 6.30am-5pm Mon-Sat. **£**. No credit cards. **Café**.

The classic East End caff. A former favourite of the Krays, it's been in the same family since Edwardian times, but the art deco marquetry interior was created in 1946. Friendly service makes it a firm favourite with the locals, and its menu extends beyond the usual fry-ups to salads, grills, chops and sarnies.

Golden Heart

110 Commercial Street, Spitalfields, E1 6LZ (7247 2158). Liverpool Street tube/rail. **Open** 11am-11pm Mon-Sat; 11am-10.30pm Sun. **Pub**.

A trad, dark wood boozer with a roaring fire in the saloon bar. Its enduring popularity is due to landlady Sandra Esqulant, confidante and surrogate mother of many BritArt enfants terribles (including Tracey Emin and Gilbert & George). With Spitalfields Market opposite, things are always busy; the scruffy Ten Bells (no.84) and flamboyant Commercial Tavern (no.142) are also worth a visit.

Hawksmoor

NEW *157 Commercial Street, Spitalfields, E1 6BJ (7247 7392/ www.thehawksmoor.com). Liverpool Street tube/rail.* **Open** 5pm-1am Tue-Sat; 5pm-midnight Sun. *Meals served* 6-11pm Tue-Sat; 6-10pm Sun. **£££**. **Bar/steakhouse**.

An understated American restaurant with a bar dedicated to the art of fine cocktail making. With the same owners as nearby tequila bar/restaurant Green & Red (51 Bethnal Green Road, 7749 9670, www.greenred.co.uk), the joint fizzes with bonhomie. From a cocktail menu that covers juleps, sours, fizzes, daisies, punches and 'expat' classics, the

LONDON BY AREA

crew mix up an explosion of fabulous, well-tempered flavours. Friendly, fun, professional and distinctly un-posey.

Les Trois Garçons

1 Club Row, Brick Lane, E1 6JX (7613 1924/www.lestroisgarcons.com). Liverpool Street tube/rail/8, 388 bus. **Open** 7-10.30pm Mon-Thur; 7-11pm Fri, Sat. **££££. French.**
This former corner pub is now a stupendously theatrical mix of antique bar fittings, vintage handbags (dangling from the ceiling) and ornamental taxidermy. However, it's far from a case of style over content: the kitchen delivers an immaculate French-slanted menu to Shoreditch sophisticates. It isn't cheap, but you get what you pay for.

Loungelover

1 Whitby Street, Spitalfields, E2 7DP (7012 1234/www.loungelover.co.uk). Liverpool Street tube/rail. **Open** 6pm-midnight Tue-Thur; 6pm-1am Fri; 7pm-1am Sat; 6pm-midnight Sun. **Bar.**
London's campest and most divinely decadent bar, swish Loungelover has a wealth of extravagantly theatrical fixtures, fittings and accessories – hippo's head, religious fresco, coloured perspex lighting, faux Regency chairs, fabulous chandeliers. You'll need to book to bag a seat in any of the nooks.

Narrow

NEW *44 Narrow Street, Limehouse, E14 8DP (7592 7950/www.gordon ramsay.com). Limehouse DLR.* **Open** 10am-11pm Mon-Sat; noon-10.30pm Sun. **££. Gastropub.**
Gordon Ramsay's first gastropub is a handsome former dockmaster's house, with a large terrace that overlooks the Thames. The posh pub bit serves real ale, a huge range of bottled beer, an extensive wine list and fine cocktails, while the next door dining room serves wonderful retro-modern food: herring roe on toast, faggots and exemplary public school puds. The drawback? If you want to eat at a sensible time, you'll have to book a month ahead. Gordon's second gastro opens in Maida Vale's Warrington Hotel in late 2007.

Plateau

Canada Place, Canada Square, Docklands, E14 5ER (7715 7100/ www.conran.com). Canary Wharf tube/DLR. **Open** *Bar & grill* noon-10.45pm Mon-Sat; noon-4pm Sun. *Restaurant* noon-3pm, 6-10.15pm Mon-Fri; 6-10.15pm Sat. **£££. French.**
Dramatic floor-to-ceiling windows run the length of the fourth floor of Canada Place, where white curves and statement lighting beautifully complement the views across Canada Square. Plateau is vast, with restaurant, bar-grill and open-roofed terrace at various degrees of formality, but none very casual. Super-attentive service, rigorous attention to detail and an economically unfettered menu.

St John Bread & Wine

94-96 Commercial Street, Spitalfields, E1 6LZ (7251 0848/www.stjohnbread andwine.com). Aldgate East tube/ Liverpool Street tube/rail. **Open** 9am-10.30pm Mon-Fri; 10am-10.30pm Sat; 10am-5pm Sun. **£££. British.**
You either appreciate the pared-down nature of the St John aesthetic or you don't. The airy room is painted white, and, when it comes to the menu, what it says is exactly what you get, be it beetroot, sorrel and boiled egg, or grilled sprats with horseradish. There's the occasional lapse in the kitchen, but staff are professional and unponcey, and there's no pressure to spend money – you can have just one dish and a glass of wine, or simply pop in to buy some excellent baked goods. The wine list is nicely priced.

Tea Smith

NEW *8 Lamb Street, Spitalfields, E1 6EA (7247 1333/www.teasmith.co.uk). Liverpool Street tube/rail.* **Open** 11am-5.30pm daily. **£. Tearoom.**
Tea Smith is aimed at tea drinkers who want something more than a cup of builder's brew. The interior has a recognisably Japanese aesthetic, and at the counter you can try a score of teas, expertly prepared and accompanied by a few fabulous cakes. Masterclasses in tea appreciation are planned.

Is green the new red?

Ken Livingstone unveils his new eco-friendly buses.

Having only waved goodbye to their iconic red, double-decker Routemaster buses in 2005, Londoners are now having to adjust to a quieter, leafier-looking vehicle – yes, it's time to say 'hello' to the hybrid.

In early 2007 Ken Livingstone, London's mayor, introduced the world's first double-decker hybrid, which joins the six single deckers already being road-tested around the city. These new, greener buses use a combination of diesel and electricity, which cuts the carbon and noise produced by each bus by 40 per cent and 30 per cent respectively.

The aim is to introduce 500 hybrids each year, making steady progress towards the ultimate objective of having an entirely green fleet. Should the mayor be successful, the new buses will reduce London's carbon emissions by 200,000 tonnes each year – a significant step towards his goal of making this one of the world's most sustainable cities.

For the time being, you'll only find the double-decker hybrid on route 141, which runs through Old Street, Bank and Monument, but you might spot the single-deck versions on route 360 between Elephant & Castle and Kensington. How will you know? Watch out for the distinctive green sycamore leaf design – and listen 30 per cent harder as it drives past.

LONDON BY AREA

Shopping

For the new Rough Trade megastore, see box p183.

A Butcher of Distinction

11 Dray Walk, Old Truman Brewery, off Brick Lane, Spitalfields, E1 6QL (7770 6111/www.butcherofdistinction. com). Liverpool Street tube/rail. **Open** 10am-7pm daily.

This is a haven of impeccable fashion. The butcher theme (porcelain tiles, meat hooks, framed joint charts) offsets the clothes to perfection; labels are a good mix of old and new.

Chica

NEW *14 Market Street, Spitalfields, E1 6DT (7247 9700/www.chicaboutique online.com). Liverpool Street tube/rail.* **Open** 11am-7pm Mon-Fri; 11am-6pm Sat, Sun.

Expect a riot of colour, frills, sequins and flounce at this boutique. A refreshing departure from 1980s-style vintage, Chica offers more than 50 collections from designers from across the globe.

Columbia Road Market

Columbia Road, Bethnal Green, E2. Liverpool Street tube/rail then 26, 48, bus/Old Street tube/rail then 55, 243 bus. **Open** 8.30am-2pm Sun.

This Sunday morning fixture is a beautiful flower market. If you aren't that interested in buying blooms, a little retail community has grown up around the market: Treacle (no.160) sells groovy crockery and dinky cup cakes; Angela Flanders (no.96) is a quaint perfume shop; Bob & Blossom (no.140) sells lovely children's toys and clothes; Marcos & Trump (no.146) is a treasure trove for vintage fashion. Refuel at Jones Dairy (23 Ezra Street) for artisanal cheeses, bagels and coffee or, on Columbia Road itself, Laxeiro (no.93) for tapas and Fleapit (no.49) for cakes.

Ella Doran Design

46 Cheshire Street, off Brick Lane, E2 6EH (7613 0782/www.elladoran.co.uk). Bethnal Green tube/Liverpool Street tube/rail. **Open** 10am-6pm Tue-Fri; noon-5pm Sat; 11am-6pm Sun.

Ella Doran's iconic kitsch placemats and coasters featuring striking photographic images (a kiwi fruit, artichokes, a Tokyo street scene) are all available in this showroom/studio. But other objects also get the Doran treatment including cushions, purses and notebooks, well priced at £10-£65.

Junky Styling

NEW *12 Dray Walk, Old Truman Brewery, 91-95 Brick Lane, E1 6RF (7247 1883/www.junkystyling.co.uk). Aldgate East tube.* **Open** 10.30am-6.30pm Mon-Fri; 11am-6.30pm Sat, Sun.
A whole new fabulous take on second-hand clothing. Owners Kerry Seager and Anni Saunders take two or more formal garments (a pinstripe suit and a tweed jacket, say) and recycle them into an entirely new piece (skirts £50-£200, jackets £120-£350), sharply tailored, usually with a hint of grunge.

Labour & Wait

18 Cheshire Street, off Brick Lane, E2 6EH (7729 6253/www.labourandwait. co.uk). Liverpool Street tube/rail. **Open** 1-5pm Sat; 10am-5pm Sun.
Labour & Wait is devoted to all things timeless, solid and simple. Stout brooms and body brushes, enamel milk jugs and balls of twine line the shelves, reminiscent of by turns a Victorian pantry and a 1950s kitchen.

Spitalfields Market

Commercial Street, E1 (7247 8556/ www.visitspitalfields.com). Liverpool Street tube/rail. **Open** *General* 10.30am-4.30pm Mon-Fri; 9.30am-5pm Sun. *Antiques* 8am-3.30pm Thur. *Food* 10am-5pm Thur, Fri, Sun. *Fashion* 10am-4pm Fri. *Records & books* 10am-4pm 1st & 3rd Wed of month.
Though a third of its original size, following redevelopment, Spitalfields is well worth a visit. Clothes range from creations by up-and-coming designers to second-hand glad rags. Also in the mix are crafts, jewellery and antiques. The western edge of the market has had a glossy makeover: now called Crispin Place, there's a thrice-weekly market of gourmet food stalls,

enhanced by a cluster of permanent shops selling upmarket clothes, cosmetics, homeware and gourmet olive oil. Canteen presides over the cluster of eating options.

Three Threads

NEW *47-49 Charlotte Road, Shoreditch, EC2A 3QT (7749 0503/www.thethree threads.com). Old Street tube/rail.* **Open** 11am-7pm Mon-Sat; 2-5pm Sun.
Unintimidating, laid-back, unique and super-stylish, this menswear shop serves free beer, has a free jukebox stocked with dad rock, and features conveniently placed bar stools at the till. Expect cult labels such as Japan's Tenderloin or Sweden's Fjall Raven, and T-shirts by Loki including the slogan 'Pan Pipe Music Is Shit'.

Nightlife

Bistrotheque (p176) hosts impressive variety shows in its cabaret room, while **Catch** (p176) and **dreambagsjaguarshoes** (p177) have great DJs.

Bardens Boudoir

38-44 Stoke Newington Road, N16 7XJ (7249 9557/www.bardensbar. co.uk). Dalston Kingsland rail/67, 76, 149, 243 buses. **Open** *Gigs* 8pm. No credit cards.
Having resolved a few licensing issues (it didn't have one), this basement space is back open for business. The space is something of a shambles: the room is at least three times wider than it is deep, and the stage isn't really a stage at all. But none of that bothers the often out-there line-ups and the hipsters that love them.

Bar Music Hall

134-146 Curtain Road, Shoreditch, EC2A 3AR (7729 7216). Old Street tube/rail. **Open** 9am-midnight Mon-Thur, Sun; 9am-1am Fri; 10am-1am Sat.
The huge central bar takes centre stage here. There's plenty of seating, though this is largely ignored at weekends when a top-notch roster of DJs – and pleasing lack of door tax – sees the

Ella Doran Design p180

place rammed with crazed dancefloor kids. During the week, things are much more sedate: gossip office groups sprawl across the black leather banquettes, while laptop-wielding creatives nap in the quiet corners

Bethnal Green Working Men's Club

42-44 Pollard Row, Bethnal Green, E2 6NB (7739 2727/www.workersplaytime. net). Bethnal Green tube. **Open** 8pm-2am Thur-Sat; 10.30am-2am Sun. **Admission** £5-£12 after 8pm Fri, Sat. What was once a run-down East End working men's club threatened with closure is now one of London's coolest clubs. The sticky red carpet and broken lampshades perfectly suit the quirky lounge, retro rock 'n' roll and fancy-dress burlesque parties. The mood is friendly and the air one of playful mischief. See box p134.

Cargo

Kingsland Viaduct, 83 Rivington Street, Shoreditch, EC2A 3AY (7739 3440/www.cargo-london.com). Old Street tube/rail. **Open** 11am-1am Mon-Thur; 11am-1am Fri; 6pm-3am Sat; 1pm-midnight Sun.
Cargo has cemented its position as an essential East End music space by hosting some terrific gigs, everything from Manchester's Friends&Family hip-hop crew to Oscar Fullone's Mish Mash – which offers pretty much what it says on the label. The restaurant serves tapas-style street food.

Favela Chic

91-93 Great Eastern Street, Shoreditch, EC2A 3HZ (7613 5228/www.favela chic.com). Old Street tube/rail. **Open** 6pm-1am Tue-Thur; 6pm-2am Fri, Sat. **Admission** free.
Favela Chic is fun. Once struggling along as the beautiful Grand Central bar, it was refurbished – apparently out of skips – to evoke a Brazilian shanty town. By 11pm the bar/club/restaurant is often packed, with a long queue outside, and the music settles into modern Brazilian beats, baile funk and samba 'n' bass.

93 Feet East

150 Brick Lane, Spitalfields, E1 6QL (7247 3293/www.93feeteast.co.uk). Shoreditch or Aldgate East tube or Liverpool Street tube/rail. **Open** 5-11pm Mon-Thur; 5pm-1am Fri; noon-1am Sat; noon-10.30pm Sun.

With three rooms, a balcony and a giant wrap-around courtyard, 93 Feet East manages to overcome the otherwise crippling lack of a late licence with exciting clubnights: It's Bigger Than is like a student house party, and we love Rock 'n' Roll Cinema combines films with local ska and rockabilly.

Plastic People

147-149 Curtain Road, Shoreditch, EC2A 3QE (7739 6471/www.plastic people.co.uk). Old Street tube/rail. **Open** 10pm-2am Mon-Thur; 10pm-3.30am Fri, Sat; 7.30pm-midnight Sun.

What Plastic People lacks in size and decoration, it makes up for in sound quality. Some of London's most progressive nights are held here, among them Afro-jazz, hip hop and Latin at Balance, and dubstep and grime at FWD, a forward-thinking urban night.

T Bar

Tea Building, 56 Shoreditch High Street, Shoreditch, E1 6JJ (7729 2973/www.t barlondon.com). Liverpool Street tube/rail. **Open** times vary, phone for details.

Straddling the DJ bar/club divide, the T offers stellar DJs for no money whatsoever. Damian Lazarus hosts his filthy electro party Stink here, while the hilarious Gay Bingo takes over the bunker warehouse space once a month.

Arts & leisure

LSO St Luke's

161 Old Street, EC1V 9NG (7490 3939/ Barbican box office 7638 8891/www. lso.co.uk/lsostlukes). Old Street tube/rail. A Grade I-listed church recently renovated and converted by the London Symphony Orchestra into a rehearsal room and concert hall. The programme takes in lunchtime recitals (some free), evening chamber concerts, and occasional jazz and rock events.

In-store gigs

In the bitter fight against cheap online music sales, London's record stores might have found their secret weapon. Almost every night of the week now in London, you can see a chart-topping act playing for nothing at the back of a shop.

One of the most striking and successful adaptations the Oxford Street behemoths Virgin and HMV made in the face of haemorrhaging sales to the internet has been embracing the free, live in-store appearance. Even seven years ago, gigs in record stores (independents such as Rough Trade and Pure Groove excepted) were an unusual, somehow even embarrassing – think Spinal Tap's promotional no-show.

Now London is getting specially designed, shop-cum-venues. The path was blazed by **Fopp** (p147), whose Tottenham Court Road flagship store was specifically designed with a 250-capacity space for live shows, but 30-year-old independent **Rough Trade** isn't far behind, with a megastore planned to arrive near Brick Lane in spring 2007. Since both the original Notting Hill shop (130 Talbot Road, 7229 8541) and its Covent Garden offshoot (16 Neal's Yard, 7240 0105) have illustrious histories of in-store appearances, Rough Trade can claim history is on its side. 'It's part of making the shop environment more attractive to the consumer,' admits founder Geoff Travis. 'And I'm all for record stores!'

■ www.roughtrade.com

T Bar p183

South London

South London's tourist attractions don't end with the South Bank. To the east is **Greenwich**, laden with centuries of royal and maritime heritage – and in 2007 celebrating its tenth anniversary as a World Heritage Site. Further along the Thames is the ill-fated Millennium Dome, perhaps finding its function as the O₂ Arena. South-west are magnificent Hampton Court Palace and Kew's Royal Botanic Gardens. Between them are residential districts of rather different character: boisterous Afro-Caribbean **Brixton** has long been a nightlife centre, while residential **Clapham** and **Battersea** have developed a rather handsome portfolio of bars and restaurants.

Sights & museums

Cutty Sark

King William Walk, SE10 9HT (www.cuttysark.org.uk). Cutty Sark DLR/Greenwich DLR/rail.

Built to last 30 years when launched on the Clyde in 1869, the world's last surviving tea clipper went some 130 years before almost collapsing completely. Sat in Greenwich dry dock as a tourist sight, the *Cutty Sark* was enjoying a complete overhaul when a terrible fire interrupted proceedings in May 2007. We await news of precisely how it will affect the restoration, although the £25 million budget and 2008 reopening are both surely in jeopardy, not to mention the exhibition centre that was to explain the work, complete with live webcams. Navigational instruments, memorabilia related to Robert Burns (whose poem gave the ship her name) and a colourful collection of merchant figureheads (donated when she opened to the public in 1957) may yet form part of the temporary exhibition.

Hampton Court Palace

East Molesey, Surrey KT8 9AU (0870 751 5175/24hr information 0870 752 7777/advance tickets 0870 753 7777/ www.hrp.org.uk). Hampton Court rail/ riverboat from Westminster or Richmond to Hampton Court Pier (Apr-Oct). **Open** *Palace* Apr-Oct 10am-6pm daily. Nov-Mar 10am-4.30pm daily. *Park* dawn-dusk daily. **Admission** £12.30; free-£10 reductions. *Maze only* £3.50; £2.50 reductions. *Gardens only* £4; £2.50-£3 reductions.

This spectacular palace, once owned by Henry VIII, was built in 1514 by Cardinal Wolsey, but Henry liked it so much he seized it for himself in 1528. For the next 200 years, it was the focal point of English history: Elizabeth I was imprisoned in one of the towers by her jealous and fearful elder sister Mary I; Shakespeare gave his first performance to James I here in 1604; and, after the Civil War, Lord Protector Oliver Cromwell was so besotted by the place he ditched his puritanical principles and moved in to enjoy its luxuries. Centuries later, the rosy walls of the palace still dazzle. Its vast size can be daunting, so take advantage of the costumed guided tours. King Henry VIII's State Apartments include the

Great Hall, noted for its splendid hammer-beam roof, beautiful stained-glass windows and elaborate religious tapestries; in the Haunted Gallery, the ghost of Catherine Howard – Henry's fifth wife – can reputedly be heard shrieking. The King's Apartments, added in 1689 by Sir Christopher Wren, are notable for a splendid mural of Alexander the Great. The Tudor Kitchens are great fun, with their giant cauldrons and blood-spattered walls. More spectacular sights await outside, where the exquisitely landscaped gardens include perfectly sculpted trees, peaceful Thames views, and the famous Hampton Court maze (in which it's virtually impossible to get lost).

Museum of Rugby/ Twickenham Stadium

Twickenham Rugby Stadium, Rugby Road, Twickenham, Middx TW1 1DZ (8892 8877/www.rfu.com). Hounslow East tube then 281 bus/Twickenham rail. **Open** *Museum* 10am-5pm Tue-Sat; 11am-5pm Sun (last entry 4.30pm). *Tours* 10.30am, noon, 1.30pm, 3pm Tue-Sat; 1pm, 3pm Sun. **Admission** £10; £7 reductions.

The impressive Twickenham Stadium is the home of English rugby union. Tickets for international matches are extremely hard to come by, although the £80 million new South Stand, increasing capacity to more than 80,000, might alleviate matters. Tours of the stadium take in the England dressing room, the players' tunnel and the Royal Box, while the museum has a permanent collection of memorabilia that charts the game's development from the late 19th century.

National Maritime Museum

Romney Road, Greenwich, SE10 9NF (8858 4422/information 8312 6565/ tours 8312 6608/www.nmm.ac.uk). Cutty Sark DLR/Greenwich DLR/rail. **Open** *July, Aug* 10am-6pm daily. *Sept-June* 10am-5pm daily. **Admission** free. No credit cards.

Opened in 1937, this colonnaded complex comprises the National Maritime Museum, Queen's House and the Royal Observatory and Planetarium (p186). The nation's seafaring history is covered in great depth over three floors, including the world's largest store of maritime art, cartography, ship's models, flags, instruments and costumes. Of the permanent galleries, 'Explorers' is devoted to pioneers of sea travel and includes a chilling *Titanic* display, where grainy launch footage is juxtaposed with ghostly wreck images; 'Passengers' is a history of the cruise holiday, with a cabin mock-up and hilarious old footage of luxury ocean travel. Upstairs, the 'All Hands' gallery provides interactive fun.

Royal Botanic Gardens (Kew Gardens)

Kew, Richmond, Surrey TW9 3AB (8332 5655/information 8940 1171/www.kew.org). Kew Gardens tube/rail/Kew Bridge rail/riverboat to Kew Pier. **Open** *Apr-Aug* 9.30am-6.30pm Mon-Fri; 9.30am-7.30pm Sat, Sun. *Sept-Oct* 9.30am-6pm daily. *Nov-Jan* 9.30am-4.15pm daily. *Feb-Mar* 9.30am-5.30pm daily. **Admission** £11.75; free-£8.75 reductions.

Kew's lush, landscaped beauty represents the pinnacle of our national gardening obsession. From the early 1700s until 1840, when the gardens were given to the nation, these were the grounds for two royal residences – the White House and Richmond Lodge. The 18th-century residents Henry II and Queen Caroline were enthusiastic gardeners; Caroline was particularly fond of exotic plants brought back by voyaging botanists. In the mid 1700s Lancelot 'Capability' Brown began designing an organised layout for the property, using the plants Caroline had collected. Thus began this extraordinary collection, covering more than half a square mile. Any visit to Kew should take in the two huge 19th-century greenhouses: the Palm House holds tropical tamarind, mango, fragrant hibiscus and frangipani, while the Temperate House has the *Pendiculata sanderina* orchid, with its 3ft petals. The Princess of Wales

Conservatory has ten climate zones under a single roof. For an interesting perspective on 17th-century life, head to Kew Palace – the smallest royal palace in Britain, its lovely structure is now open after years of renovation. Also open 'for the first time in recent memory' is the 163ft pagoda, completed in 1762. Those who climb the 253 steps (it costs £3) are rewarded with fine views. Queen Charlotte's Cottage has a dazzling bluebell garden in spring, while the Rose and Woodland gardens are the stuff of fairytales.

Event highlights 'Henry Moore at Kew Gardens' (15 Sept 2007-30 Mar 2008).

Royal Observatory & Planetarium

NEW *Greenwich Park, SE10 9NF (8312 6565/www.rog.nmm.ac.uk). Cutty Sark DLR/Greenwich DLR/rail.* **Open** 10am-5pm daily. **Admission** free.

The Observatory – built by Wren for Charles II in 1675 – straddles the Prime Meridian Line, with one foot in each hemisphere. A new, state-of-the-art planetarium should be open by the time you read this, offering a gallery dedicated to space and once again giving access to the largest refracting telescope in Britain. The exhibition in the historic building is a history of celestial study and its relation to sea travel, part of a £15 million project entitled 'Time and Space', launched in 2006. Among the astrolabes and sextants are timepieces belonging to John Harrison, who discovered accurate measurement of longitude thanks to work here with Astronomer Royal Edmund Halley, of comet fame. The building also has London's only public camera obscura.

Wimbledon Lawn Tennis Museum

Centre Court, All England Lawn Tennis Club, Church Road, SW19 5AE (8946 6131/www.wimbledon.org/museum). *Southfields tube/39, 93, 200, 493 bus.* **Open** 10.30am-5pm daily. **Admission** (incl tour) £14.50; free-£13 reductions. Highlights at this popular museum on the history of tennis include a 200°

cinema screen that allows you to find out what it's like to play on Centre Court and a re-creation of a 1980s men's dressing room, complete with a 'ghost' of John McEnroe. Visitors can also get to grips with rackets, check changing tennis fashions and enjoy a behind-the-scenes tour. Seeing the action at the Wimbledon tournament (late June/early July each year) requires forethought – or serious queuing for the small allocation of on-the-day tickets (8946 2244, www.wimbledon.org).

Eating & drinking

Brixton Bar & Grill

15 Atlantic Road, Brixton, SW9 8HX (7737 6777/www.bbag.me.uk). Brixton tube/rail. **Open** 4.30pm-midnight Tue, Wed; 4.30pm-1am Thur; 4.30pm-2am Fri, Sat; 3.30-11pm Sun. **Bar**.

A class act – friendly but slickly run, with an excellent drinks list running to fine bottled beers, wines and cocktails. The decor is Spanish-influenced, and the tapas-style menu offers the likes of spiced sweet potato chips or lamb cutlets. Candlelight softens the atmosphere in the evenings, and a DJ plays soul and funk at the weekend.

Inn at Kew Gardens

292 Sandycombe Road, Kew, Surrey TW9 3NG (8940 2220/www.theinnat kewgardens.com). Kew Gardens tube. **Open** 11am-11pm Mon-Thur, Sun; 11am-midnight Fri, Sat. **££**.

Gastropub.

A rustic bistro feel dominates the main dining room at the back of this tastefully refurbished boozer. The menu features confidently executed gastropub classics (ribeye, Toulouse sausages) and sensational fish and charcuterie platters. Well-kept draught beer and a notable wine list complete the picture.

Inside

19 Greenwich South Street, Greenwich, SE10 8NW (8265 5060/www.inside restaurant.co.uk). Greenwich rail/DLR. **Open** noon-2.30pm, 6.30-11pm Tue-Fri; 11am-2.30pm, 6.30-11pm Sat; noon-3pm Sun. **££**. **Modern European**.

Set among run-down shops near the station, Inside is a little gem. Service from the sole waitress is faultlessly attentive and the menu offers plenty of spring-like flavours alongside Middle Eastern influences. Classic brunch dishes available on Saturday.

Living

443 Coldharbour Lane, Brixton, SW9 8LN (7326 4040/www.living bar.co.uk). Brixton tube/rail. **Open** noon-2am Mon-Thur, Sun; noon-4am Fri, Sat. **Admission** £5 after 10pm Fri, Sat. **Bar**.

If you're looking for a lively, up-for-it bar bang in the centre of Brixton, this two-floor venue delivers the goods. Bhangra, Cuban or house DJs play out every night – and it gets pretty raucous on a Friday and Saturday night.

Lost Society

697 Wandsworth Road, Battersea, SW8 3JF (7652 6526/www.lost society.co.uk). Clapham Common tube/Wandsworth Road rail. **Open** 5pm-1am Tue-Thur; 4pm-2am Fri; 11am-2am Sat; 11am-1am Sun. **Bar**.

This stunning venue has been flamboyantly decorated with a subtle art deco theme running throughout. Spread over two floors, the bar offers visitors a host of nooks and crannies to linger in, ranging from a little garden terrace to a decadent indoor bar complete with giant chandelier. The food and drink are in very good taste – expert cocktails and well-priced wines matched with plates to share – and DJs play Thursday to Saturday.

Sea Cow

57 Clapham High Street, Clapham, SW4 7TG (7622 1537). Clapham Common or Clapham North tube. **Open** noon-11pm Tue-Sat; noon-9pm Sun. **Fish & chips**.

Part of a small south London chain (it's also in Dulwich and Fulham) and one of the very few chippies to offer organic food. Trendy minimal design complements unusual fish options such as swordfish, red snapper and a daily special. Is Sea Cow the future of fish and chips? We certainly hope so.

Trinity

NEW *4 The Polygon, Clapham, SW4 0JG (7622 1199). Clapham Common tube.* **Open** 12.30-3pm, 6.30-10.30pm daily. **£££**. **French**.

The new venture Adam Byatt, of much-mourned local eaterie Thyme, has found great staff – the service on our visit was faultlessly smiling and professional – and is focused on the classical, French-based cooking he does best. From a pie based on the century-old dish *dôme d'or* to an exquisite soup served in a dish shaped like an empty crab shell, precision is evident in all the cooking – served in cheekily deconstructed presentations.

Nightlife

Dogstar

389 Coldharbour Lane, Brixton, SW9 8LQ (7733 7515/www.thedogstar.com). Brixton tube/rail. **Open** 4pm-2am Mon-Thur; noon-4am Fri, Sat; noon-2am Sun.

A Brixton institution, Dogstar is a big street-corner pub that exudes the urban authenticity so loved by clubbers. The atmosphere can be pretty intense, but it's never less than vibrant. It's something of a training ground for the DJ stars of tomorrow, so the quality of music is often very high. The clientele of trendy-trainered hip-hopsters, suede-heads and indie girls remains loyal, talking of past glories as they drink under the opera-style curtains that hang above the bar.

Fire

39-41 Parry Street, Vauxhall, SW8 1RT (www.allthingsorange.com). Vauxhall tube/rail. No credit cards.

Fire is the heart of the notorious day/night club culture of Vauxhall 'gay village'. A:M, from late Friday to mid-morning Saturday, kicks things off with three rooms of DJs playing funky, chunky tech house. Then there's Later, from noon Sunday, followed by Orange, the essential Vauxhall Sunday night/Monday morning club – house music, bare torsos, poppers… hey, doesn't anyone have a job round here?

Brixton Bar & Grill p186

Plan B

*418 Brixton Road, Brixton, SW9 7AY
(7733 0926/www.plan-brixton.co.uk).
Brixton tube/rail.* **Open** 5pm-6am Fri,
Sat; 7pm-4am Thur, Sun.
It may be small, but DJ bar Plan B
punches well above its weight thanks
to a constant flow of hip hop and funk
stars at 'never knowingly under-
souled' Fidgit on Fridays and plenty of
house fare on Saturdays, with Norman
Jay a regular behind the decks.

Royal Vauxhall Tavern

*372 Kennington Lane, SE11 5HY
(7582 0833/www.theroyalvauxhall
tavern.co.uk). Vauxhall tube/rail.*
Open 9pm-2am Sat; 2pm-midnight
Sun. No credit cards.
A Victorian boozer that proclaims itself
the beating heart of Vauxhall – it's
been a key influence on London's gay
scene since World War II. The numerous tables and raised platform hark
back to the place's music hall roots: the
stage is trod most nights, with adored
avant-garde club Duckie on Saturday,
and Vauxhall, a spit-and-sawdust
cabaret, every Thursday. See box p134.

Arts & leisure

BAC (Battersea Arts Centre)

*Lavender Hill, Battersea, SW11 5TN
(7223 2223/www.bac.org.uk). Clapham
Common tube/Clapham Junction rail/
77, 77A, 345 bus.*
The forward-thinking BAC plays alma
mater to new writers and theatre companies. Expect the latest in quirky, fun
and physical theatre, particularly after
the Edinburgh festival when excited
BAC talent scouts return with their
next big things in tow. Artistic director David Jubb's track record includes
starting the Scratch programme, which
shows work in progress to progressively larger audiences until it's finished and polished. In 2007, the BAC
celebrated its 25th birthday with a 'theatre summit' that sought to inspire the
next 25 years – then learnt of funding
cuts that put its own future at risk.

O₂

NEW *Peninsula Square, Greenwich,
SE10 0DX (www.theo2.co.uk). North
Greenwich tube.* **Open** 10am-late daily.

In July 2007, the ill-fated Dome reopens as O₂, 'Europe's biggest entertainment destination'. Lord Rogers' building was always impressive (the size of 72 tennis courts, we're told), but will the contents finally measure up to the quality of the architecture? The focus is the 23,000-seat Arena, which showcases major musicians (Prince, Bon Jovi, Justin Timberlake, Barbra Streisand) and sporting events (boxing, ice hockey, tennis, even NBA). Surrounding the Arena, the Entertainment District will have an 11-screen cinema, restaurants, bars, shops and the purpose-built, 2,350-seat music venue IndigO₂ (www.theindigo2.com), hosting 'a fantastic club night' (details to be announced) and the likes of pianist Jools Holland and Youssou N'Dour. There's also a two-level exhibition space, which opens in November 2007 with the return of the Tutankhamun treasure for the first time in 30 years – and the last time they will leave Egypt. With a fleet of Thames Clipper boats laid on for additional transport, the organisers have been careful with the details – but will it be enough?

Event highlights 'Tutankhamun and the Golden Age of the Pharaohs' (from 15 Nov 2007).

West London

The triangle between **Notting Hill Gate**, **Ladbroke Grove** and **Westbourne Park** tube stations contains some lovely squares, grand houses and fine gardens, along with the shops, bars and restaurants that serve the kind of bohemian who can afford to live here. Notting Hill Gate isn't an attractive high street, but a turn north into Pembridge Road takes you towards the boutique streets of Westbourne Grove and Ledbury Road. On Saturday, don't miss **Portobello Road** market; it's a proper shopping street during the week too. **Shepherd's Bush** to the west and riverside **Hammersmith** have a much more lived-in feel.

Sights & museums

Louise T Blouin Institute

NEW *3 Olaf Street, Shepherd's Bush, W11 4BE (7985 9600/www. ltbfoundation.org). Latimer Road tube.* **Open** 10am-6pm Mon-Fri; noon-5pm Sat, Sun. **Admission** £10.

Louise T Blouin MacBain opened this 35,000sq ft non-profit art gallery in October 2006 to explore the connections between visual art and neuroscience – a lot less dry than it sounds judging by the dramatic inaugural exhibition of light works by James Turrell. Housed over three storeys of a 1920s coachworks, the Institute has two floors of galleries and a somewhat severe minimalist conservatory café.

Eating & drinking

Café García

248-250 Portobello Road, Ladbroke Grove, W11 1LL (7221 6119). Ladbroke Grove tube. **Open** 9am-5pm Mon-Thur; 8am-11pm Fri, Sat; 10am-7pm Sun. **££. Spanish**.

Annexed to veteran Spanish supermarket/importers R Garcia & Son, this place is basic. There is no table service: you point out your tapas choices from under the glass counters and take a seat. The selection isn't huge, but everything is freshly prepared and it's just perfect for market day refuelling.

Clarke's

124 Kensington Church Street, Kensington, W8 4BH (7221 9225/ www.sallyclarke.com). Notting Hill Gate tube. **Open** 12.30-2pm Mon; 12.30-2pm, 7-10pm Tue-Fri; 11am-2pm, 7-10pm Sat. **£££. Modern European**.

Inspired by her stint at Chez Panisse, Sally Clarke has stayed at the cutting edge of culinary trends since the 1980s with her no-choice evening menu: three courses of char-grills and salads, using seasonal ingredients, carefully sourced. The drinks list has one of Europe's best selections of unusual New World wines. If you can't get a booking, check out her lovely bread shop at no.122.

LONDON BY AREA

Cow

*89 Westbourne Park Road, Westbourne
Park, W2 5QH (7221 0021). Royal Oak
or Westbourne Park tube.* **Open** noon-
11pm Mon-Thur; noon-midnight Fri,
Sat; noon-10.30pm Sun. **£££**.
Gastropub.

We can't fault the Cow. Upstairs from
one of the best pubs in London, the dining room has a menu that's simple,
inventive and deftly dispatched. Like
the bar, the restaurant is compact,
squeezing into an awkward trapezium-
shaped room with a 1950s, retro feel.
Oysters are a speciality.

E&O

*14 Blenheim Crescent, Notting Hill,
W11 1NN (7229 5454/www.eando.nu).
Ladbroke Grove or Notting Hill Gate
tube.* **Open** noon-3pm, 6-10.30pm
Mon-Sat; 12.30-3.30pm, 6-10pm Sun.
£££. Asian.

Lauded as the star among Will Ricker's
uniformly excellent restaurants, E&O
boasts a dark wood and fuchsia-walled
bar full of gorgeous people sipping
delicious cocktails and nibbling dim
sum. The calmer, cream-walled dining
room offers a pan-Asian menu so full
of exotic names a glossary is enclosed.

Gate

*51 Queen Caroline Street,
Hammersmith, W6 9QL (8748 6932/
www.thegate.tv). Hammersmith tube.*
Open noon-2.45pm, 6-10.45pm Mon-
Fri; 6-10.45pm Sat. **££. Vegetarian**.

This well-heeled, artistically decorated
venue is one of the capital's leading
vegetarian restaurants. The mainly
Mediterranean menu also incorporates
exotica such as Caribbean curry or
aubergine teriyaki. Be sure to book.

Ledbury

*127 Ledbury Road, Notting Hill,
W11 2AQ (7792 9090/www.the
ledbury.com). Westbourne Park tube.*
Open noon-2pm, 6.30-10.15pm Mon-
Fri; noon-2.30pm, 6.30-10.15pm Sat,
Sun. **£££. French**.

Everything about the Ledbury is
delightful. Staff are unfailingly helpful,
the dining room is smart without being

intimidating, and the food, cooked by
Australian Brett Graham, is exceptional – fine seasonal ingredients; a few
dashes of Ferran Adria-style technology; ravishing presentation; sublime
tastes and textures.

Notting Hill Brasserie

*92 Kensington Park Road, Notting Hill,
W11 2PN (7229 4481). Notting Hill
Gate tube.* **Open** noon-3pm, 7-11pm
Mon-Sat; noon-3pm Sun. **£££**.
Brasserie.

NHB's casual-posh style is bang on for
Notting Hill's chi-chi bohemianism.
The elegant cuisine offers sensitively
cooked fish mains and some marvellous roast meats, at prices that dis-
courage the riff-raff. There's live jazz
in the bar nightly.

River Café

*Thames Wharf, Rainville Road,
Hammersmith, W6 9HA (7386 4200/
www.rivercafe.co.uk). Hammersmith
tube.* **Open** 12.30-3pm, 7-9.30pm Mon-
Sat; 12.30-3pm Sun. **££££. Italian**.

High summer is the best time to visit
the hip and terrific River Café: it's easier to get a table and the table is likely
to be in the pretty courtyard. You'll
encounter exquisite ingredients (at pre-
mium prices) and a sensibly priced
wine list that makes other establishments look greedy. Chocolate fans
should opt for the famous Nemesis.

Tea Palace

*175 Westbourne Grove, Notting Hill,
W11 2SB (7727 2600/www.teapalace.
co.uk). Bayswater or Notting Hill Gate
tube.* **Open** 10am-7pm daily. **££**.
Tearoom.

Half teashop, half smart café, this
peaceful, white tableclothed sanctuary
specialises in the kind of prim afternoon teas so beloved of big London
hotels. The event is a little less starchy
and expensive here, though the tiered
trays filled with scones, cakes and finger sandwiches should satisfy any crit-
ical-eyed regular at the Dorchester.
There are brunch and lunch menus, but
most space – 16 pages of options – is
dedicated to tea. Which is fine by us.

Portobello Road Market p192

Shopping

Aimé

32 Ledbury Road, Notting Hill, W11 2AB (7221 7070/www.aimelondon. com). Notting Hill Gate tube. **Open** 10.30am-7pm Mon-Sat.

There's an understated Parisian cool to this airy, two-floor shop. You'll find casual separates, nostalgic ballet flats and romantic silver jewellery, inscribed with French poetry. There are also delicately packaged bath products and hard-to-resist home accessories.

Appleby

95 Westbourne Park Villas, Westbourne Park, W2 5ED (7229 7772/www.appleby vintage.com). Royal Oak tube. **Open** 11am-6pm Mon-Sat.

This bright and airy vintage boutique is unusually spacious and minimal. The contents range from the 1920s to the 1980s, with a particularly strong collection of dresses. In addition to classics from vintage design legends such as Pucci, Hardy Amies and Ossie Clark, the shop has a rocking assortment of bags, shoes and jewellery.

Honest Jon's

278 Portobello Road, Notting Hill, W10 5TE (8969 9822/www.honestjons.com). Ladbroke Grove tube. **Open** 10am-6pm Mon-Sat; 11am-5pm Sun.

Honest Jon's found its way here in 1979, where it was reportedly the first place in London to employ a Rastafarian. You'll find jazz, hip hop, soul, broken beat, reggae and Brazilian music on the shelves.

Miller Harris

14 Needham Road, Notting Hill, W11 2RP (7221 1545). Notting Hill Gate tube. **Open** 10am-6pm Mon-Sat.

Lyn Harris has one of the most sought-after noses in the business. She stocks high-class perfume, body products and candles, made with quality natural extracts and oils; our personal favourites are the stunning sweet-yet-not-overpowering Noix de Tubéreuse, and Coeur d'Eté.

One

*30 Ledbury Road, Notting Hill, W11
2AB (7221 5300/www.onlyOne.com).
Notting Hill Gate tube.* **Open** 10am-
6pm Mon-Fri; 10am-6.30pm Sat.

Everything for sale in this incongruous
two-storey building – which resembles
a modernist beach house – is unique.
The customised vintage pieces are
strikingly beautiful – and you can
guarantee no one else will be wearing
the same thing as you. Some of these
garments are suffused with history –
the shop recently acquired a carefully
preserved cache from a fashion con-
sultant and private collector, including
a Chanel coat worn by Coco herself.

Portobello Road Market

*Portobello Road, W10 & W11 (7229
8354/www.portobelloroad.co.uk).
Ladbroke Grove or Notting Hill Gate
tube.* **Open** 8am-6pm Mon-Wed; 9am-
1pm Thur; 7am-7pm Fri, Sat. *Antiques*
4am-4pm Sat.

Portobello Road is several excellent
markets rolled into one. The antiques
start at the Notting Hill end; further up
are food stalls, and under the Westway
flyover and along the walkway to
Ladbroke Grove you'll find emerging
designer and vintage clothes.

Sera of London

NEW *3 Lonsdale Road, Notting Hill,
W11 2BY (7467 0799/www.seraof
london.com). Notting Hill Gate or
Westbourne Park tube.* **Open** 10am-
6pm Mon-Sat.

Spread over three bijou levels, this
shop is decked out with day-beds piled
with pouffy velvet and leopard-print
cushions, and overblown bordello wallpaper. The downstairs is devoted to
towering platforms and fetishy mules.
But it's the fabulous accessories that
dazzle. Great for glamourpuss gifts.

Nightlife

Notting Hill Arts Club

*21 Notting Hill Gate, Notting Hill,
W11 3JQ (7460 4459/www.nottinghill
artsclub.com). Notting Hill Gate tube.*
Open 6pm-1am Mon-Wed; 6pm-2am

Thur, Fri; 4pm-2am Sat; 4pm-1am Sun.
Admission £5-£8; free before 8pm.

This small basement club almost sin-
gle-handedly keeps west London on
the cool clubbing radar with nights
such as YoYo, the weekly Thursday
soul- and funkfest that kept booking
LilyAllen in 2006 resulting in queues
practically across town, and Radio
Gagarin, doing for Balkan music what
Pete Doherty did for the Priory.

Shepherd's Bush Empire

*Shepherd's Bush Green, W12 8TT
(8354 3300/box office 0870 771 2000/
www.shepherds-bush-empire.co.uk).
Shepherd's Bush tube.*

This former BBC theatre remains
London's best mid-sized venue. The
sound is decent, the staff are among
London's friendliest and booking policy takes in everything from the Roots
to Bonzo Dog Doo-Dah Band. The only
irritation is the lack of decent sight
lines from the stalls for concert-goers
less than 6ft tall; things are a lot more
comfortable on the all-seated balconies.

Arts & leisure

Electric Cinema

*191 Portobello Road, Notting Hill, W11
2ED (7908 9696/www.the-electric.co.
uk). Ladbroke Grove or Notting Hill
Gate tube.*

One of the city's oldest cinemas – and
one of the most lavish, with leather
armchairs and two-seater sofas for the
deep-pocketed. Just next door is the
excellent Electric Brasserie.

Lyric Hammersmith

*King Street, Hammersmith, W6 0QL
(0870 050 0511/www.lyric.co.uk).
Hammersmith tube.*

The Lyric has a knack for vibrant, offbeat scheduling and it also offers good
kids' theatre. The hideous façade, built
when concrete was still regarded as the
architectural panacea for all building
ills, hides a 19th-century gem of an
auditorium that was conceived by the
Victorian theatre-design supremo
Frank Matcham. The smaller Lyric
Studio houses short-run shows.

Essentials

Brown's p200

Hotels

Not so long ago, finding a bed for the night in London meant turning a blind eye to one of two things: a credit card receipt of heart-stopping proportions or acres of chintz. The bad news is, London's hotels are the most expensive in western Europe – according to www.hotels.com, the average rate for a night here at the end of 2006 was £107… £22 more than an average night in legendarily expensive Oslo. The price rise over the course of 2006 amounted to more than 20 per cent.

Time for some good news, eh? One of the most refreshing recent developments has been the appearance of stylish budget hotels. Check out the likes of the **Hoxton**, **B&B Belgravia** and the **Mayflower Hotel** for simple but chic fittings, decent service and reassuringly low price tags. Likewise, the **Yotel** (www.yotel.com) hotels, planned for London's airports, offer bargain pods with plenty of style. If comfort isn't your bag, there's even **easyHotel** threatening to redefine the term 'no frills'.

It's still the boutique hotels, though, that rightly gain the plaudits, and Kit Kemp remains the boss. The Charlotte Street, Covent Garden, Number Sixteen and the Soho are all great, but her seventh venue, the **Haymarket Hotel**, looks likely to better them all. And it should be open by the time you read this. It seems now is the time for high-end hotels: developers are snapping grand buildings all over town, transforming courthouses, railway hotels and office blocks into luxury places to stay (see box p207). And even an old stager like the **Connaught** is getting in on the act, with their extensive transformation due for completion in late 2007.

Money matters

Hotels are constantly offering special deals, particularly for weekends: always check websites or ask about special rates when booking. Also check discount hotel websites – for example www.alpharooms.com and www.london-discount-hotel.com – for prices that can fall well below the rack rates.

Many high-end hotels exclude VAT from room prices. Check this before booking.

The South Bank

Premier Travel Inn London County Hall

County Hall, Belvedere Road, SE1 7PB (0870 238 3300/www.premier travelinn.com). Waterloo tube/rail. **£.**
A room in a landmark building on the Thames, next to the London Eye, for less than £100? County Hall's former tenant, the Greater London Council, has been gone for over two decades, but the prices at this outpost of the Premier Travel Inn chain are more in line with the 1980s. Just don't expect the opulence of the exterior to carry on inside, or any Thames views.

Southwark Rose

47 Southwark Bridge Road, SE1 9HH (7015 1480/www.southwarkrose hotel.co.uk). London Bridge tube/rail. **££.**
The name may make it sound like a faux-Tudor guesthouse, but the Southwark Rose (handily placed for Tate Modern and Borough Market) is the antithesis: a slick, purpose-built, budget-conscious property with all the elements that have become shorthand for 'modern luxury hotel'.

SHORTLIST

Best new
- Haymarket Hotel (p203)
- Montagu Place (p204)
- Rockwell (p199)

Best new bargains
- Clink Hostel (p200)
- Hoxton Hotel (p208)

All-round winners
- Covent Garden Hotel (p203)
- Malmaison (p208)
- One Aldwych (p205)
- Rookery (p208)

Glossy mag faves
- Brown's (p200)
- Haymarket (p203)
- Rockwell (p199)
- Sanderson (p206)

Budget style
- Harlingford Hotel (p203)
- Hoxton Hotel (p208)
- Montagu Place (p204)

Finest dining
- Brunello at the Baglioni (p196)
- Gordon Ramsay at Claridge's (p200)
- Nahm at the Halkin (p199)
- Nobu at the Metropolitan (p204)

Best bars
- Bonds Bar at the Threadneedles (p208)
- Donovan Bar at Brown's (p200)
- Library at the Lanesborough (p199)
- Lobby Bar at One Aldwych (p205)

Quality B&B
- B&B Belgravia (p196)
- Number Sixteen (p199)
- 22 York Street (p206)

Cheap choices
- easyHotel (p197)
- Piccadilly Backpackers (p205)

ESSENTIALS

Westminster & St James's

B&B Belgravia

64-66 Ebury Street, SW1W 9QD (7823 4928/www.bb-belgravia.com). Victoria tube/rail. **££**.

This is one of the most attractive B&Bs we've seen. The black and white lounge could be straight out of *Elle Decoration*. And it's liveable as well as lovely: in the communal lounge you'll find a laptop with free internet and, above it, toys to keep the kids entertained, plus a collection of DVDs. The bedrooms are chic and predominantly white, with flatscreen TVs and sleek bathrooms with power showers.

City Inn

30 John Islip Street, SW1P 4DD (7630 1000/www.cityinn.com). Pimlico tube. **£££**.

There's nothing flashy about this hotel, apart from some modern art in the airy lobby, but it is well located for the Westminster landmarks and, notably, Tate Britain. There are decent added extras (CD/DVD libraries, with players in the rooms, plus broadband and LCD TVs) and service is efficient. On-site facilities include the Millbank Lounge, with its impressive 'library' of 75 whiskies, and you can sit on a Ron Arad chair outside the City Café.

Trafalgar

2 Spring Gardens, SW1A 2TS (7870 2900/www.hilton.co.uk/trafalgar). Charing Cross tube/rail. **££££**.

Part of the Hilton group, the Trafalgar dropped the branding in favour of designer decor. The building is imposing, but the mood inside is young and dynamic. The rooms have a masculine feel with minimalist walnut furniture, and the bathtubs are made for sharing with the tap in the middle. The location is its biggest draw: corner rooms overlook Trafalgar square and the small rooftop bar has lovely panoramic views. Ground-level bar Rockwell offers over 100 bourbons.

Windermere Hotel

142-144 Warwick Way, SW1V 4JE (7834 5163/www.windermere-hotel. co.uk). Victoria tube/rail. **££**.

Minutes from Victoria Station, Warwick Way is lined with small hotels and B&Bs. The Windermere edges ahead of the competition with good facilities (satellite TV, free internet, power showers), smart rooms that are light on the chintz and a hospitable atmosphere coupled with terrific levels of service (11 staff for just 20 rooms).

South Kensington & Chelsea

Aster House

3 Sumner Place, SW7 3EE (7581 5888/www.asterhouse.com). South Kensington tube. **££**.

This award-winning B&B bravely attempts to live up to its upmarket address. In reality, the lobby – with its pink faux marble and gold chandeliers – is more kitsch than glam, but the effect is still charming. So is the lush garden, with its pond and wandering ducks, and the palm-filled conservatory, where guests eat breakfast. The bedrooms are comfortable, if floral, with smart marble bathrooms (ask for one with a power shower).

Baglioni

60 Hyde Park Gate, SW7 5BB (7368 5700/www.baglionihotellondon.com). High Street Kensington or Gloucester Road tube. **££££**.

The Baglioni is hard to beat for exciting designer style. Occupying a Victorian mansion just across from Kensington Palace, it has none of the sniffy formality of some of its deluxe English counterparts. The swanky Italian restaurant and bar has black chandeliers, gold ceilings and gigantic vases. The chic bedrooms are more subdued: black floorboards, taupe and gold-leaf walls, dark wood furniture enlivened by jewel-coloured cushions and soft throws. Baglioni brings a welcome touch of bling to the boutique scene.

Base2Stay

25 Courtfield Gardens, Earl's Court, SW5 OPG (0845 262 8000/www.base2 stay.com). Earl's Court tube. **££**.

The new Base2Stay – a cross between a hotel and serviced apartments – looks good, with its modernist limestone and taupe tones. The prices are agreeable, though it should be noted that the so-called 'kitchenette' is actually little more than a microwave and sink, squeezed into a cupboard. But as long as you don't mind having to do everything yourself, then Base2Stay is an affordable way to have a clean room less than ten minutes from the tube station.

Blakes

33 Roland Gardens, SW7 3PF (7370 6701/www.blakeshotels.com). South Kensington tube. **££££**.

The original London boutique hotel doesn't get that much press any more – and that's exactly how its publicity-shy devotees like it. Blakes has a maximalist decor that has stood the test of time, becoming a sort of living case-book for interior design students. Each room is in a different style, with influences from Italy, India, Turkey and China. Unsurprisingly, given its off-the-beaten-track location and romantic decor, the hotel's popular for honeymoons; you can get married on site.

Cadogan

75 Sloane Street, SW1X 9SG (7235 7141/www.steinhotels.com/cadogan). Sloane Square tube. **£££**.

Louche secrets lurked behind the doors of this terribly British hotel. Edward VII visited his mistress Lillie Langtry here when it was her private home, and Oscar Wilde was arrested in room 118. Bedrooms boast leather headboards and rich, couture-inspired fabrics. Guests are permitted access to the secluded gardens and tennis courts opposite.

easyHotel

14 Lexham Gardens, Earl's Court, W8 5JE (www.easyhotel.com). Earl's Court tube. **£**.

The latest venture to which airline entrepreneur Stelios Haji-Ioannou has applied his no-frills approach is this compact hotel for compact wallets. The 34 rooms come in three sizes – small, really small and tiny. The rooms come with a bed, a bathroom and that's it. There's no wardrobe, no lift and no breakfast, and you only get a window if you pay extra for it. Check-in and check-out are at a less than generous 4pm and 10am respectively.

Gore

189 Queen's Gate, SW7 5EX (7584 6601/www.gorehotel.com). South Kensington tube. **£££**.

Clink Hostel p200

"Brilliant, this is genius" "Definitely, the best hotel booking tool I've ever seen" **"Superb, really useful and easy to use"** "This is an awesome tool!" **"I LOVE this feature!"** "This is the best interactive map of London" **"I have travelled all over the world but never seen such a service"** "The functionality of your hotel map is OUTSTANDING!" **"Best interactive map I have ever used on the web"** "Absolutely great!" **"This is excellent - a genuinely useful tool"**

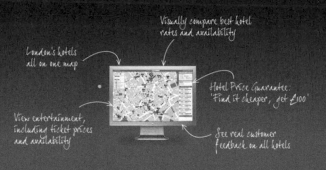

Visually compare best hotel rates and availability

London's hotels all on one map

Hotel Price Guarantee: 'Find it cheaper, get £100'

View entertainment, including ticket prices and availability

See real customer feedback on all hotels

full screen, fully interactive

The new hotel map on LondonTown.com
www.londontown.com/hotelmap

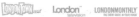

A stay at the Gore is possibly the next best thing to having a rich and eccentric titled earl as an uncle. It's a classy, creaky period piece housed in a couple of grand Victorian townhouses. The place is crammed with old paintings and antiques, and the bedrooms have fantastic 19th-century carved oak beds (some so high they need library steps), sumptuous drapes and shelves of old books. Hyde Park, the Royal Albert Hall and the museums are all just a few minutes' walk away.

Halkin

Halkin Street, SW1X 7DJ (7333 1000/ www.halkin.como.bz). Hyde Park Corner tube. **££££**.
Popular with affluent businessmen and publicity-shy Hollywood stars, the Halkin is a gracious, hype-free hideaway. You'd never guess the world's only Michelin-starred Thai restaurant, Nahm, is behind its discreet Georgian-style façade, down a Belgravia back street. Its subtle design – a successful marriage of European luxury and oriental serenity – still looks more current than hotels half its age. A peaceful, unpretentious place to be cocooned in luxury and comfort.

Lanesborough

Lanesborough Place, Hyde Park Corner, SW1X 7TA (7259 5599/ www.lanesborough.com). Hyde Park Corner tube. **££££**.
That the Lanesborough came late to the ranks of London's historic luxury hotels – in 1991 – has been no bar to its competing at the top level. It occupies an 1820s Greek Revival building by National Gallery designer William Wilkins and its luxurious guest rooms are traditionally decorated, boasting antique furniture and lavish marble bathrooms. Obviously, you pay a seriously hefty price for all this, but, hey, personal butler service is thrown in for free.

Mayflower Hotel

26-28 Trebovir Road, Earl's Court, SW5 9NJ (7370 0991/www.mayflower-group.co.uk). Earl's Court tube. **££**.

At the forefront of the budget-hotel style revolution, the Mayflower Hotel has given Earl's Court – once a far from glamorous B&B wasteland – a kick up the backside. Following a spectacular makeover a couple of years back, the Mayflower proves cheap really can be chic. The wooden-floored rooms are furnished in an Eastern style with hand-carved beds and sumptuous fabrics. At such low rates, marble bathrooms, CD players and dataports are hitherto unheard-of luxuries.

myhotel chelsea

35 Ixworth Place, SW3 3QX (7225 7500/www.myhotels.com). South Kensington tube. **£££**.
Pink walls, a floral sofa and a plate of scones in the lobby offer a posh English foil to the feng shui touches here. The rooms have dusky pink wallpaper, white wicker headboards and velvet cushions. There's also pampering courtesy of Aveda and a Cape Cod-styled bar.

Number Sixteen

16 Sumner Place, SW7 3EG (7589 5232/www.firmdale.com). South Kensington tube. **£££**.
This may be Kit Kemp's most affordable hotel but there's no slacking in style or comforts. Bedrooms are decorated with tasteful floral patterns and muted creams, greens and mauves, making them feminine but far from frilly. It's all utterly relaxing and feels like a real retreat from the city. Sumner Place itself is an appealing row of white stucco townhouses a minute away from South Kensington tube station and just around the corner from the museums.

Rockwell

NEW *181 Cromwell Road, SW5 0SF (7244 2000/www.therockwellhotel.com). Earl's Court tube.* **£££**.
On a busy road, what the Rockwell might lack in peaceful location it more than compensates for in style. Set in two converted houses, its 40 rooms have a sleek, contemporary feel (complete with flatscreen TVs and White Company toiletries) and the public spaces (there's a stylish bar and dining

ESSENTIALS

room) are bright and sophisticated. The garden terrace, with its giant pots and sunny aspect, is particularly lovely. Prices are very good value for what's on offer – note, however, that you'll find showers rather than large extravagant bathrooms here.

Twenty Nevern Square

20 Nevern Square, Earl's Court, SW5 9PD (7565 9555/www.twentynevern square.co.uk). Earl's Court tube. **££**.
Tucked away in a secluded garden square, this immaculate boutique hotel feels far away from its less-than-lovely locale. The modern-colonial style was created by its well-travelled owner, who personally sourced many of the exotic furnishings. Rooms are clad in a mixture of Eastern and European antique furniture and sumptuous silk curtains. The beds are the real stars, though, from elaborately carved four-posters to Egyptian sleigh styles, all with luxurious handmade mattresses.

West End

Arosfa

83 Gower Street, WC1E 6HJ (tel/fax 7636 2115/www.arosfalondon.com). Goodge Street tube. **£**.
Arosfa means 'place to stay' in Welsh, but we reckon this townhouse B&B sells itself short. The accommodation is fairly spartan, but it's spotless, and all rooms have en suite shower/WC (albeit tiny). It has a great Bloomsbury location and a pleasing walled garden.

Ashlee House

261-265 Gray's Inn Road, WC1X 8QT (7833 9400/www.ashleehouse.co.uk). King's Cross tube/rail. **£**.
This is a rare beast: a youth hostel with a bit of style. The funky lobby is decorated with sheepskin-covered sofas, and all the handy hostel stuff is on site: internet, TV room, luggage storage, laundry and kitchen. No curfew, either.

Brown's

33 Albemarle Street, W1S 4BP (7493 6020/www.roccofortehotels.com). Green Park tube. **££££**.

Brown's was the quintessential London hotel, opened in 1837 by Lord Byron's butler, James Brown. In 2003, Rocco Forte added it to his portfolio and embarked on a top-to-toe refurb. The public spaces remain gloriously old English (particularly the Tea Room) and the expanded Donovan Bar is sheer class. The bedrooms, however, are less impressive: large and extremely comfortable, they lack character.

Charlotte Street Hotel

15-17 Charlotte Street, W1T 1RJ (7806 2000/www.firmdale.com). Goodge Street or Tottenham Court Road tube. **£££**.
Designer Kit Kemp, doyenne of the city's boutique hotels, pioneered the 'modern English' decorative style. This gorgeous hotel is a fine exponent, fusing traditional English furnishings with avant-garde art. Bedrooms mix English understatement with bold flourishes: soft beiges and greys spiced up with plaid-floral combinations. The Oscar restaurant and bar are classy, and on Sunday nights you can combine a meal with a screening of a classic film in the mini-cinema (booking advisable).

Claridge's

55 Brook Street, W1K 4HR (7629 8860/www.claridges.co.uk). Bond Street tube. **££££**.
A favourite with everyone from A-list actors to presidents and even royalty, Claridge's is synonymous with history and class. The hotel dates back in its present form to 1898 and a signature art deco redesign but, despite the place as whole having remained traditional in feel, its bars and restaurant (Gordon Ramsay, no less) are actively fashionable. The rooms divide equally between deco original and Victorian; both are luxurious, with period touches like deco loo flushes in the marble bathrooms plus mod cons such as bedside panels controlling everything at the touch of a button.

Clink Hostel

NEW *78 King's Cross Road, WC1X 9QG (7837 0479/www.clinkhostel.com). King's Cross tube/rail.* **£**.

Weardowney Guesthouse p206

Due to open in June 2007, the latest venture from Ashlee House (p200) is a converted 18th-century courthouse.

Connaught

NEW *16 Carlos Place, W1K 2AL (7499 7070/www.theconnaughthotel london.com). Bond Street tube.* **££££**.
The well-bred and equally well-located Connaught was undergoing an extensive multimillion pound restoration as this guide went to press. Set to reopen at the end of 2007, the revamp promises luxury spa facilities, a contemporary new wing (complete with 'green' roof carpeted with plants) and a full decor overhaul.

Covent Garden Hotel

10 Monmouth Street, WC2H 9LF (7806 1000/www.firmdale.com). Covent Garden or Leicester Square tube. **££££**.
Of all Kit Kemp's gilt-edged portfolio of hotels, the Covent Garden remains most people's favourite. It's snug and stylish, and its location on London's sexiest street ensures that it continues to attract far more than its fair share of starry customers. In the guest rooms Kemp's modern English style mixes traditional touches – pinstriped wallpaper, pristine white quilts, floral upholstery – with bold, contemporary elements. The ground-floor Brasserie Max, with its retro zinc bar, buzzes.

Dorchester

53 Park Lane, W1A 2HJ (7629 8888/ www.thedorchester.com). Hyde Park Corner tube. **££££**.
One of the grandes dames of the London hotel scene, the Dorchester is a perennial favourite with celebs. Despite its opulence – it has the grandest lobby in town, complete with Liberace's piano – staff are down to earth, and there's no hint of fustiness. The hotel continually upgrades older rooms to the same high standard as the rest, with floral (but not chintzy) decor, antiques and lavish marble bathrooms; some boast views of Hyde Park. Similarly, it's all change on the food and drink front: the

revamped bar was a resounding success, now Alain Ducasse is breezing in to set up a restaurant.

Harlingford Hotel

61-63 Cartwright Gardens, WC1H 9EL (7387 1551/www.harlingfordhotel.com). Russell Square tube/Euston tube/rail. **££**.
On the corner of a Georgian crescent lined with cheap hotels, the Harlingford is a stylish trailblazer in this Bloomsbury B&B enclave. The tasteful guests' lounge, scattered with trendy light fittings and modern prints, almost makes you forget this is a budget hotel. But while staff are eager to please, don't expect a porter to carry your bags upstairs and do turn a blind eye to the odd suitcase scuff on the paintwork. An adjacent garden and tennis court are available to guests.

Haymarket Hotel

NEW *1 Suffolk Place, SW1Y 4BP (7470 4000/www.haymarkethotel.com). Piccadilly Circus tube.* **£££**.
To say Kit Kemp's latest venture was eagerly anticipated is a criminal understatement – *Condé Nast Traveller* was only one of the publications confident enough to rate it among the world's coolest hotels *prior* to opening. It should live up to the hype, with a fabulous West End location (next to the Theatre Royal, handy for the National Gallery and Soho) and John Nash building (the man behind most of Regency London) complemented by Kemp's usual attention to design detail. There are 50 individual bedrooms and suites with super-luxe bathrooms – granite, glass and oak, cast-iron tubs, inset TVs. Downstairs the Italian restaurant and bar will be open to the public, but resident-only spaces offer a welcome retreat. Best of all, we reckon, is the promise of a fabulous 50ft swimming pool downstairs – how good will that 'spectacular lighting scheme' be?

Hazlitt's

6 Frith Street, W1D 3JA (7434 1771/ www.hazlittshotel.com). Tottenham Court Road tube. **£££**.

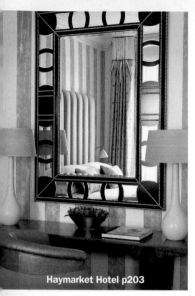
Haymarket Hotel p203

This idiosyncratic Georgian townhouse hotel – named after 18th-century essayist William Hazlitt, who died here – maintains an impressive literary pedigree: it was immortalised in Bill Bryson's *Notes from a Small Island* and the library contains signed first editions from such guests as Ted Hughes and JK Rowling. Rooms are as true to period as possible, with fireplaces, carefully researched colour schemes and clawfoot bathtubs. But don't worry: 21st-century comforts are also present and correct.

Metropolitan

19 Old Park Lane, W1K 1LB (7447 1000/www.metropolitan.como.bz). Hyde Park Corner tube. **££££**.
This modern upstart caused quite a stir when it joined the old guard on Park Lane in 1997 with its minimalist rooms. The standard doubles are actually quite small, although the hotel has an upgrade policy when larger ones are available. Still, the rooms have recently been refurbished, so everything is pristine, and you can't beat the views on the park side. Upstairs, Nobu remains a destination dining spot and massages are available in the COMO Shambhala Urban Escape.

Montagu Place

NEW *2 Montagu Place, W1H 2ER (7467 2778/www.montagu-place.co.uk). Baker Street tube.* **££**.
The Montagu is a stylish, small hotel, located in a Grade II-listed Georgian townhouse. Catering primarily for the midweek business traveller, its 16 rooms are divided into Comfy, Fancy and Swanky categories, the difference being size – Swanky are the largest, with enormous bathrooms, while Comfy are smallest and situated at the back of the building. All rooms have deluxe pocket-sprung beds, as well as cafetières with freshly ground coffee and flatscreen TVs. The look is boutique-hotel sharp and prices are affordable.

Morgan Hotel

24 Bloomsbury Street, WC1B 3QJ (7636 3735/www.morganhotel.co.uk). Tottenham Court Road tube. **££**.
Imagine *EastEnders* transplanted to Bloomsbury. The three Shoreditch-bred Ward siblings have been running this cheap and cheerful hotel since the 1970s. While it doesn't aspire to boutique status, rooms have extras beyond basic B&B standard: modern headboards with inbuilt reading lamps, air-con and new bathrooms with granite sinks. The cosy breakfast room, with its framed London memorabilia, is the perfect setting for a 'full English'. The hotel's annexe of spacious flats is one of London's best deals.

No.5 Maddox Street

5 Maddox Street, W1S 2QD (7647 0200/www.living-rooms.co.uk). Oxford Circus tube. **£££**.
Blink and you'll miss the entrance of this discreet bolthole just off Regent Street. Instead of rooms, accommodation is in chic flats, done up in the East-meets-West style that was all the

rage when it opened in the late 1990s: bamboo floors and dark wood furniture, sable throws and crisp white sheets. There's no bar, but Soho's nearby and Patara, a decent Thai restaurant, is on the ground floor. The kitchens are stocked with saintly organic as well as naughty treats, and room service will even shop for you.

One Aldwych

1 Aldwych, WC2B 4RH (7300 1000/ www.onealdwych.com). Covent Garden/ Temple tube/Charing Cross tube/rail. **££££**.

Despite weighty history – the 1907 building is by the architects responsible for the Ritz and was later the HQ of the *Morning Post* – One Aldwych is a thoroughly modern, luxury hotel. Everything from the Frette linen, B&B Italia chairs and Bang & Olufsen sound systems in the bedrooms to the environmentally friendly loo-flushing system and chemical-free REN toiletries in the bathrooms has been chosen with care. There's a private cinema with sumptuous Italian seats (dinner-and-a-movie packages are available), a spa, two great restaurants and a well-equipped gym, but the *pièce de résistance* is the shimmering 18m pool, complete with music piped into the water.

Piccadilly Backpackers

12 Sherwood Street, W1F 7BR (7434 9009/www.piccadillybackpackers.com). Piccadilly Circus tube. **£**.

Piccadilly Backpackers has two great things going for it: rates (from £12 per night in pod-style dorms) and location. The accommodation is basic, but with good common facilities (widescreen TV lounge, laundrette, 24-hour internet café), and ten rooms feature 'pods' – six beds arranged three up, three down.

Ritz

150 Piccadilly, W1J 9BR (7493 8181/ www.theritzlondon.com). Green Park tube. **££££**.

The reputation of this lavish 100-year-old establishment precedes it – what other hotel has spawned an adjective

meaning 'ostentatiously luxurious and glamorous'. The high-ceilinged, Louis XVI-style rooms have been painstakingly renovated to their former glory in a range of restrained pastel colours. Less restrained are the swanky 24-carat gold leaf features and the magnificently heavy curtains. The real show-stopper, however, is the ridiculously ornate Long Gallery, an orgy of chandeliers, rococo mirrors and marble columns. In spring 2007, the hotel received planning permission for an expansion that will bring the total number of rooms to nearly 200; an annexe is to be built on the site of a grizzly office block on nearby Arlington Street.

St Martins Lane Hotel

45 St Martin's Lane, WC2N 4HX (7300 5500/reservations 0800 634 5500/7300 5500/www.stmartins lane.com). Leicester Square tube/ Charing Cross tube/rail. **££££**.

When it arrived in 2000, St Martins was the toast of the town. The flamboyant lobby was always buzzing; the Light Bar was filled with celebrities, and guests giggled at Philippe Starck's playful decor. The novelty has worn off slightly but it remains a bolthole for high-profile guests seeking a high-profile refuge. The all-white bedrooms have comfortable minimalism down to a T, with floor-to-ceiling windows, soft throws, gadgetry secreted in sculptural cabinets and modern free-standing tubs in the limestone bathrooms. St Martins Lane is set for a fresh injection of high-profile style, probably in late 2007, when an outpost of New York celeb hangout Bungalow 8 opens here.

St Margaret's Hotel

26 Bedford Place, WC1B 5JL (7636 4277/www.stmargaretshotel.co.uk). Holborn or Russell Square tube. **£**.

This sprawling townhouse hotel has 64 rooms, but retains its cosy ambience thanks to the Marazzi family, who have run it for six decades. The rooms are simple, comfy and relatively spacious. Costs are kept down with shared, scrupulously clean bathrooms (only a dozen are en suite), and cooked breakfasts are served in an old-fashioned chandeliered dining room.

Sanderson

50 Berners Street, W1T 3NG (7300 1400/www.morganshotelgroup.com). Oxford Circus tube. **£££**.

Design hotels may be two a penny in London these days, but this modish Schrager/Starck creation is still a knock-out, partly because it combines modern minimalism with a playful, theatrical style. The pricey Long Bar and brand-new Suka restaurant fill nightly with fashionable types. There's also a suitably fashionable spa.

Sherlock Holmes Hotel

108 Baker Street, W1U 6LJ (7486 6161/www.sherlockholmeshotel.com). Baker Street tube. **££**.

How do you transform a dreary, chintz-filled Hilton into a hip boutique hotel? Hype up the Baker Street address, banish the bland decor and create a sleek lobby bar. That's what the Park Plaza chain did when it snapped up the Sherlock Holmes a few years ago. The rooms resemble hip bachelor pads: beige and brown colour scheme, leather headboards, pinstripe scatter cushions and spiffy bathrooms. The inevitable memorabilia ranges from expressionist paintings of Holmes and Watson in Sherlock's Grill to magnifying glasses.

Soho Hotel

4 Richmond Mews (off Dean Street), W1D 3DH (7559 3000/www.firmdale.com). Tottenham Court Road tube. **£££**.

Located in the heart of Soho, this is Kit Kemp's most edgy creation yet. Some say Kemp brings the country house to the city but the savvy urban aesthetic here is a very long way indeed from the shires. Bedrooms exhibit a contemporary edge, with modern furniture, industrial-style windows and all mod cons (Tivoli PAL digital radios, flatscreen TVs), although there are classic Kemp touches (bold pinstripes,

traditional florals, plump sofas) throughout. It's all very cool, but also thoroughly calming and comfortable.

Sumner

54 Upper Berkeley Street, W1H 7QR (7723 2244/www.thesumner.com). Marble Arch tube. **££**.

The end of its lease forced the team behind the highly regarded Five Sumner Place to relocate to this fine old Georgian townhouse around the corner from Marble Arch. Top interior designers have gone to work on the public spaces, which are cool and Nordic in shades of slate and grey. Depending on your predilections, the results are either hip and minimal or reminiscent of a Harley Street surgery waiting room. The 20 bedrooms are entirely different in feel, feeling much more like home.

22 York Street

22-24 York Street, W1U 6PX (7224 2990/www.22yorkstreet.co.uk). Baker Street tube. **££**.

There's no sign on the door; people usually discover Liz and Michael Callis's immaculately kept B&B by word of mouth. Unpretentious and comfortable, it's perfect for those who loathe hotels and are uncomfortable in designer interiors. The rooms are subtly tasteful, with wooden floorboards, antique pieces and French quilts. Most are en suite; all have an exclusively allocated bathroom.

Weardowney Guesthouse

9 Ashbridge Street, NW8 8DH (7725 9694/guesthouse@weardowney.com). Marylebone tube/rail. **£**.

Amy Wear and Gail Downey – models turned knitwear designers – recently moved out of the house they'd shared for ten years above their boutique and opened it to paying guests. The seven rooms (two en suite) are adorned with hand-knitted throws and curtains, and with prints and artwork from the pair's creative associates. It's very cosy and attractive, but a long way from a hotel stay: it feels like you're staying over at a friend's house.

The shock of the old

St Pancras

New York's hippest developer has developed a penchant for historic London real estate: Andre Balazs, saviour of LA's Chateau Marmont, proprietor of New York's Mercer and off/on companion of Uma Thurman, has been sniffing around London with a view to opening his first London hotel. He was outbid at his first attempt, but he confirms he's still looking.

It seems that if a building is imposing and central, sooner or later someone turns it into a hotel. For years there has been none more inviting than the magnificent **St Pancras Chambers**, the Victorian red-brick pile that looms over Euston Road. Long a favourite backdrop for period films, it's now undergoing a more permanent transformation. Some time during 2009, the long redundant (and Grade I-listed) former railway hotel reopens its doors to paying guests.

Responsible for the building's rebirth is the Marriott chain, which will attach its prestige Renaissance label to the 245-room hotel. The timing is shrewd: the opening of the Channel Tunnel rail link into St Pancras station, scheduled for November 2007, is already transforming King's Cross from a seedy backwater into a major international gateway. And the reworked hotel should be as sympathetic as it is impressive, with the project supported by both English Heritage and the Victorian Society.

Pipping the Renaissance to the post, though, will be **Bow Street Magistrates Court**. Previous occupants have included Oscar Wilde and East End gangster Reggie Kray – inmates at Irish developer Gerry Barrett's 80-room boutique hotel should prove rather more enthusiastic about their stay.

ESSENTIALS

The City

Great Eastern Hotel
*40 Liverpool Street, EC2M 7QN
(7618 5000/www.great-eastern-
hotel.co.uk). Liverpool Street tube/rail.*
££££.
Once a faded railway hotel, the Great
Eastern is now a mammoth urban
style mecca, with a design sympathetic to the glorious Victorian building. Bedrooms wear the regulation
style mag uniform: Eames chairs,
chocolate shagpile rugs and Frette
linens. And you'll never go hungry or
thirsty – there are seven restaurants
and bars, of good quality but no
longer Conran-run. The hotel recently
became a Hyatt.

Hoxton Hotel
NEW *81 Great Eastern Street, EC2A
3HU (7550 1000/www.hoxtonhotels.
com). Old Street tube/rail.* **££.**
With the Hoxton Hotel, located just
beyond the bounds of the City in hip
Shoreditch, Sinclair Beecham – the
man behind Pret a Manger – sets out
to prove budget needn't be boring. The
large glass front wall maintains a link
between the streetlife and the busy
double-height foyer with its lounge
seating. A large and well-designed bar
and restaurant increases the buzz.
Rooms are a little poky and the finish-
es are cheap, but you get Frette linen,
a flatscreen TV (unlimited movies, £5),
free Wi-Fi and a free Pret-lite breakfast
– all for under £60 at the weekend, less
if you book well in advance.

Malmaison
*Charterhouse Square, EC1M 6AH
(7012 3700/www.malmaison.com).
Barbican tube/Farringdon tube/rail.*
££.
Part of a UK-wide chain, Malmaison
London still manages to feel like a one-
off. The location is an absolute dream
– overlooking a semi-private, leafy
square by Smithfield Market, with its
array of restaurants and bars. The
decor is striking but comfortable, with
lots of distinctive touches, such as

black bathrobes and specially commissioned photos of London. Clientele
are predominantly drawn from the hipper end of City business.

Rookery
*12 Peter's Lane, Cowcross Street,
EC1M 6DS (7336 0931/www.rookery
hotel.com). Farringdon tube/rail.*
£££.
Tucked down an alleyway just north
of Smithfield Market, the Rookery is
straight out of a Dickens novel. The 33-
room hotel has been converted from a
row of 18th-century buildings and is
crammed with antiques: Gothic oak
beds, plaster busts and clawfoot bathtubs. It's equipped with all the modern
creature comforts too. The rooms vary
in size, but are all characterful.

Threadneedles
*5 Threadneedle Street, EC2R
8AY (7657 8080/www.theeton
collection.com). Bank tube/DLR.* **£££.**
Occupying the former HQ of the
Midland Bank, Threadneedles success-
fully integrates modern design with a
monumental space (including a gorgeous stained-glass dome over the
lobby). The decor is soothingly neutral,
with Korres natural toiletries in the
serene limestone bathrooms. Little
stress-busting comforts reflect its
business-friendly location, such as
fleecy throws, a scented candle lit at
turndown, a 'movie treats' menu.

Zetter
*86-88 Clerkenwell Road, EC1M 5RJ
(7324 4444/www.thezetter.com).
Farringdon tube/rail.* **££.**
True to its trendy Clerkenwell location, the Zetter is a bone fide loft hotel
in a converted Victorian warehouse,
with a soaring atrium, exposed brick
and funky 1970s furniture. Instead of
minibars, vending machines in the
corridors dispense everything from
dental kits to champagne. Rooms are
sleek and functional but cosied up
with homely comforts like hot-water
bottles and old Penguin paperbacks.
Prices beat anything in the West
End hands down.

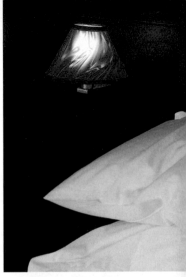

Hoxton Hotel

Getting Around

Airports

Gatwick Airport

0870 000 2468/www.baa.co.uk/ gatwick. About 30 miles south of central London, off the M23.

Of the three rail services that link Gatwick to London, the quickest is the **Gatwick Express** (0845 850 1530, www.gatwickexpress.co.uk) to Victoria Station, which takes about 30 minutes and runs from 3.30am to 12.30am daily. Tickets cost £14 single, £13.20 day return (after 9.30am) and £24 for an open period return (valid for 30 days). Under-15s are £6.50 single, half-price open and cheap day returns; under-5s go free.

Southern (0845 748 4950, www.southernrailway.com) also runs a rail service between Gatwick and Victoria, with trains every 15-20 minutes (or around hourly 1-4am). It takes about 35 minutes, at £9 for a single, £9.30 for a day return (after 9.30am) and £18 for an open period return (valid for one month). Under-16s get half-price tickets; under-5s go free.

If you're staying in the King's Cross or Bloomsbury area, consider the **Thameslink** service (0845 748 4950, www.firstcapitalconnect.co.uk) via London Bridge, Blackfriars, Farringdon and King's Cross; journey times vary. Tickets cost £10 single (after 9.30am), £10.10 day return and £20.20 for a 30-day open return.

Hotelink offers a shuttle service (01293 532244, www.hotelink.co.uk) at £19 each way (£22 online). A **taxi** costs about £100 and takes ages.

Heathrow Airport

0870 000 0123/www.baa.co.uk/ heathrow. About 15 miles west of central London, off the M4.

The **Heathrow Express** (0845 600 1515, www.heathrowexpress.co.uk) runs to Paddington every 15 minutes 5.10am-11.25am daily, and takes 15-20 minutes. The train can be boarded at either of the airport's two tube stations. Tickets cost £14.50 single or £27 return; under-16s go half-price. Many airlines have check-in desks at Paddington.

A longer but cheaper journey is by tube. Tickets for the 50- to 60-minute **Piccadilly Line** ride into central London cost £4 one-way (£2 under-16s). Trains run every few minutes from about 5am to 11.57pm daily except Sunday, when they run from 6am to 11pm.

National Express (0870 580 8080, www.nationalexpress.com) runs daily coach services to London Victoria between 7am and 0.15am daily, leaving Heathrow Central bus terminal around every 30 minutes. For a 90-minute journey to London, you can expect to pay £4 for a single (£2 under-16s) or £8 (£4 under-16s) for a return.

As at Gatwick, **Hotelink** offers an airport-to-hotel shuttle service for £17 per person each way. A **taxi** will cost roughly £100 and take an hour or more, depending on traffic.

London City Airport

7646 0000/www.londoncityairport.com. About 9 miles east of central London.

The **Docklands Light Railway** (DLR) now includes a stop for London City Airport. The journey to Bank in the City takes around 20 minutes, and trains run 5.30am-12.30am Mon-Sat or 7am-11.30pm Sun.

Many people still use the blue **Shuttlebus**, a 25-minute ride to Liverpool Street Station via Canary Wharf. It leaves every 15 minutes from 6.30am to 9.30pm, when the terminal closes. Tickets to Liverpool Street cost £6.50 one-way, or £3.50 to Canary Wharf. Have cash ready to pay the driver. A **taxi** costs around £20 to central London; less to the City or Canary Wharf.

Luton Airport

01582 405100/www.london-luton.com.
About 30 miles north of central
London, J10 off the M1.

Luton Airport Parkway Station is
close to the airport, but not in it: there's
still a short shuttle-bus ride. The
Thameslink service (p211) calls at
many stations (King's Cross and City,
on Ludgate Hill, among them); it has a
journey time of 35-45 minutes. Trains
leave every 15 minutes or so and cost
£11.10 single one-way and £20.60
return, or £11.20 for a cheap day return
(after 9.30am Monday to Friday, weekends). Luton–King's Cross trains run
at least hourly through the night.

The Luton to Victoria journey takes
60-90 minutes by coach. **Green Line**
(0870 608 7261, www.greenline.co.uk)
runs a 24-hour service every 30
minutes or so at peak times. A single
is £10.50, £7 for under-16s, while
returns cost £15 and £11. A **taxi** costs
upwards of £50.

Stansted Airport

0870 000 0303/www.stansted
airport.com; www.baa.co.uk/stansted.
About 35 miles north-east of central
London, J8 off the M11.

The quickest way to get to London is
on the **Stansted Express** train (0845
748 4950) to Liverpool Street Station;
the journey time is 40-45 minutes.
Trains leave every 15-45 minutes
depending on the time of day, and tickets cost £15 single, £25 return; under-
16s travel half-price, under-5s free.

The **Airbus** (0870 580 8080,
www.nationalexpress.com) coach service from Stansted to Victoria takes at
least an hour and 20 minutes and runs
24 hours. Coaches run roughly every
30 minutes. A single is £10 (£5 for
under-16s), return is £16 (£8 for under-
16s). A **taxi** is about £80.

Arriving by rail

Eurostar

St Pancras International Terminal,
NW1 (0870 518 6186/www.eurostar.
com). King's Cross tube/rail.

From November 2007, Eurostar trains
will no longer arrive at Waterloo
Station but instead hustle into the
brand new St Pancras International.

Mainline stations

For information on train times and
ticket prices, call 08457 484950 or
www.nationalrail.co.uk. You can get
timetable and price information, and
buy tickets, for any train operator in
the UK via www.thetrainline.com.

All London's major rail stations are
served by the tube.

Arriving by coach

Eurolines

Victoria Coach Station, 164
Buckingham Palace Road, SW1W 9TQ
(01582 404511/www.eurolines.com).
Services to continental Europe from
Victoria coach station.

Public transport

Details on public transport times and
other information can be found online at
www.tfl.gov.uk, or by calling 7222 1234.
Alternatively, see www.journeyplan-
ner.org to help you find the best route.
TfL's **Travel Information Centres**
provide maps and information about
the tube, buses and Docklands Light
Railway (DLR; p214). You can find them
in the stations listed below. Call 7222
5600 for more information.

Heathrow Airport Terminals 1, 2
& 3 *Underground station.* Open
6.30am-10pm daily.
Liverpool Street Open *7.15am-9pm*
Mon-Sat; 8.15am-8pm Sun.
Victoria Open *7.15am-9pm Mon-Sat;*
8.15am-8pm Sun.

London Underground

Delays are common. Escalators are often
out of action. Some lines close at weekends for engineering. It's hot, smelly and
crowded in rush hour (roughly 8am to
9.30am and 4.30pm to 7pm Mon-Fri).
Nevertheless, 'the tube' is still the quickest way to get around London.

Using the Underground

The single **fare** across the network is £4. Using Oyster pay-as-you-go, the fare varies by zone: zone 1 costs £1.50; zones 1-2 costs £1.50 or £2, depending on the time you travel; the zones 1-6 single fare is £2 or £3.50. The single fare for children is £2 for any journey including travel in zone 1 and £1.50 for any journey not including zone 1.

To enter and exit the tube using an Oyster card, simply touch it to the yellow reader, which will open the gates. Make sure you also touch the card to the reader when you exit, otherwise you will be charged a higher fare when you next use your Oyster card to enter a station.

To enter using a **paper ticket**, place it in the slot with the black magnetic strip facing down, then pull it out of the top to open the gates. Exiting the system at your destination is done in much the same way, though if you have a single journey ticket, it will be retained by the gate as you leave.

There are 12 tube lines, colour-coded on the tube map on the back flap.

Oyster card

Oyster, a pre-paid travel smart-card, is the cheapest way of getting around on buses, tubes and the DLR. There is a £3 refundable deposit payable for the card. Any tube journey within zone 1 using Oyster to pay-as-you-go costs £1.50 (50p for under-16s). A single tube journey within zone 2, 3, 4, 5 or 6 costs £1 (50p for under-16s). Single tube journeys from zones 1-6 using Oyster are £3.50 (7am-7pm Mon-Fri); £2 at other times and £1 for children. You can charge up at tube stations, London Travel Information Centres (p212), some rail stations and at newsagents. For more details contact www.tfl.gov.uk/oyster or 0870 849 9999.

Travelcards

Using Oyster to pay as you go will always be 50p cheaper than the equivalent Day Travelcard. If you are also using National Rail services, Oyster may not be accepted: opt for a Day Travelcard. Peak Day Travelcards can be used all day, Monday to Friday (except public holidays). They cost from £6.20 for zones 1-2 (£3.10 child), up to £12.40 for zones 1-6 (£6.20 child). All tickets are valid for journeys started before 4.30am the next day. Most people are happy with the Off-Peak Day Travelcard, which allows you to travel from 9.30am (Mon-Fri) and all day Saturday, Sunday and public holidays. They cost from £5.10 for zones 1-2, rising to £6.70 for zones 1-6.

Up to four under-11s can travel free on the tube (from 9.30am Mon-Fri; all day Sat, Sun and public holidays) as long as they are accompanied by a fare-paying adult. Another four can travel with an adult for £1 each (a Day Travelcard is issued) at the same times.

If you plan to spend a few days charging around town, you can buy a 3-Day Travelcard. Again the off-peak version will meet most visitors' needs. It costs £20.10 for zones 1-6. The peak version can be used all day Monday to Friday on the start date and for any journey that starts before 4.30am on the day following the expiry date; it's available for £16.40 (zones 1-2) or £39.60 (zones 1-6).

Travelling with children

Under-14s travel free on buses and trams without the need to provide any proof of identity; 14- and 15-year-olds can also travel free, but need to get an Under-16 Oyster photocard. For details, visit www.tfl.gov.uk/fares or call 0845 330 9876. A 14-15 Oyster photocard is needed by 11- to 15-year-olds to pay as they go on the tube or DLR or to buy 7-Day, monthly or longer period Travelcards and by 11- to 15-year-olds if using the tram to/from Wimbledon. Photocards are not required for adult rate 7-Day Travelcards, Bus Passes or for any adult rate Travelcard or Bus Pass charged on an Oyster card. For details of how to obtain under-14, 14-15 or 16-17 Oyster photocards contact www.tfl.gov.uk/fares or 0845 330 9876.

Underground timetable

Tube trains run daily from around 5.30am (except Sunday, when they start an hour or two later). The only exception is Christmas Day, when there is no service. Generally, you should not have to wait more than ten minutes for a train, and during peak times services should run every two or three minutes. Last trains from central stations leave between 11.30pm-midnight, 30 minutes earlier on a Sunday; weekend tubes began running a little later in May 2007: until 1am on Friday and Saturday. Other than on New Year's Eve, when the tubes run all night, the only all-night public transport is by night bus.

Docklands Light Railway

Docklands Light Railway (DLR) trains (7363 9700, www.tfl.gov.uk/dlr) run from Bank or Tower Gateway. At Westferry DLR the line splits east and south via Island Gardens to Greenwich and Lewisham; a change at Poplar can take you north to Stratford. The easterly branch forks after Canning Town to either Beckton or London City Airport. Trains run from 5.30am to 12.30am Monday to Saturday and 7am to 11.30pm Sunday.

The adult single **fares** on DLR are the same as for the tube (p212), except a DLR-only zones 2-3 journey, which costs £1.50 (£1 Oyster pay-as-you-go) or, for kids, 70p (50p pay-as-you-go).

Buses

All London buses are now low-floor and easily accessible to wheelchair-users and passengers with buggies; the only exceptions are Heritage routes 9 and 15, operated by the world-famous and much-loved open-platform Routemaster buses (p73). You *must* have a ticket or valid pass before getting on: inspectors patrol and board buses at random, and can fine you £20. You can buy a ticket (or 1-Day Bus Pass) from pavement ticket machines, although, frustratingly, they're often out of order. Better to travel armed with an Oyster card or some other pass (p213).

Using Oyster pay-as-you-go, the **single fare** is £1 a trip and the most you will pay a day will be £3. Paying with cash at the time of travel costs £2 for a single trip. Under-16s travel for free (using an Under-14 or 14-15 Oyster photocard as appropriate; p213). A 1-Day Bus Pass gives unlimited bus and tram travel for £3.50. A book of six Saver tickets costs £6 and can be bought at some newsagents and tube stations.

Many buses run 24 hours a day, seven days a week. There are also some special **night buses** with an 'N' prefix to the route number, which operate from about 11pm to 6am. Most night services run every 15 to 30 minutes, but many busier routes have a bus around every ten minutes.

Water transport

Most river services operate every 20 minutes to hour from 10.30am to 5pm; see www.tfl.gov.uk for schedules. **Thames Clippers** (www.thamesclippers.com) runs a commuter fleet, which was doubled in 2007 to accommodate anticipated traffic to the O_2 Arena. Piers to board the Clippers from are: Savoy (a short walk east of Embankment tube), Blackfriars, Bankside (for the Globe), London Bridge and St Katharine's (Tower Bridge).

Taxis

If a **black taxi**'s orange 'For Hire' sign is switched on, it can be hailed. If a taxi stops, the cabbie must take you to your destination, if it's within seven miles. It can be hard to find an unoccupied cab, especially just after the pubs close or when it rains. Rates are higher after 8pm on weekdays and at weekends. You can book cabs in advance; both **Radio Taxis** (7272 0272) and **Dial-a-Cab** (7253 5000; credit cards only) run 24-hour services (booking fee £2).

Minicabs (saloon cars) are generally cheaper than black cabs, but only use licensed firms (look for the yellow disc) and avoid those who tout for business. They'll be unlicensed, uninsured, possibly dangerous, probably not know the route, and will charge huge rates.

There are, happily, plenty of trustworthy and licensed local minicab firms. Londonwide firms include **Lady Cabs** (7272 3300), which employs only women drivers, and **Addison Lee** (7387 8888). If you want a licensed minicab firm, text HOME to 60835 – Transport of London will send you the phone numbers of the two nearest. Always ask the price when you book and confirm it with the driver.

Driving

Congestion charge

Everyone driving in central London – an area defined as within King's Cross (N), Old Street roundabout (NE), Aldgate (E), Old Kent Road (SE), Elephant & Castle (S), Vauxhall, Chelsea, South Kensington (SW), Kensington, Holland Park, North Kensington, Bayswater, Paddington (W), Marylebone and Euston (N) – between 7am and 6pm Monday to Friday, has to pay an £8 fee. Expect a fine of £50 if you fail to do so (rising to £150 if you delay payment). Passes can be bought from newsagents, garages and NCP car parks, as well as online; the scheme is enforced by CCTV cameras. You can pay any time during the day of entry, even afterwards, but it's an extra £2 after 10pm. Payments will be accepted until midnight on the next charging day after a vehicle has entered the zone. For more information, phone 0845 900 1234 or go to www.cclondon.com.

Parking

Parking on a single or double yellow line, a red line or in residents' parking areas during the day is illegal, and you may end up being fined, clamped or towed. However, in the evening (from 6pm or 7pm in much of central London) and at various times at weekends, parking on single yellow lines is legal and free. If you find a clear spot on a single yellow line during the evening, look for a sign giving the regulations for that area. Meters also become free at certain times during evenings and weekends. Parking on double yellow lines and red routes is illegal at all times.

NCP 24-hour **car parks** (0870 606 7050, www.ncp.co.uk) around London are numerous but pricey (£6-£10 for two hours). Central ones include Arlington House, Arlington Street, St James's, W1; Snowsfield, Southwark, SE1, and 4-5 Denman Street, Soho, W1.

Vehicle removal

If your car has disappeared, the chances are (assuming it was legally parked) it's been stolen; if not, it's probably been taken to a car pound. A release fee of £200 is levied for removal, plus £25 per day from the first midnight after removal. To add insult to injury, you'll also probably get a parking ticket of £60-£100 when you collect the car (which will be reduced by a 50% discount if paid within 14 days). To find out how to retrieve your car, call the Trace Service hotline (7747 4747).

Vehicle hire

Easycar's online-only service, at www.easycar.com, offers competitive rates, just so long as you don't mind driving a branded car around town. Otherwise, try **Alamo** (0870 400 4508, www.alamo.com), **Budget** 0844 581 9999, www.budget.co.uk) and **Hertz** (0870 599 6699, www.hertz.co.uk).

Cycling

Call **Transport for London** (7222 1234) for cycling maps that indicate cycle paths and quieter routes. **Go Pedal!** (07850 796320, www.gopedal.co.uk) delivers and collects a bicycle and accessories, while the **London Bicycle Tour Company** (1A Gabriel's Wharf, 56 Upper Ground, South Bank, SE1 9PP, 7928 6838, www.londonbicycle.com) rents out bikes, tandems and rickshaws.

ESSENTIALS

Resources A-Z

Accident & emergency

In the event of a serious accident, fire or other incident, call **999** – free from any phone, including payphones – and ask for an ambulance, the fire service or police. The following central London hospitals each have a 24-hour Accident & Emergency department.

Chelsea & Westminster Hospital *369 Fulham Road, Chelsea, SW10 9NH (8746 8000). South Kensington tube.*

Guy's Hospital *St Thomas Street (entrance Snowsfields), Borough, SE1 9RT (7188 7188). London Bridge tube/rail.*

Royal London Hospital *Whitechapel Road, Whitechapel, E1 1BB (7377 7000). Whitechapel tube.*

St Mary's Hospital *Praed Street, Paddington, W2 1NY (7886 6666). Paddington tube/rail.*

St Thomas's Hospital *Lambeth Palace Road, Lambeth, SE1 7EH (7188 7188). Westminster tube/Waterloo tube/rail.*

University College *Hospital Grafton Way, Fitzrovia, WC1E 3BG (7387 5798). Euston Square or Warren Street tube.*

Credit card loss

American Express *01273 696933.*
Diners Club *01252 513500.*
MasterCard/Eurocard *0800 964767.*
Switch *0870 600 0459.*
Visa/Connect *0800 895082.*

Customs

For allowances, see www.hmrc.gov.uk.

Dental emergency

Dental care is free for resident students, under-18s and people on benefits. All other patients must pay. NHS-eligible patients pay on a subsidised scale.

Dental Emergency Care Service *Guy's Hospital, St Thomas Street, Bankside, SE1 9RT (7188 0511). London Bridge tube/rail.* **Open** 9am-5pm Mon-Fri.

Queues start forming at 8am; arrive by 10am if you're to be seen at all.

Disabled

London is a difficult city for disabled visitors, though legislation is gradually improving access and facilities. The bus fleet is more wheelchair-friendly, but the tube remains extremely escalator-dependent. The *Tube Access Guide* booklet is available free of charge; call the Travel Information line for more information (7222 1234).

Most major visitor attractions and hotels offer good accessibility, though provision for the hearing- and sight-disabled is patchier. *Access in London* is an invaluable reference for disabled travellers, available from Access Project (www. accessproject-phsp.org).

Artsline

54 Chalton Street, Somers Town, NW1 1HS (tel/textphone 7388 2227/ www.artslineonline.com). Euston tube/rail. **Open** 9.30am-5.30pm Mon-Fri. Information on disabled access to London's arts and entertainment events.

Electricity

The UK uses the standard European 220-240V, 50-cycle AC voltage and three-pin plugs.

Embassies & consulates

American Embassy *24 Grosvenor Square, Mayfair, W1A 1AE (7499 9000/www.usembassy.org.uk). Bond*

Street or Marble Arch tube.
Open 8.30am-5.30pm Mon-Fri.
Australian High Commission
Australia House, Strand, Holborn,
WC2B 4LA (7379 4334/www.australia.
org.uk). Holborn or Temple tube. **Open**
9.30am-3.30pm Mon-Fri.
Canadian High Commission
38 Grosvenor Street, Mayfair, W1K
4AA (7258 6600/www.canada.org.uk).
Bond Street or Oxford Circus tube.
Open 8-11am Mon-Fri.
Embassy of Ireland *17 Grosvenor*
Place, Belgravia, SW1X 7HR (7235
2171/passports and visas 7225 7700).
Hyde Park Corner tube. **Open** 9.30am-
1pm, 2.30-5pm Mon-Fri.
New Zealand High Commission
New Zealand House, 80 Haymarket,
St James's, SW1Y 4TQ (7930 8422/
www.nzembassy.com). Piccadilly Circus
tube. **Open** 9am-5pm Mon-Fri.
South African High Commission
South Africa House, Trafalgar
Square, St James's, WC2N 5DP
(7451 7299/www.southafrica
house.com). Charing Cross tube/rail.
Open 9am-5pm Mon-Fri.

Internet

Most hotels have at least a modem
plug-in point (dataport) in each room,
if not broadband or wireless access.
Those that don't have either usually
offer some other form of surfing. There
are also lots of cybercafés around town,
including the easyInternetCafé chain.
You'll also find terminals in public
libraries. For others, check www.cyber-
cafes.com. For wireless access, check
with your provider or visit www.wi-
fihotspotlist.com

easyInternetCafé

456-459 Strand, Trafalgar Square,
WC2R ORG (www.easyinternetcafe.
com). Charing Cross tube/rail. **Open**
8am-11pm daily. **Terminals** 393.
Locations throughout the city.

Left luggage

The threat of terrorism has meant that
London bus and train stations tend to
have left-luggage desks rather than

lockers; to find out if a train station
offers this facility, call 0845 748 4950.
Gatwick Airport *South Terminal*
01293 502014/North Terminal
01293 502013.
Heathrow Airport *Terminal 1*
8745 5301/Terminals 2-3 8759
3344/Terminal 4 8897 6874.
London City Airport *7646 0162.*
Stansted Airport *01279 663213.*

Opening hours

Banks 9am-4.30pm (some close
at 3.30pm, some 5.30pm) Mon-Fri;
sometimes also Saturday mornings.
Businesses 9am-5pm Mon-Fri.
Pubs & bars 11am-11pm Mon-Sat;
noon-10.30pm Sun.
Shops 10am-6pm Mon-Sat; some to
8pm. Many are also open on Sunday,
usually 11am-5pm or noon-6pm.

Pharmacies

Also called 'chemists' in the UK. Larger
supermarkets and all branches of
Boots (www.boots.com) have a phar-
macy, and there are independents on
most of London's high streets. Staff are
qualified to advise on over-the-counter
medicines. Most pharmacies are open
9am-6pm and are closed on Sunday).

Police

Look under 'Police' in the phone book
or call 118 118/500/888 if none of the
following are convenient.
Charing Cross Police Station
Agar Street, Covent Garden, WC2N 4JP
(7240 1212). Charing Cross tube/rail.
Marylebone Police Station
1-9 Seymour Street, Marylebone, W1H
7BA (7486 1212). Marble Arch tube.
West End Central Police Station
27 Savile Row, Mayfair, W1X 2DU
(7437 1212). Piccadilly Circus tube.

Post

Post offices usually open 9am to
5.30pm Monday to Friday and 9am to
noon Saturday, with the exception of
Trafalgar Square Post Office (24-

28 William IV Street, WC2N 4DL, open 8.30am-6.30pm Mon-Fri; 9am-5.30pm Sat). For general enquiries, call 0845 722 3344 or visit www.post office.co.uk.

Smoking

On 1 July 2007, a new law was due to come into force that prohibits smoking in all enclosed public spaces, including pubs, bars, clubs, restaurants and shops, as well as on public transport. Hotels can still offer smoking rooms.

Telephones

London's dialling code is 020. If you're calling from outside the UK, dial your international access code, then the UK code, 44, then the full London number, omitting the first 0 from the code. To dial abroad from the UK, first dial 00, then the relevant country code (Australia 61; Canada 1; New Zealand 64; Republic of Ireland 353; South Africa 27; USA 1).

US cellphone users will need a tri-or quad-band handset.

Public payphones take coins and/or credit cards. The minimum cost is 40p. International calling cards, offering bargain minutes via a freephone number, are widely available.

Tickets

With the exception of the major cultural institutions, which have in-house box offices, most venues subcontract their ticketing to agencies. Ticketmaster (www.ticketmaster.co.uk, 0870 534 4444, +44 161 385 3211 international) and TicketWeb (www.ticketweb.co.uk, 0870 060 0100) cover most places.

tkts
Clocktower building, Leicester Square, WC2H 7NA (www.officiallondontheatre. co.uk). Leicester Square tube. **Open** 10am-7pm Mon-Sat; noon-3pm Sun.
A non-profit-making organisation selling reduced-price tickets for West End shows on a first-come, first-served basis on the day of the performance only.

Time

London operates on Greenwich Mean Time (GMT), which is five hours ahead of the US's Eastern Standard time. In autumn (28 October 2007, 26 October 2008) the UK puts its clocks to GMT. In spring (30 March 2008) the clocks go forward by one hour to what is called 'British Summer Time'.

Tipping

Tip in taxis, minicabs, restaurants, hotels, hairdressers and some bars (not pubs). Ten per cent is normal, with some restaurants adding as much as 15 per cent. Watch out for places that include service, then leave the space for a gratuity on your credit card slip blank.

Tourist information

Visit London (7234 5800, www.visit london.com) is the city's official tourist information company. There are also tourist offices in Greenwich, Leicester Square and next to St Paul's.

Britain & London Visitor Centre
1 Lower Regent Street, Piccadilly Circus, SW1Y 4XT (8846 9000/ www.visitbritain.com). Piccadilly Circus tube. **Open** 9.30am-6.30pm Mon-Sat; 10am-4.30pm Sun.

Visas

EU citizens don't need a visa to visit the UK; US citizens, Canadians, Australians, South Africans and New Zealanders need only a passport for tourist visits. *Always* check the current situation at www.ukvisas.gov.uk well before you travel.

What's on

Time Out magazine, available from central London newsagents from Tuesday each week, contains up-to-date listings on all aspects of London life and entertainment. For gay listings, also look out for freesheets *Boyz* and *QX*.

ESSENTIALS

Index

Sights & areas

ESSENTIALS

Eating & drinking

ESSENTIALS